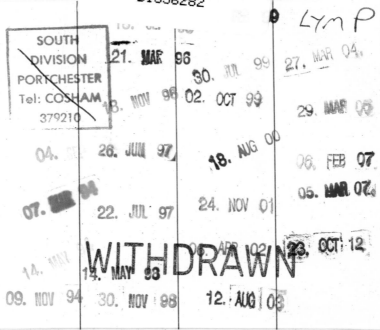

This book is due for return on or before the last date shown
above; it may, subject to the book not being reserved by
another reader, be renewed by personal application, post, or
telephone, quoting this date and details of the book.

EVERYMAN,
I WILL GO WITH THEE,
AND BE THY GUIDE,
IN THY MOST NEED
TO GO BY THY SIDE

WILLIAM SHAKESPEARE

The Sonnets and
Narrative Poems

EVERYMAN'S LIBRARY

91

First included in Everyman's Library, 1906
These poems are published by arrangement with New American
Library, a division of Penguin Books USA Inc.
Complete Sonnets: Copyright © 1964, 1989 by William Burto.
Introduction copyright © 1964 by W. H. Auden. Copyright © 1963,
1988 by Sylvan Barnet
Narrative Poems: Copyright © 1968 by William Burto. Copyright ©
1963, 1989 by Sylvan Barnet
Introduction, Bibliography and Chronology © David Campbell
Publishers Ltd., 1992
Typography by Peter B. Willberg

ISBN 1-85715-091-0

A catalogue record for this book is available from the British Library

Published by David Campbell Publishers Ltd., 79 Berwick Street,
London W1V 3PF

Distributed by Random House (UK) Ltd.,
20 Vauxhall Bridge Road, London SW1V 2SA

Printed and bound in Germany

CONTENTS

Introduction   vii

Select Bibliography   xxx

Chronology   xxxii

The Sonnets   3

Textual Note   82

Index of First Lines   83

Narrative Poems   87

   Venus and Adonis   89

   The Rape of Lucrece   131

   The Phoenix and the Turtle   197

   The Lover's Complaint   201

   The Passionate Pilgrim   213

Textual Note   223

Appendix

Introduction to the Sonnets by W. H. Auden   . .   227

INTRODUCTION

William Shakespeare (1564-1616) was already known as a playwright and actor before he published, in 1593 and 1594, his two narrative poems *Venus and Adonis* and *Lucrece* (usually known by its subtitle *The Rape of Lucrece*), both dedicated to Henry Wriothesley, third Earl of Southampton. These long and accomplished poems suggest a sustained period of verse-writing which must have preceded them, and that period may have included some of Shakespeare's sonnets. The sonnets are first mentioned in 1598 by Francis Meres; it is possible that the extended compositional period of the 154 sonnets both preceded and followed the long narrative poems, though the sonnets as a group were not published until 1609 (together with the long poem called *A Lover's Complaint*). The 1609 *Sonnets* lacks an authorial dedication of the sort found in *Venus* and *Lucrece*, and it has been conjectured that the volume was published without Shakespeare's authorization.

In 1599 a volume called *The Passionate Pilgrim*, ascribed to Shakespeare, was published by a dubious publisher called William Jaggard. This book contains five poems known to be by Shakespeare, of which I and II are versions of sonnets 138 and 144, III and IV are versions of sonnets included in *Love's Labour's Lost*, and XVI is a variant on a short poem in *Love's Labour's Lost*. Four poems (VII, XI, XIX, and XX) are known to be by contemporaries of Shakespeare, and the other eleven poems are of uncertain authorship (IV, VI, and IX concern Venus and Adonis). Finally, in 1601, in a volume called *Love's Martyr*, there appeared, among other poems appended to the title poem by Robert Chester, a poem by Shakespeare called 'The Phoenix and [the] Turtle', celebrating the funeral of a married pair of birds, a (female) phoenix and a (male) turtle-dove, martyrs to their marital love (the phoenix does not rise again, but dies with her mate).

To sum up: by 1593, when he was twenty-nine, Shakespeare was capable of writing a poem as confident, sophisticated, and elaborate as *Venus and Adonis*; his poetic production may have continued up to the issuing of the 1609 *Sonnets* (when Shakespeare was forty-five), though similarities between some of the plays and certain sonnets suggest that most of the sonnets were written in the 1590s, between Shakespeare's late twenties and mid-thirties. These, then, are chiefly the poems of a young man. Problems of love and sexuality dominate the poems thematically, and problems of genre-investigation and stanza-exploitation dominate them formally.

The narrator of *Venus and Adonis* is alternately amused and full of compunction with respect to the story he tells – the goddess Venus' unsuccessful pursuit of the beautiful boy Adonis, who, though he foils the amorous goddess hunting him, is himself killed – sexually gored – by the boar he hunts. Though the putative motive for the story is to explain the origin of the anemone (into which Adonis, after his death, is changed), this myth of explanation is given short shrift by Shakespeare, occupying only a few lines at the end of the poem. For Shakespeare, the true culmination of the story is the long lament of Venus over the body of Adonis, and her concluding prophecy, in lines 1135–64, that human love will thenceforth be corrupted:

> It shall be fickle, false, and full of fraud;
> Bud, and be blasted, in a breathing while;
> The bottom poison, and the top o'erstrawed
> With sweets that shall the truest sight beguile.
>   The strongest body shall it make most weak,
>   Strike the wise dumb, and teach the fool to speak . . .
>
> It shall be cause of war and dire events
> And set dissension 'twixt the son and sire,
> Subject and servile to all discontents,
> As dry combustious matter is to fire.
>   Sith in his prime death doth my love destroy,
>   They that love best their loves shall not enjoy.

The whole of *Venus and Adonis* occupies 1194 lines, making up 199 pentameter stanzas of six lines each, rhyming *ababcc*. The task for a poet in a long poem of this sort is to fill out the bare circumstance (Venus hunts Adonis; Adonis hunts the boar; Adonis is killed; Venus laments) by what the Renaissance rhetoricians called 'invention' – that is, keeping the poem afloat by sufficient incident and style to carry it through its length without wearying the reader. Shakespeare's plot has inherent, if serio-comic, erotic interest, and Shakespeare exploits to the full both Venus' experienced lust and Adonis' appalled virginity:

> Even as an empty eagle, sharp by fast,
> Tires with her beak on feathers, flesh, and bone,
> Shaking her wings, devouring all in haste,
> Till either gorge be stuffed or prey be gone –
>   Even so she kissed his brow, his cheek, his chin,
>   And where she ends she doth anew begin ...

> Look how a bird lies tangled in a net,
> So fastened in her arms Adonis lies.
> Pure shame and awed resistance made him fret,
> Which bred more beauty in his angry eyes:
>   Rain added to a river that is rank
>   Perforce will force it overflow the bank.

A characteristically Shakespearian expansion of similes – the ravenous eagle for Venus, the entangled bird for Adonis – fills out the first part of this passage, while a *sententia* (a philosophic or moral aphorism) is invented to occupy the last two illustrative lines. (*Sententiae* are employed by Shakespeare to an even greater extent in the more moral poem *Lucrece*, where the narrator and the characters alike take every opportunity to moralize in pithy ways upon lust, violence, crime, honor, and death.)

Because the story of Venus and Adonis is a fertility myth, Venus is 'in the right' in criticizing Adonis' rejection of her solicitations; in repudiating her, he is refusing the very process of sexuality and reproduction, as embodied in the goddess. The narrator, who however has considerable sympathy for the besieged Adonis, relents towards his predatory Venus enough to allow her the universal and natural claim (which appears strongly in the first part of the *Sonnets*) that beauty should not be sequestered from sexual use:

Torches are made to light, jewels to wear,
Dainties to taste, fresh beauty for the use,
Herbs for their smell, and sappy plants to bear.
Things growing to themselves are growth's abuse.
  Seeds spring from seeds, and beauty breedeth beauty.
  Thou wast begot; to get it is thy duty.

Such speeches give force to Venus' argument, but are at odds, dramatically, with her attempts to overpower, by sheer bodily force, the reluctant boy.

Any new reader of *Venus and Adonis* will be surprised to find that Shakespeare's writing kindles into its most genuine poetic originality in the astonishingly empathetic writing about animals contained in the poem. Keats quoted the passage about the snail's antennae:

... The snail, whose tender horns being hit,
Shrinks backward in his shelly cave with pain,
And there, all smoth'red up, in shade doth sit,
Long after fearing to creep forth again.

And Keats was surely thinking, when he described a limping hare in *The Eve of Saint Agnes*, of Shakespeare's hare fleeing from hounds:

Then shalt thou see the dew-bedabbled wretch
Turn, and return, indenting with the way.
Each envious brier his weary legs do scratch;
Each shadow makes him stop, each murmur stay;
  For misery is trodden on by many,
  And, being low, never relieved by any.

Shakespeare's tendency to attach allegorical meanings to his animals, visible in the conclusion of the passage on the hare, becomes even more evident in the description of Adonis' stallion. As Venus wrestles with Adonis, Adonis' horse, his reins tied to a tree, breaks his tether at the sight of a mare, and races off into the forest to couple with her, thereby giving Adonis a lesson in natural sexual behavior:

Imperiously he leaps, he neighs, he bounds,
And now his woven girths he breaks asunder; ...
    The iron bit he crusheth 'tween his teeth,
    Controlling what he was controlled with.

His ears up-pricked, his braided hanging mane
Upon his compassed crest now stand on end;
His nostrils drink the air, and forth again,
As from the furnace, vapors doth he send;
    His eye, which scornfully glisters like fire,
    Shows his hot courage and his high desire ...

Round hoofed, short-jointed, fetlocks shag and long,
Broad breast, full eye, small head, and nostril wide,
High crest, short ears, straight legs and passing
    strong,
Thin mane, thick tail, broad buttock, tender hide:
    Look what a horse should have he did not lack,
    Save a proud rider on so proud a back.

Later in the poem we meet Venus' description – Shakespeare's description – of the boar, which contains the most energetic and surreal writing in the whole poem, as the boar approaches 'like to a mortal butcher bent to kill':

    On his bow-back he hath a battle set
    Of bristly pikes that ever threat his foes;
    His eyes like glowworms shine when he doth fret;
    His snout digs sepulchers where'er he goes;
        Being moved, he strikes whate'er is in his way,
        And whom he strikes his crooked tushes slay.

Venus and Adonis is, in its successive 'inventions' and its love of paradoxes ('She's Love, she loves, and yet she is not loved'), deliberately constructed as a 'masterpiece' – an exhibition of the various elaborative talents (narrative, descriptive, mythological, classical, rhetorical) of its young author, who moralizes (through Adonis) in rather stilted and prearranged ways:

    Love comforteth like sunshine after rain,
    But Lust's effect is tempest after sun.
    Love's gentle spring doth always fresh remain;
    Lust's winter comes ere summer half be done.
        Love surfeits not, Lust like a glutton dies;
        Love is all truth, Lust full of forgèd lies.

Even Venus' normally tempestuous nature is suspended so that she can utter *sententiae*. As she says,

> Unlike myself thou hear'st me moralize,
> Applying this to that, and so to so,
> For love can comment upon every woe.

We feel that Shakespeare too can 'comment upon every woe', not only here but in the even more ambitious, if more static, poem that followed *Venus and Adonis* – *Lucrece*. Venus' pursuit of Adonis, no matter how repellent, is still allowable, since Venus is a goddess to whom all is permitted. But *Lucrece* moves us into a far darker world, the tragic world of human crime, honor, and civic and marital obligation. (The poem is composed in a seven-line pentameter stanza rhyming *ababbcc*, a more expressively flexible stanza, because of the 'extra' fifth line before the couplet, than the quatrain-plus-couplet stanza of *Venus and Adonis*.) Though *Lucrece* too is theoretically an explanatory poem (showing why Rome expelled the Tarquins and restored republican government), the myth of explanation once again concerns Shakespeare very little. Like *Venus and Adonis*, *Lucrece* is officially a narrative poem; but its 1855 lines (to *Venus'* 1194) contain an even smaller component of narrative. The poem is chiefly devoted to the long lyric speeches of Tarquin the violator and Lucrece the victim.

The story of Lucrece was a given for Shakespeare, together with its Roman setting and its Roman ethics, which approved suicide. Tarquin has raped a virtuous wife, who remains alive only long enough to tell her story, since Tarquin has threatened, if she resists him, to kill her and one of her male servants, and place their bodies in a sexually compromising position. Lucrece can make her subsequent story indubitable only by her suicide; and only by her death, as she says, can she evade possible pregnancy by Tarquin and the consequent shame to her husband of an illegitimately fathered child (lines 1062–4). It has been argued by William Empson (in his Introduction to the Signet *Poems*) that Lucrece took sexual pleasure in her violation, since she speaks of 'my trespass' (line 1070), 'my sable ground of sin' (line 1074), and notably of her 'gross blood ... stained with this abuse' (lines 1655–9). The

'contamination' of this Roman poem by Christian vocabulary
– the only moral vocabulary available to Shakespeare's
audience – may account for some of Lucrece's locutions. But it
must be remembered that to Renaissance biology the infusion
of Tarquin's semen into Lucrece's body is enough to render
her body and its corporeal spirits, such as blood, contami-
nated. Lucrece is very clear about the entire absence, during
the rape, of any 'accessary yieldings' to lust on her part (in
lines 1654-9, the very lines quoted by Empson to make his
dubious point):

> This refuge let me find:
> Though my gross blood be stained with this abuse,
> Immaculate and spotless is my mind;
> That was not forced, that never was inclined
> To accessary yieldings, but still pure
> Doth in her poisoned closet yet endure.

In using the three words Christians ascribe chiefly to the
Virgin Mary ('pure', 'spotless', and especially 'immaculate'),
Shakespeare ratifies the mental and spiritual chastity of his
heroine (as, indeed, did the originating legend). 'False' Tar-
quin's semen did indeed 'stain' that part of her blood that
issues, after her death, black and corrupted (line 1743), but
Lucrece herself had no part in the corruption.

In taking on this classic and renowned subject, Shakespeare
shows himself interested chiefly in the motives animating both
his protagonists. (Lucrece's husband Collatine's boast of his
wife's chastity, which inflames Tarquin, is the merest pretext
to get the plot going.) The greater interest attaches to
Tarquin's soliloquy, since as a Roman nobleman violating his
soldierly bond to Collatine and the bond of a guest to
Lucrece's hospitality, he is forfeiting civic honor as well as his
own self-respect. Does Shakespeare, as we might expect,
explain the lust that animates Tarquin as a vice arising from
his temperament or his 'gross blood'? On the contrary, he
ascribes Tarquin's lust to his eye – the organ of aesthetic
perception. The emphasis is insistent and repeated: though
Tarquin originally goes to Lucrece's house animated by his
ear that heard her praised (line 38) and by his envy of

Collatine (line 39), once he gets there he is rendered powerless to resist his impulse by Lucrece's beauty. As Lucrece welcomes Tarquin to her house, her 'Beauty's red and Virtue's white' (line 65) play out their chaste allegorical war in her surprised countenance:

> This silent war of lilies and of roses,
> Which Tarquin viewed in her fair face's field,
> In their pure ranks his traitor eye encloses ...

> Therefore that praise which Collatine doth owe
> Enchanted Tarquin answers with surmise,
> In silent wonder of still-gazing eyes.

Tarquin exhibits nothing 'inordinate/Save sometimes too much wonder in his eye', but Lucrece, in her innocence, could not 'moralize his wanton sight'. After the house is still, Tarquin lights a torch, 'lodestar to his lustful eye' and excuses his lust's intent by reference to his eye:

> All orators are dumb when beauty pleadeth ...

> My heart shall never countermand mine eye ...
> Desire my pilot is, beauty my prize.

The narrator continues to blame the eye: 'That eye which looks on her confounds his wits.' Lucrece lies in her bedroom as Tarquin enters 'Rolling his greedy eyeballs in his head', until, pulling apart the bedcurtains, he sees, with his 'lewd unhallowed eyes', Lucrece herself. Once again, the narrator emphasizes the lust of the eye:

> What could he see but mightily he noted?
> What did he note but strongly he desirèd?
> What he beheld, on that he firmly doted,
> And in his will his willful eye he tirèd.

Though for a moment Tarquin hesitates,

> His eye, which late this mutiny restrains,
> Unto a greater uproar tempts his veins ...

> His drumming heart cheers up his burning eye,
> His eye commends the leading to his hand.

Tarquin tells Lucrece, in fact, that her rape is her own fault, that her beauty has overcome his eyes:

> For those thine eyes betray thee unto mine ...

> Thy beauty has ensnared thee to this night ...
> By thy bright beauty was [will] newly bred ...

> [Will only] hath an eye to gaze on Beauty,
> And dotes on what he looks, 'gainst law or duty.

When we last see Tarquin's eye, just before the rape, it has become the malevolently gazing organ of a mythological beast capable of paralysing its prey – 'a cockatrice' dead-killing eye'.

Shakespeare's striking insistence on the primary criminal function of the eye is that of neither a moralist (though the narrator of the poem is certainly an active moralist) nor a psychological analyst of rape (if it were the latter, he might more properly have emphasized Tarquin's power, brutality, envy, and sadism equally with Lucrece's appearance). No: Shakespeare is here conceiving rape as the ultimate consequence of aesthetic perception, and he writes as an aesthete for whom seeing and possessing beauty is the single most compelling force in the world. The helplessness of the aesthete before beauty is projected, however inappropriately, onto Tarquin as rapist; and the entirely bizarre emphasis on Lucrece's beauty and Tarquin's compulsion under it distorts the proportions of the poem out of any reasonable telling of the story.

The poem is similarly distorted by a second visual distraction, Lucrece's contemplation (for over two hundred lines) of a painting of the fall of Troy. Dramatically speaking, this interlude allows time for Lucrece to send a messenger to summon her husband, but this function could have been covered by a line ('So with her husband speedily returned', etc.). Once again, the poem goes out of its way to emphasize vision, but the object of natural aesthetic beauty (Lucrece's face) is now replaced by an object of constructed aesthetic beauty, the painting. What is emphasized is the power of an aesthetic object to convey grief and, indirectly (since poesis was thought to be like painting, *ut pictura poesis*), the power of the very poem we are reading to convey Lucrece's tragedy to

our eyes. As Lucrece gazes at the painting, she describes it to
herself:

> So Lucrece, set awork, sad tales doth tell
>> To penciled pensiveness and colored sorrow:
>> She lends them words, and she their looks doth
>> borrow.

> She throws her eyes about the painting round.

The poem, having shown in Lucrece a Platonic beauty of form
whose outward fairness matches the chastity within, now
shows in the painting an anti-Platonic counter-beauty, that of
the fair-faced traitor Sinon, to whom Lucrece compares
Tarquin with his 'outward honesty'. Though Lucrece is a
reluctant anti-Platonist, against her will she learns, through
the rape and the painting alike, that physical beauty can
conceal moral corruption.

In short, we see here Shakespeare examining with savage
force the abject slavery to Beauty that he will explore in the
helpless speaker of the sonnets, so enthralled by the beauty of
the disingenuous young man, the 'master-mistress' (sonnet
#20) of his passion. But by the time of the sonnets, irony and
self-understanding have entered into Shakespeare's subjection
to, and fear of, his own artist-eye; with irony comes a degree of
control over his subject-matter that is not present in the lurid
portrait of Tarquin.

Stylistically, both *Venus and Adonis* and *Lucrece*, though
enormously accomplished, are inferior to most of the sonnets.
Both poems are very much concerned with elaborate local
stylizations (like Adonis' contrast between Love and Lust
quoted above). These are striking in themselves, as purple
passages, but ultimately disruptive to the narrative whole.
Such stylistic *tours de force* are especially prevalent in *Venus and
Adonis*, sometimes marked by conspicious antithesis, some-
times by repetition of different forms of the same word,
sometimes by epigram, sometimes by repeated ellipses of a
word or phrase ('Torches are made to light, jewels [are made]
to wear,/Dainties [are made] to taste', etc.), sometimes by

rapidly successive metaphors, as in the description of the clasped hands of Venus and Adonis:

> she takes him by the hand,
> A lily prisoned in a jail of snow,
> Or ivory in an alablaster band:
> So white a friend engirts so white a foe.

This is the sort of writing that Keats urged on Shelley, when he pressed him to 'load every rift with ore'. It is a writing more intent on making every line 'interesting', linguistically speaking, than in thinking of structural architecture or narrative changes of pace.

A Lover's Complaint (not always ascribed to Shakespeare) resembles *Venus and Adonis* in showing sedulous attention to local effect. When, at the beginning, the weeping and forsaken girl (who eventually voices the complaint, or lament, overheard by the narrator) gazes distractedly in all directions, the poem renders her action in such overladen verse that the putative subject is overcome by its metaphors:

> Sometimes her leveled eyes their carriage ride,
> As they did batt'ry to the spheres intend;
> Sometime diverted their poor balls are tied
> To th'orbèd earth; sometimes they do extend
> Their view right on; anon their gazes lend
> To every place at once, and, nowhere fixed,
> The mind and sight distractedly commixed.

This exercise in Spenserian language (which uses the same rhyme royal stanza as *Lucrece*), concludes as the rejected girl tells the reverend old man to whom she is confessing her plight that she would fall in love with her betrayer all over again (even knowing the extent of his infidelity), so greatly is she beguiled by his beauty. Her lover was 'one by nature's outwards so commended,/That maidens' eyes stuck over all his face.' Her lament is entirely taken up with describing her lover and his persuasive wooing, and he, like the young man of the sonnets, enchants both sexes. The closing stanza of *A Lover's Complaint* shows the same rigidly parallel metaphorical stylization evident in *Venus and Adonis* and, to a lesser extent, in *Lucrece*:

O, that infected moisture of his eye,
O, that false fire which in his cheek so glowed,
O, that forced thunder from his heart did fly,
O, that sad breath his spongy lungs bestowed,
O, all that borrowed motion, seeming owed,
Would yet again betray the fore-betrayed
And new-pervert a reconcilèd maid!

It is evident that the sonnets, too, are highly stylized, highly metaphorical, often constructed in strict parallel metaphors. Why, then, do we prefer them as poems? It is because in them, with a few exceptions (like #145, not a true sonnet and thought to be an early poem punning on hate-away/ Hathaway – the maiden name of Shakespeare's wife), Shakespeare has learned to subordinate local stylistic ornamentation to structural conception.

Though the rhyme scheme used by Shakespeare for his sonnets (*abab cdcd efef gg*) was invented by earlier English poets, none of Shakespeare's predecessors had seen the structural potential in its four-part form – three quatrains and a couplet. This structure makes the Shakespearian sonnet more flexible to permutations and combinations than the Italian sonnet, which has only two structural parts, an octave and a sestet. Because of its essentially binary form, the Italian sonnet lends itself to such structures as question/answer, problem/ solution, description/moral, assertion/retraction, and so on. It was no doubt the difficulty of reproducing the Italian octave (rhyming *abbaabba*) in English that caused Shakespeare and others to experiment with an easier rhyme form. The Shakespearian sonnet can of course be used in a two-part way, imitating the Italian sonnet by arranging itself conceptually in an eight-line beginning followed by a six-line resolution. Some of Shakespeare's sonnets do indeed follow this pattern; #119, for instance, portrays 'ill' in its octave and the 'benefit of ill' in its sestet. But more often, Shakespeare fully exploits the four-part flexibility of his form. Sometimes the octave will indeed behave like an Italian octave and set a problem; but then the third quatrain acts as a resolution, and the subsequent couplet can sum up and totalize the twelve lines that precede it (see, for instance, #129, 'The expense of spirit'). Daring experiments with structure are attempted throughout the sequence (see, for instance, #66, with its division into a one-line introduction, an eleven-line description, and a two-line recapitulation).

The most frequent form in the sonnets is one in which each of the three quatrains acts as a tooth in a gear: each nudges the poem a distinct notch forward by changing the terms of the model which the poem is developing. In #60, for example, the first model of life offered us by the poem is one of steady-state sameness from the physical world:

> Like as the waves make towards the pebbled shore,
> So do our minutes hasten to their end;
> Each changing place with that which goes before,
> In sequent toil all forwards do contend.

But the second model is one of shocking change over a lifetime; it is in fact a four-line allegory of the rise-and-fall model of the tragic drama, used so often by Shakespeare:

> Nativity, once in the main of light,
> Crawls to maturity, wherewith being crowned,
> Crooked eclipses 'gainst his glory fight,
> And Time that gave doth now his gift confound.

But this model, too, is rejected by the speaker as not having given his ultimate sense of life. He goes on, in the third quatrain, to offer a much more horrifying model altogether: here, the process that took four lines in the second quatrain happens much faster, once per line:

> Time doth transfix the flourish set on youth,
> And delves the parallels in beauty's brow,
> Feeds on the rarities of nature's truth,
> And nothing stands but for his scythe to mow.

We notice, too, that whereas Nativity was allowed a time of existence in the main of light, as well as maturity and being crowned, before its eclipse, Shakespeare now frames his clauses so that the transfixing and delving and feeding processes precede, syntactically, the youth and beauty and truth they attack; rarities are destroyed before they even attain a stable existence in the quatrain. If this is the 'real' and 'true' model of what life is like, than it obliterates, in its conceptual horror, the two that precede it. The greatest interest in reading the sonnets lies in our seeing the way Shakespeare interrogates his own conceptions, repudiates them, substitutes better ones, and then goes even further to sum up the whole perpetually self-cancelling process of thinking.

Generalizing sonnets like #60 are scattered through the sequence, and are frequently anthologized. But surely the first thing that strikes every reader of Shakespeare's sonnets is the sense of an oblique, obscure, and buried story in them. Because it has been argued that the 1609 volume may not give the poems in an order that Shakespeare established, this story has been rescripted and rearranged by many past readers and critics, but no entirely convincing total reconstruction of it can be achieved from the fragmentary evidence of the poems. It is possible that Shakespeare had many separate early sonnets in his drawer (like those included in *Love's Labour's Lost* and *Romeo and Juliet*) and inserted his earlier efforts (including the 'non-sonnets' #126 and #145) into two groups of poems written about his relations with a fair young man and a black-haired, black-eyed woman. In the order in which they were printed by the publisher, sonnets #1-126 seem to concern a fair young man. Although the male speaker of the sonnets begins by adjuring the young man to marry and produce an heir (with arguments resembling those of Venus to Adonis), this theme disappears after sonnet #17, and is replaced by the speaker's own infatuation with the young man, who betrays his trust by infidelity, and reproaches the speaker with infidelity as well. The twelve-line 'sonnet' #126, the envoi to the first part of the sequence, consists of six rhymed couplets followed (in the 1609 quarto) by two sets of brackets standing in for the missing couplet, and presumably symbolizing the young man's eventual death, foretold in the last couplet.

Sonnets #127-52 largely concern a 'dark' woman, the speaker's mistress, who plays him false with the fair young man (a triangle that some see reflected as well in sonnets #40-42 of the first group). Sonnets #153 and #154 tell two versions of the same story – how Cupid's fiery brand (a mythological version of the phallus) cannot be quenched or cooled by being plunged (by the nymphs, agents of chastity) into water, but rather will heat the very 'well' (a symbol of the vagina) into which it is dipped. These mythological poems sum up, in classical terms, the impossibility of repressing erotic desire. They glance back at the European sonnet tradition, which regularly invoked mythological personages in a way Shakespeare repudiated in his own sonnet practice.

The 'story' of the sonnets has been questioned by purists, who point out, legitimately, that most of the sonnets, since they address an unspecified and non-gendered 'you', could have been written to almost anyone at almost any time. They take on coloration by being inserted into a sequence containing gendered poems describing erotic relations among the speaker, another man, and a woman – but removed from that sequence, they would not be easily seen as telling a story. Even when a sonnet exhibits verbal links to adjoining sonnets, it can often be shown to possess equally strong verbal links to sonnets far away in the sequence. Barring a hitherto undiscovered ratification of the sonnet-order, we cannot conclusively establish it as Shakespeare's own, nor has anyone been able to propose undisputed historical names for the protagonists. Wordsworth believed the story to be true ('With this key/ Shakespeare unlocked his heart'), but Browning, master of the dramatic monologue, disputed Wordsworth's conclusion ('If so, the less Shakespeare he!'). The American poet John Berryman, adding his opinion, said of sonnet # 144, 'When Shakespeare said, "Two loves I have," Reader, he was not kidding.'

Because most scholars have been drawn to the study of Shakespeare by the plays, they have often seemed to care more about the 'plot' of the sonnets (or, for historical purposes, about the actual identities of the protagonists) than about the sonnets as distinguished lyric poems. Poems do not succeed by being little playlets, *romans à clef*, or psychological documents; poems succeed as new forms of experiment in genre, structure, and language.

How are the sonnets new in these ways? There had been many love-sonnet sequences preceding Shakespeare's, which comes late in literary history, two hundred years after Dante's

La Vita Nuova, which began the vogue continued by Petrarch, Ronsard, and others on the Continent, brought to England via the translations of Wyatt and Surrey, and perfected by Sidney (in *Astrophel and Stella*) and Spenser (in the *Amoretti*). Though poets could have several successive love-objects (like Ronsard's Marie and Hélène), any given group of sonnets normally featured a single lover and a single beloved. Shakespeare complicates his sequence by involving his three chief characters in erotic relations with each other. And he complicates it further by introducing a rival poet or poets in sonnets #78–86. Nor is the speaker guiltless, apparently, of relations with persons other than the young man and the dark lady – he accuses himself to the young man of unspecified infidelities (#109-12 and #117-21). Shakespeare has deliberately opened up the two-character form he inherited and, as the dramatist he would become, populated the love-sequence in new and drastically more interesting ways.

We find in Shakespeare's greatest poem, then, four protagonists orbiting in intersecting circles. This generic innovation opens up opportunities for the depiction of many more aspects of love and jealousy – homoerotic love (sonnet #20 declares that the homosexual desire expressed in the poems has not found sexual expression), heterosexual intercourse, upper-class/lower class relationships – than previous sequences, as well as allowing (in the rival-poet group) opportunities for aesthetic reflection and aesthetic self-description. These variations provide for many metaphorical possibilities, depending on the sex, social status, and aesthetic role of the personages. In inventive metaphorical reach alone, Shakespeare excels his predecessors. In scrapping (except for the last two sonnets) the classical apparatus so necessary to his European predecessors, and in suppressing all mention of the Christian afterlife or of Christian dogma as a whole, Shakespeare becomes distinctively modern among the sonneteers.

One wants to say that Shakespeare's chief triumph in the sonnets is the tormented speaker of these poems, successively passionate, reproachful, abject, grieving, triumphant, coarse, deranged, and classical. It has even been said, in hyperbolic praise, that in these sonnets Shakespeare invented modern subjectivity itself. But this is insufficient praise unless we explain how such a speaker is constructed in verse. Shakespeare's chief psychological invention is to make his speaker change his mind (as we saw in #60) during the course of a sonnet. This is not an entirely new technique; after all, lovers from Petrarch on had expressed remorse after expressing desire. But Shakespeare's speaker does not deal only in such direct antitheses; he frequently alters his position subtly from quatrain to quatrain, as in #129 ('Th'expense of spirit'), where we see him first in a full 'morning-after' retrospective repudiation of lust, and then watch him pass through a blame of the woman and her 'bait/On purpose laid to make the taker mad', until, by going back far enough, he is compelled to re-live his experience chronologically, as it actually occurred:

> A bliss in proof, and proved, a very woe,
> Before, a joy proposed; behind, a dream.

These four nouns – *bliss, woe, joy, dream* – are psychological nouns, whereas the nouns the speaker had begun with in describing lust – *expense, spirit, waste, shame* – were economic, theological, and moral ones, a change revealing to us how far the speaker has come from his original self-blaming position. Finally, the speaker utters his totalizing couplet:

> All this the world well knows, yet none knows well
> To shun the heaven that leads men to this hell.

The retrospective 'well knows' and the chronological 'knows well' face each other in helpless acquiescence to the inevitable repetition of lust – chronologically experienced as proposed joy and a bliss in proof, retrospectively judged as the expense of spirit in a waste of shame, and psychologically expiring in emotional woe and cognitive unreality. We are given, in #129, the two incompatible models of our experience that we live with every day: our retrospective view as we look back on an incident, and the chronological experience of it that we have as we are living it. We are also given, in the couplet, an ironic third model that cognitively embraces the previous two; this, too, is a model we live with every day. By creating a speaker who is at once living chronologically, retrospectively,

SONNETS AND POEMS

and ironically, Shakespeare makes the sonnet-voice ampler
and more psychologically convincing than ever before.

Shakespeare's speaker has more than a single-layered past.
His past has many receding planes, as we can deduce from
#30, in lines like,

> Then can I drown an eye, unused to flow,
> For precious friends hid in death's dateless night,
> And weep afresh love's long since cancelled woe.

We see the protagonist here in a condensed set of six time-
frames: 1) before he fell in love; 2) when he possessed happy
love; 3) when he then found woe in love, and wept; 4) when he
cancelled that woe, and stopped weeping; 5) the long time
during which he didn't weep (when his eyes were 'unused to
flow'); 6) the voluntary renewal of weeping described in the
sonnet. Such a protagonist seems more 'real', psychologically
speaking, than a protagonist depicted as having only a
present, or one looking back to a single past event. Also, this
protagonist represents his summoning of 'remembrance of
things past' as a habitual act, and we therefore regard him as
one who can repeat this survey of many different temporalities
in his past over and over, with different temporalities for
different events. Shakespeare's many-layered description of his
protagonist makes him a more unpredictable *persona* than, for
instance, Astrophel.

In the more public sonnets, Shakespeare discovers other
ways of introducing dynamic change as the poem evolves. In
#66, for example, the speaker watches a procession pass. At
first, he sees only a succession of victims – 'maiden virtue
rudely strumpeted', for instance. Eventually, after we have
seen several such past participles ('trimmed', 'forsworn', 'mis-
placed', 'strumpeted', 'disgraced',) we begin to ask 'Misplaced
by whom?' 'Strumpeted by whom?' As this question becomes
pressing, the procession (keeping its past participles of victi-
mage) enlarges to show victimizers along with their victims:

> And strength by limping sway disabled,
> And art made tongue-tied by authority,
> And folly (doctorlike) controlling skill.

xxiv

The next pressing questions – who gave 'limping sway' the power to disable strength? what sort of authority silences art? who put scholastic folly in control of skill? – are answered by the final tableau in the procession. The last couple arrive, and we see 'captive good attending captain ill'. 'Captain ill' is a secular version of Satan, whom Christianity had called 'the Prince of this world'. The progression of personages in the train – victims; victims accompanied by their victimizers; chief victim attending on chief victimizer – show Shakespeare in this sonnet imitating the dramatic procession in a court masque.

Once we have the hundred and fifty-four sonnets in our head, we feel – as the quatrains and couplets whirl around each other and construct a dense intertextual galaxy – that we replicate inside ourselves the creative ferment of Shakespeare's mind. And yet the enormously logical structure of each developing poem makes us recognize that not only ferment, but minute lexical discrimination, logical hierarchizing, and perpetual comparison and antithesis are going on there as well.

The pathos of the sonnets depends in large part, in fact, on the intertextual reverberations among lines and concepts. The single word 'love', in all its variants, appears in so many contexts – of bitterness, sweetness, exaltation, abjection – that human feelings like love, as we read the sonnets, undergo continual amplification, refinement, and redefinition. Indeed, as # 151 says, 'Who knows not conscience is born of love?' Yet multiplicity breeds, also, continual irony. Sonnet # 152, formally closing the sequence before the Cupid-coda, may serve here to call attention to the greatest triumph of Shakespeare in the sonnets, which is that Shakespeare the writer is always watching 'Shakespeare' the speaker, and constructing both covert and overt ironies between the coolness of writing and the heatedness of loving. The ironies are present from the beginning, as we discover that the apparently 'impersonal truth' generating the whole sequence, 'From fairest creatures we desire increase', is immediately revealed as said not by a disinterested observer, but by one who has a particular fair creature in mind. But the ironies mount to unbearable self-laceration by # 147, as not only the writer but the speaker himself sees the self-contradictions of passion:

> Past cure I am, now reason is past care,
> And frantic-mad with evermore unrest;
> My thoughts and my discourse as madmen's are,
> At random from the truth vainly expressed;
>   For I have sworn thee fair, and thought thee bright,
>   Who art as black as hell, as dark as night.

In # 152, swearing and forswearing rise to such a pitch that the speaker is self-perjured:

> For I have sworn thee fair; more perjured eye,
> To swear against the truth so foul a lie.

The 'perjured [I]' speaks *at random* from the truth, not even predictably (and therefore reassuringly) at variance from it. The trust in language that the poet-speaker once had is no longer present. And since language is his chief form of being, and norm of being, he is extinguished with the extinction of its reliability and verity.

The final erotic despair of the sonnets is strangely contradicted by the powerful allegorical poem 'The Phoenix and Turtle' (customarily called 'The Phoenix and the Turtle'), which suggests that at least one kind of love, a marital love that deliberately produces no offspring, may result in happiness. (Naturally speaking, the pair of birds, female phoenix and male turtle-dove, could not produce offspring of any describable sort.) The poem is written in a solemn and formal trochaic tetrameter, and consists of thirteen quatrains (rhyming *abba*) which constitute the narrative portion of the poem, followed by five tercets (rhyming *aaa*) for the liturgical dirge or threnody that Reason sings, mourning these 'co-supremes and stars of love', the phoenix and the turtle representing Beauty and Truth: 'Truth and Beauty buried be.' It should be noticed that both thirteen and five are prime numbers, indivisible like the phoenix and the turtle. (This poem has given impetus to many subsequent poems, among them Keats' 'Ode on a Grecian Urn' ['Beauty is Truth, Truth Beauty'] and Dickinson's 'I died for Beauty'.)

The convener of the birds who come to mourn the dead pair (a gathering that excludes demonic and predatory birds) praises the marriage of the phoenix and the turtle as a new unity, destroying division yet preserving individuality. We might call this the dream of the androgyne, resuscitated from Plato's myth:

> Reason, in itself confounded,
> Saw division grow together,
> To themselves yet either neither,
> Simple was so well compounded,
>
> That it cried, 'How true a twain
> Seemeth this concordant one!
> Love hath reason, reason none,
> If what parts can so remain.'

Perhaps the single-rhyme triplet-form of the threnody sung by Reason represents the secular trinity formed by the phoenix, the turtle, and the magical new entity formed by their love shining between them – as the Holy Spirit is said to issue from the mutal love of Father and Son:

> So between them love did shine
> That the turtle saw his right
> Flaming in the phoenix sight:
> Either was the other's mine.

Truth, Beauty, and Love could not unite in the sonnets. In this allegory – the most powerful voicing in English of Plato's dream – they kindle by sheer self-ignition into the funeral pyre where Immortality sacrifices her future to die with her chastely erotic and loyal consort, consumed 'in the mutual flame' too purely itself to exist on earth. Only Shakespeare would have had the anthem for the pair sung by Reason. Reason is a standard that, even in frenzy, he never abandoned: 'Past cure I am, now Reason is past care': what Reason did not ratify could not be consonant with full humanity. And yet what Reason does ratify is too good for this world. The phoenix will not be resurrected; there is no other world for her to live in; there is no afterlife for herself and the turtle. There is only the ideal they represent, unforsaken by Shakespeare but, as he knows, unlivable by anyone in the human sphere. As a conclusion to these poems of problematic love and sexuality – a hunt, a rape, a complaint, a vexed triangle – 'The Phoenix and the Turtle' remains both true and anguishing.

Helen Vendler

SELECT BIBLIOGRAPHY

The Shakespeare industry is not in recession or ever likely to be, and the reader will find his or her own way into – and hopefully through – some of the mass. Of general interest are E. K. Chambers, *William Shakespeare: A Study of Facts and Problems*, two vols., Clarendon Press, Oxford, 1930. Sharp biographical focus is present in Samuel Schoenbaum's *William Shakespeare: A Compact Documentary Life*, Oxford University Press, Oxford, 1977. Three periodicals are devoted to Shakespeare in English: the *Shakespeare Survey* and the *Shakespeare Annual*, both published once a year, and the *Shakespeare Quarterly*. Reference to the Sonnets and the Poems, often of article length, will be found in these continuing companions to Shakespeare studies.

TEXTS

W. G. INGRAM and THEODORE REDPATH, eds. *The Sonnets*, University of London Press, London, 1964; reprinted, Hodder & Stoughton, London, 1978. Detailed and scholarly annotation and commentary.

JOHN KERRIGAN, ed., *The Sonnets and A Lover's Complaint*, Penguin Books, London, 1986. Comprehensive introduction and copious annotation.

J. C. MAXWELL, ed. *The Poems*, Cambridge University Press, Cambridge, 1966. Very good generally but light on *A Lover's Complaint*.

F. T. PRINCE, ed. *The Poems*, Methuen, 1960. (*Venus and Adonis, Lucrece, The Passionate Pilgrim, The Phoenix and Turtle*). Excellent introduction and annotation.

MARTIN SEYMOUR-SMITH, ed. *The Sonnets*, Heinemann, London, 1963. Excellent focus on interpretation.

CRITICISM/SCHOLARSHIP

The literature here is so vast that any selection is of necessity arbitrary.

STEPHEN BOOTH, *Essay on Shakespeare's Sonnets*, Yale University Press, New Haven, 1969.

ROBERT GIROUX, *The Book Known as Q: A Consideration of Shakespeare's Sonnets*, Atheneum, New York, 1982.

GERALD HAMMOND, *The Reader and Shakespeare's Young Man Sonnets*, Macmillan, London, 1981.

EDWARD HUBLER, ed., *The Riddle of Shakespeare's Sonnets*, Routledge, London, 1962.

L. C. KNIGHTS, 'Shakespeare's Sonnets', 1934, reprinted in his *Explorations*, Chatto & Windus, London, 1946.

HILTON LANDRY, ed., *New Essays on Shakespeare's Sonnets*, AMS Press, New York, 1976.

J. B. LEISHAM, *Themes and Variations in Shakespeare's Sonnets*, Hutchinson, London, 1961.

ANTHONY LOW, *The Georgic Revolution*, Princeton University Press, Princeton, New Jersey, 1985.

M. M. MAHOOD, *Shakespeare's Wordplay*, Methuen, London, 1957

GIORGIO MELCHIORI, *Shakespeare's Dramatic Meditations: An Experiment in Criticism*, Clarendon Press, Oxford, 1976.

ARTHUR MIZENER, 'The Structure of Figurative Language in Shakespeare's Sonnets', reprinted in *Essays in Shakespearian Criticism*, ed. Calderwood and Toliver, Prentice-Hall, New Jersey, 1970.

KENNETH MUIR, *Shakespeare's Sonnets*, Allen & Unwin, London, 1979.

WINIFRED NOWOTTNY, *The Language Poets Use*, Athlone Press, London, 1962.

PAUL RAMSAY, *The Fickle Glass: A Study of Shakespeare's Sonnets*, AMS Press, New York, 1979.

GEORGE RYLANDS, 'Shakespeare the Poet', in *A Companion to Shakespeare Studies*, ed. Granville-Barker and Harrison, Cambridge University Press, Cambridge, 1941 (on 'A Lover's Complaint').

INGA STINA-EWBANK, 'Shakespeare's Poetry' in *A New Companion to Shakespeare Studies*, ed. Muir and Schoenbaum, Cambridge University Press, Cambridge, 1971.

HELEN VENDLER, 'Jacobson, Richards and Shakespeare's Sonnet CXXIX' in *I. A. Richards: Essays in his Honour*, ed. Brower, Vendler and Hollander, Oxford University Press, New York, 1973.

CHRONOLOGY

DATE	AUTHOR'S LIFE	LITERARY CONTEXT
1564	Born in Stratford, Warwickshire, the eldest surviving son of John Shakespeare, glover and occasional dealer in wool, and Mary Arden, daughter of a prosperous farmer.	Birth of Christopher Marlowe.
1565	John Shakespeare elected Alderman of Stratford.	Clinthio: *Hecatommithi.* Edwards: *Damon and Pythias.*
1566	Birth of Shakespeare's brother Gilbert.	Gascoigne: *Supposes.*
1567		Udall: *Roister Doister.* Golding: *The Stories of Venus and Adonis and of Hermaphroditus and Salamcis.*
1568	His father is elected bailiff.	Gascoigne: *Jocasta.* Wilmot: *Tancred and Gismunda.* Second Edition of Vasari's *Lives of the Artists.*
1569	Probably starts attending the petty school attached to the King's New School in Stratford. Birth of his sister Joan.	
1570	His father involved in money-lending.	
1571	John Shakespeare is elected Chief Alderman and deputy to the new bailiff.	
1572		Whitgift's *Answer* to the 'Admonition' receives Cartwright's *Reply*, beginning the first literary debate between Anglicans and Puritans.
1573		Tasso: *Aminta.*
1574	Probably enters the Upper School (where studies include rhetoric, logic, the Latin poets, and a little Greek). Birth of his brother Richard.	

Death of Michelangelo. Birth of Galileo.

Rebellion against Spain in the Netherlands. Birth of the actor Edward Alleyn.
Birth of the actor Richard Burbage.

Mary Stuart flees to England from Scotland.

Northern Rebellion.

Excommunication of Elizabeth. Baif's Academy founded in Paris to promote poetry, music and dance.
Ridolfi Plot. Puritan 'Admonition' to Parliament.

Dutch rebels conquer Holland and Zeeland. Massacre of St Bartholomew's Day in Paris.

Accession of Henry III and new outbreak of civil war in France. First Catholic missionaries arrive in England from Douai. Earl of Leicester's Men obtain licence to perform within the City of London.

DATE	AUTHOR'S LIFE	LITERARY CONTEXT
1575		*Gammer Gurton's Needle* is printed.
1576		Castiglione's *The Book of the Courtier* banned by the Spanish Inquisition. George Gascoigne: *The Steel Glass*.
1577		John Northbrooke's attack in *Treatise wherein Dicing, Dancing, Vain Plays etc are reproved*.
1578	Shakespeare family fortunes are in decline, and John is having to sell off property to pay off his increasing debts.	Sidney writes *The Lady of May* and begins the 'Old' *Arcadia*. George Whetstone: *Promos and Cassandra*. John Lyly: *Euphues, the Anatomy of Wit*. Pierre de Ronsard, leader of the Pléiade, publishes his *Sonnets pour Hélène*. He is said to have exercised a considerable influence on the English sonnet-writers of the sixteenth century.
1579		Spenser: *The Shepherd's Calendar*. North: translation of Plutarch. Gossen: *The School of Abuse, and Pleasant Invective against Poets, Pipers, Players etc*.
1580	Birth of Shakespeare's brother Edmund.	
1581		John Newton's translation of Seneca's *Ten Tragedies*. Barnaby Rich: *Apolonius and Silla*.
1582	Shakespeare marries Anne Hathaway, a local farmer's daughter, 7 or 8 years his senior, who is already pregnant with their first child.	Tasso: *Gerusalemme Liberata*. Watson: *Hekatompathia* (First sonnet sequence published in England). Whetstone: *Heptameron of Civil Discourses*. Sidney begins *Astrophel and Stella* and the 'New' *Arcadia*. Lope de Vega writing for the Corrals in Madrid.

CHRONOLOGY

HISTORICAL EVENTS

Kenilworth Revels.

Restricted by the City of London's order that no plays be performed within
the City boundaries, James Burbage of The Earl of Leicester's Men builds
The Theatre only just outside the boundaries in Shoreditch. The Blackfriars
Theatre is built. End of civil war in France. Observatory of Uraniborg built
for the Danish astronomer, Tycho Brahe. Death of Titian.
Drake's circumnavigation of the world. The Curtain Theatre built. Birth of
Rubens.

First visit to England of the duc d'Alençon as a suitor to Elizabeth,
provoking much opposition to a French match. The Corral de la Cruz built
in Madrid.

Spanish conquest of Portugal. Jesuit mission arrives in England from Rome
led by Edmund Campion and Parsons.
Stricter enforcement of treason laws and increased penalties on recusants.
Campion captured and executed. Northern provinces of the Netherlands
renounce their allegiance to Phillip II, and invite the duc d'Alençon to be
their sovereign.
Sir Walter Ralegh established in the Queen's favour. The Corral del Principe
built in Madrid.

DATE	AUTHOR'S LIFE	LITERARY CONTEXT
1583	Birth of their daughter Susanna.	
1583-4	The players' companies of the Earls of Essex, Oxford and Leicester perform in Stratford.	Giordarno Bruno visits England.
1584		Bruno publishes two works dedicated to his English patron, Sidney. Reginald Scott: *The Discovery of Witchcraft*.
1585	Birth of Shakespeare's twins Hamnet and Judith. The following years until 1592 are the 'Lost Years' for which no documentary records of his life survive, only legends such as the one of deer-stealing and flight from prosecution, and conjectures such as ones that he became a schoolmaster, travelled in Europe, or went to London to be an actor as early as the mid 1580s.	Death of Pierre de Ronsard.
1586		Timothy Bright: *A Treatise of Melancholy*.
1586-7	Five players' companies visit Stratford, including the Queen's, Essex's, Leicester's and Stafford's.	
1587		Holinshed: *Chronicles of England Scotland and Ireland*. Marlowe: First part of *Tamburlaine the Great* acted. New edition of *The Mirror for Magistrates*.
1588		Marlowe: Second part of *Tamburlaine*. Thomas Kyd: *The Spanish Tragedy*. Lope de Vega, serving with the Armada, writes some of *The Beauty of Angelica*.

CHRONOLOGY

HISTORICAL EVENTS

First meeting of the Durham House Set led by Ralegh, Northumberland and Harriot, to promote mathematics, astronomy and navigation. Archbishop Whitgift leads more extreme anti-Puritan policy. Throckmorton plot, involving the Spanish ambassador.

Death of d'Alençon. Assassination of William of Orange. The Teatro Olimpico, Vicenza, built by Palladio.

England sends military aid to the Dutch rebels under the command of Leicester. Ralegh organizes the colonization of Virginia.

Babington plot. Death of Sir Philip Sidney. Rise of the Earl of Essex. Colonization of Munster.

Execution of Mary Stuart. Drake's raid on Cadiz.

Defeat of the Armada. Death of the Earl of Leicester. The first of the Puritan Marprelate Tracts published.

DATE	AUTHOR'S LIFE	LITERARY CONTEXT
1589	The earliest likely date at which Shakespeare began composition of his first plays (1 *Henry VI*, *The Taming of the Shrew*) when he would have been working as an actor at The Theatre, with Burbage's company.	Marlowe: *The Jew of Malta*. Thomas Nashe: *The Anatomy of Absurdity*. Richard Hakluyt: *Principal Navigations, Voyages and Discoveries of the English nation*.
1590	2 *Henry VI*, 3 *Henry VI*.	Spenser: First 3 books of *The Faerie Queen*. Publication of Sidney's 'New' *Arcadia*. Nashe: *An Almond for a Parrot*, one of the Marprelate Tracts. Greene: *Menaphon*. Guarina: *The Faithful Shepherd*.
1590-1	*King John, Titus Andronicus* written.	
1590-2	Performances of *Henry VI*, parts 2 and 3, *Titus* and *The Shrew* by the Earl of Pembroke's Men.	
1591	*Richard III* and *The Comedy of Errors* written.	Spenser's *Complaints* which includes his translation of fifteen of Joachim du Bellay's sonnets – du Bellay was a member of the Pléiade and responsible for its manifesto. Sir John Harington's translation of *Orlando Furioso*. Publication of Sidney's *Astrophel and Stella*.
1592	First recorded reference to Shakespeare as an actor and playwright in Greene's attack in *The Groatsworth of Wit* describing him as 'an upstart crow'.	Samuel Daniel: *Delia*. Marlowe's *Edward II* and *Doctor Faustus* performed. *Arden of Feversham* printed. Nashe: *Strange News*.
1593	Publication of *Venus and Adonis*, dedicated to the Earl of Southampton. The *Sonnets* probably begun.	Marlowe: *Massacre of Paris*. *The Phoenix Nest*, miscellany of poems including ones by Ralegh, Lodge and Breton. Barnabe Barnes: *Parthenophil and Parthenope*. George Peele: *The Honour of the Garter*. Lodge: *Phillis*. Nashe: *Christ's Tears over Jerusalem*.

CHRONOLOGY

HISTORICAL EVENTS

Failure of the Portugal expedition. Henry III of France assassinated. English military aid sent to Henry of Navarre. Marlowe's tutor, Francis Ket, burned at the stake for atheism.

English government discovers and suppresses the Puritan printing press.

Earl of Essex given command of the English army in France. The last fight of the *Revenge* under Spanish attack.

Capture of Madre de Dios. Split in the main players' company. Shakespeare and Burbage's group remain at The Theatre, Alleyn's move to the Rose on Bankside. Plague in London: the theatres closed.

Marlowe arrested on blasphemy charges and murdered two weeks later. Kyd arrested for libel. Henry of Navarre converts to Catholicism in order to unite France.

SONNETS AND POEMS

DATE	AUTHOR'S LIFE	LITERARY CONTEXT
1593–4	*The Two Gentlemen of Verona.*	
1593–6		John Donne writing his early poems, the Satires and Elegies.
1594	*The Rape of Lucrece* dedicated to his patron Southampton. *The Comedy of Errors* and *Titus Andronicus* performed at the Rose. Shakespeare established as one of the shareholders in his company, The Chamberlain's Men, which performs before the Queen during the Christmas festivities.	Daniel: *Cleopatra.* Spenser: *Amoretti* and *Epithalamion.* Drayton: *Idea's Mirror.* Nashe: *The Terrors of the Night, The Unfortunate Traveller.* Greene: *Friar Bacon and Friar Bungay.*
1594–5	*Love's Labour's Lost* and *Romeo and Juliet* written.	
1595	*Richard II.*	Daniel: *The First Four Books of the Civil Wars between the two houses of Lancaster and York.* Sidney: *Defence of Poesy* published. Ralegh: *The Discovery of the Empire of Guiana.*
1595–6	*A Midsummer Night's Dream.*	
1596	Death of his son, Hamnet. *The Merchant of Venice.* Shakespeare living in Bishopsgate ward. His father, John, is granted a coat of arms.	Lodge: *Wits Miserle.* First complete edition of Spenser's *Faerie Queen.*
1597	*Henry IV* Part 1. First performance of *The Merry Wives of Windsor.* Shakespeare's company now under the patronage of the new Lord Chamberlain, Hunsdon. In Stratford, Shakespeare buys New Place, the second largest house in the town, with its own orchards and vines.	John Donne writes 'The Storme' and 'The Calme'. Francis Bacon: first edition of *Essays.* Jonson and Nashe imprisoned for writing *The Isle of Dogs.*
1597–8	*Henry IV* Part 2.	
1598	Shakespeare one of the 'principal comedians' with Richard Burbage, Heminge and Cordell in Jonson's *Every Man in his Humour.* For the second year, Shakespeare is listed as having failed to pay tax levied on all householders.	Publication of Sidney's *Works* and of Marlowe's *Hero and Leander* (together with Chapman's continuation). *Seven Books of the Iliads* (first of Chapman's Homeric translations). Meres: *Palladia Tamia.*

xl

HISTORICAL EVENTS

Henry of Navarre accepted as King in Paris. Rebellion in Ireland. The London theatres re-open. The Swan Theatre is built. Ralegh accused of blasphemy.

France declares war on Spain. Failure of the Indies voyage and death of Hawkins. Ralegh's expedition to Guiana.

England joins France in the war against Spain. Death of Drake. Raid on Cadiz led by Essex. In long standing power struggle with Essex, Robert Cecil is appointed Secretary of State.

Islands Voyage led by Essex and Ralegh. The government suppresses the *Isle of Dogs* at the Swan and closes the theatres. Despite the continued hostility of the City of London, they soon re-open. James Burbage builds the second Blackfriars Theatre. Death of James Burbage.

Peace between France and Spain. Death of Philip II. Tyrone defeats the English at Armagh. Essex appointed Lord Deputy of Ireland.

DATE	AUTHOR'S LIFE	LITERARY CONTEXT
1598 *cont*		New edition of Lodge's *Rosalynde*. Lope de Vega: *La Arcadia*. James VI of Scotland: *The True Law of Free Monarchies*.
1598–9	*As You Like It*.	
1598–1600	*Much Ado About Nothing*.	
1599	*Henry V, Julius Caesar*. Shakespeare one of the shareholders in the Globe Theatre. He moves lodgings to Bankside. Publication of *The Passionate Pilgrim*, a miscellany of 20 poems, at least 5 by Shakespeare.	Jonson: *Every Man out of his Humour*. Dekker: *The Shoemaker's Holiday*. Sir John Hayward: *The First Part of the Life and Reign of King Henry IV*. Greene's translation of *Orlando Furioso*.
1600		'England's Helicon'.
1600–1	*Hamlet* (Performed with Burbage as the Prince and Shakespeare as the Ghost.)	
1601	*The Phoenix and the Turtle, Troilus and Cressida*. The Lord Chamberlain's Men paid by one of Essex's followers to perform *Richard II* on the day before the rebellion. Death of John Shakespeare.	
1602	Shakespeare buys more property in Stratford.	
1602–4	*Alls Well That Ends Well*.	
1603	Shakespeare's company now under the patronage of King James. Shakespeare is one of the principal tragedians in Jonson's *Sejanus*.	Montaigne's *Essays* translated into English. Thomas Heywood: *A Woman Killed with Kindness*.
1604	Shakespeare known to be lodging in Silver Street with a Huguenot family called Mountjoy. *Othello*; first performance of *Measure for Measure*.	Chapman: *Bussy d'Ambois*. Marston: *The Malcontent*.
1604–5	Ten of his plays performed at court by the King's Men.	

The Burbage brothers, Richard and Cuthbert, pull down The Theatre and, with its timbers, build the Globe on Bankside. Essex's campaign fails in Ireland, and after returning without permission to court he is arrested. The government suppresses satirical writings, and burns pamphlets by Nashe and Harvey.

Essex released but still in disgrace. The Fortune Theatre built by Alleyn and Henslowe. Bruno executed for heresy by the Inquisition in Rome.

Essex's Rebellion. Essex and Southampton arrested, and the former executed. Spanish invasion of Ireland. Monopolies debates in Parliament.

Spanish troops defeated in Ireland.

Death of Elizabeth, and accession of James I. Ralegh imprisoned in the Tower. Plague in London. Sir Thomas Bodley re-founds the library of Oxford University.

Peace with Spain. Hampton Court Conference.

SONNETS AND POEMS

DATE	AUTHOR'S LIFE	LITERARY CONTEXT
1605	First performance of *King Lear* at the Globe, with Burbage as the King, and Robert Armin as the Fool. Shakespeare makes further investments in Stratford, buying a half interest in a lease of tithes.	Cervantes: *Don Quixote* (part one). Bacon: *The Proficience and Advancement of Learning.* Jonson and Inigo Jones: *The Masque of Blackness.* Jonson and co-authors imprisoned for libellous references to the court in *Eastward Ho.*
1605–6		Jonson: *Volpone.*
1606	First performance of *Macbeth.*	John Ford's masque *Honour Triumphant.*
1606–7	*Antony and Cleopatra.*	
1607	Susanna marries John Hall, a physician. Death of Shakespeare's brother Edmund, an actor.	Tourneur's *The Revenger's Tragedy* printed. Barnes: *The Devil's Charter.*
1607–8	*Coriolanus, Pericles.*	
1608	Shakespeare one of the Shareholders in the Blackfriars Theatre. Death of his mother.	Lope de Vega: *Peribanez.* Beaumont and Fletcher: *Philaster.* Jonson and Jones: *The Masque of Beauty.* Donne writes *La Corona.* Twelve books of Homer's *Iliad* (Chapman's translation).
1609	Publication, probably unauthorized, of the quarto edition of the *Sonnets* and *A Lover's Complaint.*	Jonson and Jones: *The Masque of Queens.* Donne's 'The Expiration' printed; 'Liturgie' and 'On the Annunciation' written. Bacon: *De Sapientia Veterum.* Lope de Vega: *New Art of Writing Plays for the Theatre.*
1609–10	*Cymbeline.*	
1610		Donne: *Pseudo-Martyr* printed and *The First Anniversarie* written. Jonson: *The Alchemist.* Beaumont and Fletcher: *The Maid's Tragedy.*
1610–11	*The Winter's Tale.*	
1611	*The Tempest* performed in the Banqueting House, Whitehall. Simon Forman records seeing performances of *Macbeth, The Winter's Tale* and *Cymbeline.*	Beaumont and Fletcher: *A King and No King, The Knight of the Burning Pestle.* Tourneur: *The Atheist's Tragedy.*

CHRONOLOGY

HISTORICAL EVENTS

Gunpowder Plot.

Monteverdi: *Orfeo*.
Bacon appointed Solicitor General.

Galileo's experiments with the telescope confirm the Copernican theory.
Kepler draws up 'Laws of Planetary Motion'. Twelve year Truce between
Spain and Netherlands.

Galileo: *The Starry Messenger*. Assassination of Henry IV of France.
Parliament submits the Petition of Grievances.

The Inquisition of Rome begins investigating Galileo.

DATE	AUTHOR'S LIFE	LITERARY CONTEXT
1611 *cont*		Jonson and Jones: *Masque of Oberon.* Authorized Version of the Bible. Sir John Davies; *The Scourge of Folly.* Donne writes the *The Second Anniversarie* and a 'A Valediction: forbidding mourning'.
1612	Shakespeare appears as a witness in a Court of Requests case involving a dispute over a dowry owed by his former landlord, Mountjoy, to his son-in-law, Belott. Death of his brother Gilbert.	Webster: *The White Devil* printed. Tourneur: *The Nobleman.* Lope de Vega: *Fuente Ovejuna.*
1613	At a performance of his last play, *Henry VIII*, the Globe Theatre catches fire and is destroyed. As part of the court celebrations for the marriage of Queen Elizabeth, The King's Men perform 14 plays, including *Much Ado, Othello, The Winter's Tale* and *The Tempest.* Death of his brother Richard.	Sir Thomas Overbury: *The Wife.* Donne: 'Good Friday' and 'Epithalamion' on Princess Elizabeth's marriage. Cervantes: *Novelas ejemplares* – a collection of short stories.
1614	In Stratford, Shakespeare protects his property interests during a controversy over a threat to enclose the common fields.	Jonson: *Bartholomew Fair.* Webster: *The Duchess of Malfi.* Ralegh: *The History of the World.*
1615	The Warwick Assizes issue an order to prevent enclosures, which ends the dispute in Stratford.	Cervantes publishes 8 plays and *Don Quixote* (part two).
1616	Marriage of his daughter Judith to Thomas Quincy, a vintner, who a month later is tried for fornication with another woman whom he had made pregnant. Death of Shakespeare (23 April).	Jonson: *The Devil is an Ass.* Jonson publishes his *Works.*
1623	The players Heminge and Condell publish the plays of the First Folio.	

CHRONOLOGY

Death of Henry, Prince of Wales.

Marriage of Princess Elizabeth to Frederick, Elector Palatine. Bacon appointed Attorney-General.

The second Globe and the Hope Theatre built.

Inquiry into the murder of Sir Thomas Overbury in the Tower implicates the wife of the King's favourite, Somerset.

Ralegh released from the Tower to lead an expedition to Guiana; on his return he is executed.

WILLIAM
SHAKESPEARE

———

THE SONNETS

Edited by William Burto

TO THE ONLY BEGETTER OF
THESE ENSUING SONNETS
MR. W. H. ALL HAPPINESS
AND THAT ETERNITY
PROMISED
BY
OUR EVER-LIVING POET
WISHETH
THE WELL-WISHING
ADVENTURER IN
SETTING
FORTH
                                    T.T.

The initials concluding the dedication are those of Thomas Thorpe, the publisher of the volume. The identity of Mr. W. H. is uncertain. Most persons who write on the subject have felt it too prosaic to hold that Mr. W. H. was simply a person who brought the poems into the publisher's hands; rather, they have sought to identify him with the friend to whom many of the poems are addressed. The favorite candidates are William Herbert, Earl of Pembroke (and one of the dedicatees of the First Folio), and Henry Wriothesley, Earl of Southampton (to whom Shakespeare dedicated *Venus and Adonis* and *Lucrece*). But it is unlikely that an earl would be addressed as "Mr." Yet another candidate is Sir William Hervey, third husband of Southampton's mother; his advocates say that Hervey was the "begetter" in the sense that he may have encouraged Shakespeare to write the sonnets urging the young man (allegedly Southampton) to wed.

THE SONNETS

I From fairest creatures we desire increase,
That thereby beauty's rose might never die,
But as the riper should by time decease,
4 His tender heir might bear his memory;
But thou contracted to thine own bright eyes,
Feed'st thy light's flame with self-substantial fuel,
Making a famine where abundance lies,
8 Thyself thy foe, to thy sweet self too cruel.
Thou that art now the world's fresh ornament,
And only herald to the gaudy spring,
Within thine own bud buriest thy content,
12 And, tender churl, mak'st waste in niggarding.
    Pity the world, or else this glutton be,
    To eat the world's due, by the grave and thee.

2 When forty winters shall besiege thy brow,
And dig deep trenches in thy beauty's field,
Thy youth's proud livery, so gazed on now,
4 Will be a tottered weed of small worth held:
Then being asked where all thy beauty lies,
Where all the treasure of thy lusty days,
To say within thine own deep-sunken eyes,
8 Were an all-eating shame and thriftless praise.
How much more praise deserved thy beauty's use,
If thou couldst answer, "This fair child of mine
Shall sum my count, and make my old excuse,"
12 Proving his beauty by succession thine.
    This were to be new made when thou art old,
    And see thy blood warm when thou feel'st it cold.

1: 5 **contracted** betrothed 6 **self-substantial fuel** fuel of your own substance 10 **only** chief 11 **thy content** what you contain, i.e., potential fatherhood 12 **niggarding** hoarding 14 **world's due** i.e., propagation of the species 14 **by the grave and thee** i.e., by dying without children

2: 2 **trenches** i.e., wrinkles 3 **livery** outward appearance 4 **tottered weed** tattered garment 6 **lusty** vigorous 8 **thriftless** unprofitable 9 **use** investment 11 **sum my count** even out my account 11 **my old excuse** excuse when I am old

3

3   Look in thy glass and tell the face thou viewest
      Now is the time that face should form another,
      Whose fresh repair if now thou not renewest,
4   Thou dost beguile the world, unbless some mother.
      For where is she so fair whose uneared womb
      Disdains the tillage of thy husbandry?
      Or who is he so fond will be the tomb
8   Of his self-love to stop posterity?
      Thou art thy mother's glass, and she in thee
      Calls back the lovely April of her prime;
      So thou through windows of thine age shalt see,
12   Despite of wrinkles, this thy golden time.
        But if thou live rememb'red not to be,
        Die single and thine image dies with thee.

4   Unthrifty loveliness, why dost thou spend
      Upon thyself thy beauty's legacy?
      Nature's bequest gives nothing but doth lend,
4   And being frank she lends to those are free.
      Then, beauteous niggard, why dost thou abuse
      The bounteous largess given thee to give?
      Profitless usurer, why dost thou use
8   So great a sum of sums yet canst not live?
      For having traffic with thyself alone,
      Thou of thyself thy sweet self dost deceive.
      Then how when Nature calls thee to be gone,
12   What acceptable audit canst thou leave?
        Thy unused beauty must be tombed with thee,
        Which, usèd, lives th' executor to be.

3: **fresh repair** youthful state 4 **unbless some mother** leave some woman unblessed with motherhood 5 **uneared** untilled 7 **fond** foolish 8 **Of** because of 13 **rememb'red not to be** only to be forgotten

4: 2 **beauty's legacy** inheritance of beauty 4 **frank ... free** (both words mean "generous") 5 **niggard** miser 7 **use** (1) invest (2) use up 8 **live** (1) make a living (2) endure 9 **traffic** commerce 14 **lives** i.e., in a son

5   Those hours that with gentle work did frame
    The lovely gaze where every eye doth dwell
    Will play the tyrants to the very same
4   And that unfair which fairly doth excel;
    For never-resting Time leads summer on
    To hideous winter and confounds him there,
    Sap checked with frost and lusty leaves quite gone,
8   Beauty o'ersnowed and bareness everywhere.
    Then, were not summer's distillation left
    A liquid prisoner pent in walls of glass,
    Beauty's effect with beauty were bereft,
12 Nor it nor no remembrance what it was.
      But flowers distilled though they with winter meet,
      Leese but their show, their substance still lives sweet.

6   Then let not winter's ragged hand deface
    In thee thy summer ere thou be distilled.
    Make sweet some vial; treasure thou some place
4   With beauty's treasure ere it be self-killed.
    That use is not forbidden usury
    Which happies those that pay the willing loan;
    That's for thyself to breed another thee,
8   Or ten times happier be it ten for one.
    Ten times thyself were happier than thou art,
    If ten of thine ten times refigured thee:
    Then what could death do if thou shouldst depart,
12 Leaving thee living in posterity?
      Be not self-willed, for thou art much too fair,
      To be death's conquest and make worms thine heir.

5: 1 **hours** (disyllabic) 2 **gaze** object gazed on 4 **unfair** make ugly
4 **fairly** in beauty 6 **confounds** destroys 9 **summer's distillation**
perfumes made from flowers 11 **Beauty's effect** i.e., the perfume 12 **Nor
... nor** (there would be) neither ... nor 14 **Leese but their show** lose only
their outward form

6: 1 **ragged** rough 3 **treasure** enrich 5 **use** lending money at interest
6 **happies ... loan** makes happy those who willingly pay the loan 9 **happier**
luckier 10 **refigured** represented

7   Lo, in the orient when the gracious light
    Lifts up his burning head, each under eye
    Doth homage to his new-appearing sight,
4   Serving with looks his sacred majesty;
    And having climbed the steep-up heavenly hill,
    Resembling strong youth in his middle age,
    Yet mortal looks adore his beauty still,
8   Attending on his golden pilgrimage;
    But when from highmost pitch, with weary car,
    Like feeble age he reeleth from the day,
    The eyes, 'fore duteous, now converted are
12 From his low tract and look another way:
        So thou, thyself outgoing in thy noon,
        Unlooked on diest unless thou get a son.

8   Music to hear, why hear'st thou music sadly?
    Sweets with sweets war not, joy delights in joy.
    Why lov'st thou that which thou receiv'st not gladly,
4   Or else receiv'st with pleasure thine annoy?
    If the true concord of well tunèd sounds,
    By unions married, do offend thine ear,
    They do but sweetly chide thee, who confounds
8   In singleness the parts that thou shouldst bear.
    Mark how one string, sweet husband to another,
    Strikes each in each by mutual ordering;
    Resembling sire, and child, and happy mother,
12 Who all in one, one pleasing note do sing;
        Whose speechless song, being many, seeming one,
        Sings this to thee, "Thou single wilt prove none."

7: 1 **orient** east 1 **light** sun 2 **under** i.e., earthly 7 **looks** onlookers 9 **highmost pitch** zenith 9 **car** chariot (of Phoebus) 11 **converted** turned away 12 **tract** track 14 **get** beget

8: 1 **Music to hear** you who are music to hear 1 **sadly** gravely 7–8 **confounds ... bear** i.e., destroys by playing singly the multiple role (of husband and father) that you should play 9 **sweet husband to another** i.e., tuned in unison (so that when struck, its partner vibrates) 14 **none** nothing

9   Is it for fear to wet a widow's eye
That thou consum'st thyself in single life?
Ah, if thou issueless shalt hap to die,
4   The world will wail thee like a makeless wife;
The world will be thy widow and still weep,
That thou no form of thee hast left behind,
When every private widow well may keep,
8   By children's eyes, her husband's shape in mind.
Look what an unthrift in the world doth spend,
Shifts but his place, for still the world enjoys it;
But beauty's waste hath in the world an end,
12   And kept unused, the user so destroys it:
     No love toward others in that bosom sits
     That on himself such murd'rous shame commits.

10   For shame, deny that thou bear'st love to any
Who for thyself art so unprovident.
Grant if thou wilt, thou art beloved of many,
4   But that thou none lov'st is most evident;
For thou art so possessed with murd'rous hate,
That 'gainst thyself thou stick'st not to conspire,
Seeking that beauteous roof to ruinate,
8   Which to repair should be thy chief desire.
O, change thy thought, that I may change my mind.
Shall hate be fairer lodged than gentle love?
Be as thy presences is, gracious and kind,
12   Or to thyself at least kind-hearted prove.
     Make thee another self for love of me,
     That beauty still may live in thine or thee.

9: 3 **issueless** childless 3 **hap** happen, chance 4 **makeless** mateless
5 **still** always 7 **private** individual 9 **Look what** whatever 9 **unthrift**
prodigal 10 **his** its 14 **murd'rous shame** shameful murder

10: 6 **thou stick'st** you scruple 7 **roof** i.e., body (which houses the spirit)
11 **presence** appearance 14 **still** always

7

11   As fast as thou shalt wane, so fast thou grow'st
      In one of thine, from that which thou departest;
      And that fresh blood which youngly thou bestow'st
4   Thou mayst call thine, when thou from youth convertest.
      Herein lives wisdom, beauty, and increase;
      Without this, folly, age, and cold decay.
      If all were minded so, the times should cease,
8   And threescore year would make the world away.
      Let those whom Nature hath not made for store,
      Harsh, featureless, and rude, barrenly perish.
      Look whom she best endowed, she gave the more;
12   Which bounteous gift thou shouldst in bounty cherish.
          She carved thee for her seal, and meant thereby
          Thou shouldst print more, not let that copy die.

12   When I do count the clock that tells the time,
      And see the brave day sunk in hideous night;
      When I behold the violet past prime,
4   And sable curls are silvered o'er with white;
      When lofty trees I see barren of leaves,
      Which erst from heat did canopy the herd,
      And summer's green, all girded up in sheaves,
8   Borne on the bier with white and bristly beard;
      Then of thy beauty do I question make,
      That thou among the wastes of time must go,
      Since sweets and beauties do themselves forsake,
12   And die as fast as they see other grow,
          And nothing 'gainst Time's scythe can make defense,
          Save breed, to brave him when he takes thee hence.

11: 3 **youngly** in youth   4 **Thou ... convertest** you ... change   6 **Without
this** beyond this course of action   7 **times** generations of men   9 **for store**
as stock to draw upon   10 **featureless, and rude** ugly and unrefined.
11 **Look whom** whomever   13 **seal** stamp

12: 2 **brave** splendid   4 **sable** black   6 **erst** formerly   9 **question make**
entertain doubt   14 **Save breed, to brave** except offspring, to defy

13   O, that you were yourself, but, love, you are
      No longer yours than you yourself here live;
      Against this coming end you should prepare,
4   And your sweet semblance to some other give.
      So should that beauty which you hold in lease
      Find no determination, then you were
      Yourself again after your self's decease,
8   When your sweet issue your sweet form should bear.
      Who lets so fair a house fall to decay,
      Which husbandry in honor might uphold
      Against the stormy gusts of winter's day
12   And barren rage of death's eternal cold?
        O, none but unthrifts! Dear my love, you know,
        You had a father; let your son say so.

14   Not from the stars do I my judgment pluck,
      And yet methinks I have astronomy;
      But not to tell of good or evil luck,
4   Of plagues, of dearths, or seasons' quality;
      Nor can I fortune to brief minutes tell,
      Pointing to each his thunder, rain, and wind,
      Or say with princes if it shall go well
8   By oft predict that I in heaven find.
      But from thine eyes my knowledge I derive,
      And, constant stars, in them I read such art
      As truth and beauty shall together thrive
12   If from thyself to store thou wouldst convert:
        Or else of thee this I prognosticate,
        Thy end is truth's and beauty's doom and date.

13: 3 **Against** in expectation of   5 **in lease** i.e., for a term   6 **determination** end   8 **issue** offspring   10 **husbandry** (1) thrift (2) marriage   13 **unthrifts** prodigals

14: 1 **pluck** derive   2 **astronomy** astrology   5 **fortune to brief minutes tell** i.e., predict the exact time of each happening   6 **Pointing** appointing   6 **his** its   8 **oft predict** that frequent prediction of what   10 **art** knowledge   11 **As** as that   12 **store** fertility   12 **convert** turn   14 **doom and date** end, Judgment Day

15 When I consider everything that grows
    Holds in perfection but a little moment,
    That this huge stage presenteth naught but shows
4   Whereon the stars in secret influence comment;
    When I perceive that men as plants increase,
    Cheerèd and checked even by the selfsame sky,
    Vaunt in their youthful sap, at height decrease,
8   And wear their brave state out of memory;
    Then the conceit of this inconstant stay
    Sets you most rich in youth before my sight,
    Where wasteful Time debateth with Decay,
12 To change your day of youth to sullied night;
        And, all in war with Time for love of you,
        As he takes from you, I engraft you new.

16 But wherefore do not you a mightier way
    Make war upon this bloody tyrant Time?
    And fortify yourself in your decay
4   With means more blessèd than my barren rhyme?
    Now stand you on the top of happy hours,
    And many maiden gardens, yet unset,
    With virtuous wish would bear your living flowers,
8   Much liker than your painted counterfeit.
    So should the lines of life that life repair,
    Which this time's pencil, or my pupil pen,
    Neither in inward worth nor outward fair
12 Can make you live yourself in eyes of men.
        To give away yourself keeps yourself still,
        And you must live, drawn by your own sweet skill.

15: 4 **in secret influence comment** i.e., exert a silent influence   6 **Cheerèd and checked** encouraged and rebuked   7 **Vaunt** boast   8 **wear their brave state out of memory** wear out their handsome condition until it is forgotten   9 **conceit** idea   9 **stay** duration   11 **debateth** contends   14 **engraft** i.e., with eternizing poetry

16: 6 **unset** unplanted   8 **counterfeit** portrait   9 **lines of life** lineal descendants   10 **time's pencil** artist of the present day   11 **fair** beauty   13 **give away yourself** i.e., to beget children   13 **keeps** preserves

17 Who will believe my verse in time to come
    If it were filled with your most high deserts?
    Though yet heaven knows it is but as a tomb
4   Which hides your life and shows not half your parts.
    If I could write the beauty of your eyes,
    And in fresh numbers number all your graces,
    The age to come would say "This poet lies,
8   Such heavenly touches ne'er touched earthly faces."
    So should my papers, yellowed with their age,
    Be scorned, like old men of less truth than tongue,
    And your true rights be termed a poet's rage
12 And stretchèd meter of an antique song:
        But were some child of yours alive that time,
        You should live twice, in it and in my rhyme.

18 Shall I compare thee to a summer's day?
    Thou art more lovely and more temperate.
    Rough winds do shake the darling buds of May,
4   And summer's lease hath all too short a date.
    Sometime too hot the eye of heaven shines,
    And often is his gold complexion dimmed;
    And every fair from fair sometime declines,
8   By chance, or nature's changing course, untrimmed;
    But thy eternal summer shall not fade,
    Nor lose possession of that fair thou ow'st,
    Nor shall Death brag thou wand'rest in his shade,
12 When in eternal lines to time thou grow'st.
        So long as men can breathe or eyes can see,
        So long lives this, and this gives life to thee.

17: 2 **deserts** (rhymes with "parts") 4 **parts** good qualities 6 **numbers** verses 8 **touches** (1) strokes of pencil or brush (2) traits 11 **true rights** due praise 11 **rage** inspiration 12 **stretchèd meter** poetic exaggeration

18: 4 **lease** allotted time 4 **date** duration 7 **fair from fair** beautiful thing from beauty 8 **untrimmed** divested of ornament 10 **thou ow'st** you possess

19   Devouring Time, blunt thou the lion's paws,
      And make the earth devour her own sweet brood;
      Pluck the keen teeth from the fierce tiger's jaws,
4   And burn the long-lived phoenix in her blood;
      Make glad and sorry seasons as thou fleets,
      And do whate'er thou wilt, swift-footed Time,
      To the wide world and all her fading sweets;
8   But I forbid thee one most heinous crime,
      O, carve not with thy hours my love's fair brow,
      Nor draw no lines there with thine antique pen.
      Him in thy course untainted do allow,
12 For beauty's pattern to succeeding men.
        Yet do thy worst, old Time; despite thy wrong,
        My love shall in my verse ever live young.

20   A woman's face, with Nature's own hand painted,
      Hast thou, the master mistress of my passion;
      A woman's gentle heart, but not acquainted
4   With shifting change, as is false women's fashion;
      An eye more bright than theirs, less false in rolling,
      Gilding the object whereupon it gazeth;
      A man in hue all hues in his controlling,
8   Which steals men's eyes and women's souls amazeth.
      And for a woman wert thou first created,
      Till Nature as she wrought thee fell a-doting,
      And by addition me of thee defeated,
12 By adding one thing to my purpose nothing.
        But since she pricked thee out for women's pleasure,
        Mine be thy love, and thy love's use their treasure.

19: 4 **phoenix** mythical bird that periodically is consumed in flames and arises renewed (symbol of immortality) 4 **in her blood** alive 10 **antique** (1) old (2) grotesque, antic 11 **untainted** untouched

20: 1 **Nature's** i.e., not Art's 2 **master mistress** supreme mistress (some editors hyphenate, indicating that in this case the "mistress" is a "master") 2 **passion** love (or possibly love poems) 5 **rolling** i.e., roving from one to another 7 **hue** appearance (both complexion and form) 11 **defeated** defrauded 13 **pricked thee out** (1) marked you out (2) added a phallus (cf. line 12)

21 So is it not with me as with that Muse,
   Stirred by a painted beauty to his verse,
   Who heaven itself for ornament doth use,
4 And every fair with his fair doth rehearse;
   Making a couplement of proud compare
   With sun and moon, with earth and sea's rich gems,
   With April's first-born flowers, and all things rare
8 That heaven's air in this huge rondure hems.
   O, let me true in love but truly write,
   And then believe me, my love is as fair
   As any mother's child, though not so bright
12 As those gold candles fixed in heaven's air:
        Let them say more that like of hearsay well;
        I will not praise that purpose not to sell.

22 My glass shall not persuade me I am old,
   So long as youth and thou are of one date,
   But when in thee Time's furrows I behold,
4 Then look I death my days should expiate.
   For all that beauty that doth cover thee
   Is but the seemly raiment of my heart,
   Which in thy breast doth live, as thine in me.
8 How can I then be elder than thou art?
   O, therefore, love, be of thyself so wary
   As I, not for myself, but for thee will,
   Bearing thy heart, which I will keep so chary
12 As tender nurse her babe from faring ill.
        Presume not on thy heart when mine is slain;
        Thou gav'st me thine, not to give back again.

21: 1 **Muse** poet 2 **Stirred** inspired 4 **fair** beautiful thing 4 **Rehearse**
mention, i.e., compare 5 **couplement** combination 5 **compare** com-
parison 8 **rondure** sphere, world 8 **hems** encircles 13 **that like of
hearsay well** who delight in empty talk 14 **that** who

22: 2 **of one date** of the same age 4 **expiate** end 11 **chary** carefully
13 **Presume not on** do not lay claim to

23 As an unperfect actor on the stage,
    Who with his fear is put besides his part,
    Or some fierce thing replete with too much rage,
4   Whose strength's abundance weakens his own heart;
    So I, for fear of trust, forget to say
    The perfect ceremony of love's right,
    And in mine own love's strength seem to decay,
8   O'ercharged with burden of mine own love's might.
    O, let my books be then the eloquence
    And dumb presagers of my speaking breast,
    Who plead for love, and look for recompense,
12 More than that tongue that more hath more expressed.
        O, learn to read what silent love hath writ.
        To hear with eyes belongs to love's fine wit.

24 Mine eye hath played the painter and hath steeled
    Thy beauty's form in table of my heart;
    My body is the frame wherein 'tis held,
4   And perspective it is best painter's art,
    For through the painter must you see his skill,
    To find where your true image pictured lies,
    Which in my bosom's shop is hanging still,
8   That hath his windows glazèd with thine eyes.
    Now see what good turns eyes for eyes have done:
    Mine eyes have drawn thy shape, and thine for me
    Are windows to my breast, wherethrough the sun
12 Delights to peep, to gaze therein on thee.
        Yet eyes this cunning want to grace their art,
        They draw but what they see, know not the heart.

23: 5 **for fear of trust** fearing to trust myself   6 **right** (pun on "rite")
9 **books** (possibly it should be emended to "looks," i.e., though silent, he
hopes his looks will speak for him)   10 **dumb presagers** silent foretellers
12 **more expressed** more often expressed   14 **wit** intelligence

24: 1 **steeled** engraved   2 **table** tablet, picture   4 **perspective** (perhaps the
idea is that the **frame**, in line 3, contributes to the perspective of the picture it
encloses; some editors put a colon after **perspective**)   8 **his** its   8 **glazèd**
covered as with glass   13 **cunning** ability   13 **want** lack

25 Let those who are in favor with their stars
    Of public honor and proud titles boast,
    Whilst I whom fortune of such triumph bars,
4   Unlooked for joy in that I honor most.
    Great princes' favorites their fair leaves spread
    But as the marigold at the sun's eye,
    And in themselves their pride lies burièd,
8   For at a frown they in their glory die.
    The painful warrior famousèd for might,
    After a thousand victories once foiled,
    Is from the book of honor rasèd quite,
12 And all the rest forgot for which he toiled.
        Then happy I that love and am beloved
        Where I may not remove, nor be removed.

26 Lord of my love, to whom in vassalage
    Thy merit hath my duty strongly knit,
    To thee I send this written ambassage,
4   To witness duty, not to show my wit.
    Duty so great, which wit so poor as mine
    May make seem bare, in wanting words to show it,
    But that I hope some good conceit of thine
8   In thy soul's thought, all naked, will bestow it;
    Till whatsoever star that guides my moving
    Points on me graciously with fair aspect,
    And puts apparel on my tottered loving
12 To show me worthy of thy sweet respect.
        Then may I dare to boast how I do love thee;
        Till then, not show my head where thou mayst prove me.

25: 4 **Unlooked for joy in that** unexpectedly enjoy that which   6 **But**
only   9 **painful** painstaking   11 **rasèd quite** erased entirely

26: 3 **written ambassage** message   4 **wit** mental powers   6 **wanting**
lacking   7 **conceit** thought   8 **all naked, will bestow** it will accept (give
lodging to) my bare statement   9 **moving** life   10 **aspect** astrological
influence   11 **tottered** tattered   14 **prove** test

27 Weary with toil, I haste me to my bed,
  The dear repose for limbs with travel tired,
  But then begins a journey in my head
4 To work my mind when body's work's expired;
  For then my thoughts, from far where I abide,
  Intend a zealous pilgrimage to thee,
  And keep my drooping eyelids open wide,
8 Looking on darkness which the blind do see;
  Save that my soul's imaginary sight
  Presents thy shadow to my sightless view,
  Which like a jewel hung in ghastly night,
12 Makes black night beauteous and her old face new.
   Lo, thus, by day my limbs, by night my mind,
   For thee, and for myself, no quiet find.

28 How can I then return in happy plight
  That am debarred the benefit of rest,
  When day's oppression is not eased by night,
4 But day by night and night by day oppressed,
  And each, though enemies to either's reign,
  Do in consent shake hands to torture me,
  The one by toil, the other to complain
8 How far I toil, still farther off from thee?
  I tell the day, to please him, thou art bright
  And dost him grace when clouds do blot the heaven;
  So flatter I the swart-complexioned night,
12 When sparkling stars twire not, thou gild'st the even.
   But day doth daily draw my sorrows longer,
   And night doth nightly make grief's length seem stronger.

27: 2 **travel** (1) labor (2) journeying 4 **To work** to set at work 6 **Intend** set out upon 9 **imaginary** imaginative 10 **shadow** image

28: 6 **shake hands** unite 7 **the other to complain** i.e., the night causes me to complain 10 **dost him grace** i.e., shine for him 11 **swart-complexioned** dark complexioned 12 **twire** twinkle (?) 12 **thou gild'st the even** you brighten the evening

29   When, in disgrace with Fortune and men's eyes,
        I all alone beweep my outcast state,
        And trouble deaf heaven with my bootless cries,
4   And look upon myself and curse my fate,
        Wishing me like to one more rich in hope,
        Featured like him, like him with friends possessed,
        Desiring this man's art, and that man's scope,
8   With what I most enjoy contented least;
        Yet in these thoughts myself almost despising,
        Haply I think on thee, and then my state,
        Like to the lark at break of day arising
12   From sullen earth, sings hymns at heaven's gate;
           For thy sweet love rememb'red such wealth brings,
           That then I scorn to change my state with kings.

30   When to the sessions of sweet silent thought
        I summon up remembrance of things past,
        I sigh the lack of many a thing I sought,
4   And with old woes new wail my dear Time's waste.
        Then can I drown an eye, unused to flow,
        For precious friends hid in death's dateless night,
        And weep afresh love's long since canceled woe,
8   And moan th' expense of many a vanished sight;
        Then can I grieve at grievances foregone,
        And heavily from woe to woe tell o'er
        The sad account of fore-bemoanèd moan,
12   Which I new pay as if not paid before.
           But if the while I think on thee, dear friend,
           All losses are restored and sorrows end.

29: 1 **disgrace** disfavor 3 **bootless** useless 6 **like him, like him** like a second man, like a third man 7 **art** skill 7 **scope** mental power 10 **Haply** perchance 10 **state** i.e., condition 12 **sullen** gloomy

30: 1 **sessions** sittings of a court or council 4 **new wail** newly bewail 4 **my dear Time's waste** Time's destruction of things dear to me 6 **dateless** endless 7 **canceled** i.e., because paid in full 8 **expense** loss 9 **foregone** former 10 **tell** count

31 Thy bosom is endearèd with all hearts
Which I by lacking have supposèd dead;
And there reigns love and all love's loving parts,
4 And all those friends which I thought burièd.
How many a holy and obsequious tear
Hath dear religious love stol'n from mine eye,
As interest of the dead, which now appear
8 But things removed that hidden in there lie.
Thou art the grave where buried love doth live,
Hung with the trophies of my lovers gone,
Who all their parts of me to thee did give;
12 That due of many now is thine alone.
    Their images I loved I view in thee,
    And thou, all they, hast all the all of me.

32 If thou survive my well-contented day,
When that churl Death my bones with dust shall cover,
And shalt by fortune once more resurvey
4 These poor rude lines of thy deceasèd lover,
Compare them with the bett'ring of the time,
And though they be outstripped by every pen,
Reserve them for my love, not for their rhyme,
8 Exceeded by the height of happier men.
O, then vouchsafe me but this loving thought:
"Had my friend's Muse grown with this growing age,
A dearer birth than this his love had brought,
12 To march in ranks of better equipage;
    But since he died, and poets better prove,
    Theirs for their style I'll read, his for his love."

31: 1 endearèd made more precious 5 obsequious funereal 6 religious worshipful 7 interest right 7 which who 10 trophies memorials 11 parts shares 12 That due of many that which was due to many

32: 1 my well-contented day i.e., my day of death whose arrival will content me 5 bett'ring improved poetry 7 Reserve preserve 8 happier more gifted 12 of better equipage better equipped

33 Full many a glorious morning have I seen
    Flatter the mountain tops with sovereign eye,
    Kissing with golden face the meadows green,
4   Gilding pale streams with heavenly alchemy;
    Anon permit the basest clouds to ride
    With ugly rack on his celestial face,
    And from the forlorn world his visage hide,
8   Stealing unseen to west with this disgrace.
    Even so my sun one early morn did shine,
    With all triumphant splendor on my brow;
    But out alack, he was but one hour mine,
12 The region cloud hath masked him from me now.
        Yet him for this my love no whit disdaineth;
        Suns of the world may stain when heaven's sun staineth.

34 Why didst thou promise such a beauteous day,
    And make me travel forth without my cloak,
    To let base clouds o'ertake me in my way,
4   Hiding thy brav'ry in their rotten smoke?
    'Tis not enough that through the cloud thou break,
    To dry the rain on my storm-beaten face,
    For no man well of such a salve can speak,
8   That heals the wound, and cures not the disgrace.
    Nor can thy shame give physic to my grief;
    Though thou repent, yet I have still the loss.
    Th' offender's sorrow lends but weak relief
12 To him that bears the strong offense's cross.
        Ah, but those tears are pearl which thy love sheeds,
        And they are rich and ransom all ill deeds.

33: 2 **Flatter ... eye** i.e., the sun, like a monarch's eye, flatters all that it rests upon   5 **Anon** soon   5 **basest** darkest   6 **rack** vapory clouds   7 **forlorn** forsaken   11 **out alack** alas   12 **region cloud** clouds of the upper air   14 **stain** grow dim

34: 3 **base** dark   4 **brav'ry** finery   4 **rotten smoke** unwholesome vapors   9 **physic** remedy   13 **sheeds** sheds   14 **ransom** atone for

35   No more be grieved at that which thou hast done:
       Roses have thorns, and silver fountains mud,
       Clouds and eclipses stain both moon and sun,
4   And loathsome canker lives in sweetest bud.
       All men make faults, and even I in this,
       Authorizing thy trespass with compare,
       Myself corrupting, salving thy amiss,
8   Excusing thy sins more than thy sins are;
       For to thy sensual fault I bring in sense—
       Thy adverse party is thy advocate—
       And 'gainst myself a lawful plea commence.
12   Such civil war is in my love and hate
         That I an accessory needs must be
         To that sweet thief which sourly robs from me.

36   Let me confess that we two must be twain,
       Although our undivided loves are one.
       So shall those blots that do with me remain,
4   Without thy help, by me be borne alone.
       In our two loves there is but one respect,
       Though in our lives a separable spite,
       Which though it alter not love's sole effect,
8   Yet doth it steal sweet hours from love's delight.
       I may not evermore acknowledge thee,
       Lest my bewailèd guilt should do thee shame;
       Nor thou with public kindness honor me,
12   Unless thou take that honor from thy name.
         But do not so; I love thee in such sort
         As, thou being mine, mine is thy good report.

35: 3 **stain** darken   4 **canker** cankerworm (that destroys flowers)   6 **Authorizing** justifying   6 **with compare** by comparison   7 **salving thy amiss** palliating your misbehavior   8 **Excusing ... are** i.e., offering excuses more abundant than your sins (?)   9 **to thy ... sense** perhaps: to your physical fault I add reason ("sense"); possibly, however, "in sense" is a pun on "incense," i.e., my reason sweetens your sins   13 **accessory** accomplice   14 **sourly** bitterly

36: 5 **but one respect** only one regard   6 **separable spite** spiteful separation   7 **sole** unique   13-14 **But do ... report** (this couplet is repeated in Sonnet 96)   14 **report** reputation

37 As a decrepit father takes delight
To see his active child do deeds of youth,
So I, made lame by Fortune's dearest spite,
4 Take all my comfort of thy worth and truth.
For whether beauty, birth, or wealth, or wit,
Or any of these all, or all, or more,
Entitled in their parts do crownèd sit,
8 I make my love engrafted to this store.
So then I am not lame, poor, nor despised
Whilst that this shadow doth such substance give
That I in thy abundance am sufficed
12 And by a part of all thy glory live.
Look what is best, that best I wish in thee.
This wish I have, then ten times happy me!

38 How can my Muse want subject to invent,
While thou dost breathe, that pour'st into my verse
Thine own sweet argument, too excellent
4 For every vulgar paper to rehearse?
O, give thyself the thanks, if aught in me
Worthy perusal stand against thy sight;
For who's so dumb that cannot write to thee
8 When thou thyself dost give invention light?
Be thou the tenth Muse, ten times more in worth
Than those old nine which rhymers invocate;
And he that calls on thee, let him bring forth
12 Eternal numbers to outlive long date.
If my slight Muse do please these curious days,
The pain be mine, but thine shall be the praise.

37: 3 **dearest** most grievous   4 **of** from   5 **wit** intelligence   7 **Entitled in ... sit** sit as kings entitled to their places   8 **engrafted to this store** i.e., fused with and nourished by this abundance   13 **Look what** whatever

38: 1 **want subject to invent** lack subject matter for creation   2 **that** who   3 **argument** subject   4 **vulgar paper** ordinary composition   4 **rehearse** repeat   5 **in me** of my writings   6 **stand against thy sight** meet your eyes, i.e., be written for you   7 **dumb** mute   8 **invention** imagination   10 **invocate** invoke   12 **numbers** verses   12 **long date** a distant era   13 **curious** critical   14 **pain** trouble

39 O, how thy worth with manners may I sing,
When thou art all the better part of me?
What can mine own praise to mine own self bring,
4 And what is't but mine own when I praise thee?
Even for this, let us divided live,
And our dear love lose name of single one,
That by this separation I may give
8 That due to thee which thou deserv'st alone.
O, absence, what a torment wouldst thou prove,
Were it not thy sour leisure gave sweet leave
To entertain the time with thoughts of love,
12 Which time and thoughts so sweetly dost deceive,
And that thou teachest how to make one twain
By praising him here who doth hence remain.

40 Take all my loves, my love, yea take them all;
What hast thou then more than thou hadst before?
No love, my love, that thou mayst true love call;
4 All mine was thine, before thou hadst this more.
Then if for my love thou my love receivest,
I cannot blame thee for my love thou usest;
But yet be blamed, if thou this self deceivest
8 By willful taste of what thyself refusest.
I do forgive thy robb'ry, gentle thief,
Although thou steal thee all my poverty;
And yet love knows it is a greater grief
12 To bear love's wrong than hate's known injury.
Lascivious grace, in whom all ill well shows,
Kill me with spites; yet we must not be foes.

39: 1 **with manners** i.e., without self-praise 5 **for** because of 11 **entertain** pass

40: 6 **for** because 6 **thou usest** you are intimate with 7 **this self** i.e., your other self, the poet ("this self" is, however, often emended to "thy self") 8 **willful taste** capricious enjoyment 10 **my poverty** the little I have 12 **known** open 13 **Lascivious grace** i.e., you who have such grace even when lascivious

41   Those pretty wrongs that liberty commits,
When I am sometime absent from thy heart,
Thy beauty and thy years full well befits,
4   For still temptation follows where thou art.
Gentle thou art, and therefore to be won;
Beauteous thou art, therefore to be assailed;
And when a woman woos, what woman's son
8   Will sourly leave her till she have prevailed?
Ay me, but yet thou might'st my seat forbear,
And chide thy beauty and thy straying youth,
Who lead thee in their riot even there
12   Where thou art forced to break a twofold truth:
    Hers, by thy beauty tempting her to thee,
    Thine, by thy beauty being false to me.

42   That thou hast her, it is not all my grief,
And yet it may be said I loved her dearly;
That she hath thee is of my wailing chief,
4   A loss in love that touches me more nearly.
Loving offenders, thus I will excuse ye:
Thou dost love her, because thou know'st I love her,
And for my sake even so doth she abuse me,
8   Suff'ring my friend for my sake to approve her.
If I lose thee, my loss is my love's gain,
And losing her, my friend hath found that loss:
Both find each other, and I lose both twain,
12   And both for my sake lay on me this cross.
    But here's the joy: my friend and I are one;
    Sweet flattery! Then she loves but me alone.

41: 1 **pretty** petty (?) 1 **liberty** licentiousness **4 still** always **9 seat** place 11 **Who** which 11 **riot** revels 12 **truth** duty

42: 3 **of my wailing chief** chief cause of my grief **4 nearly** closely 7 **abuse** deceive 8 **approve** test, experience sensually 9 **love's** mistress'

43   When most I wink, then do mine eyes best see,
     For all the day they view things unrespected,
     But when I sleep, in dreams they look on thee
4   And, darkly bright, are bright in dark directed.
     Then thou, whose shadow shadows doth make bright,
     How would thy shadow's form form happy show
     To the clear day with thy much clearer light,
8   When to unseeing eyes thy shade shines so!
     How would, I say, mine eyes be blessèd made,
     By looking on thee in the living day,
     When in dead night thy fair imperfect shade
12 Through heavy sleep on sightless eyes doth stay!
       All days are nights to see till I see thee,
       And nights bright days when dreams do show thee me.

44   If the dull substance of my flesh were thought,
     Injurious distance should not stop my way,
     For then despite of space I would be brought,
4   From limits far remote, where thou dost stay.
     No matter then although my foot did stand
     Upon the farthest earth removed from thee;
     For nimble thought can jump both sea and land,
8   As soon as think the place where he would be.
     But, ah, thought kills me that I am not thought,
     To leap large lengths of miles when thou art gone,
     But that so much of earth and water wrought,
12 I must attend time's leisure with my moan,
       Receiving naught by elements so slow
       But heavy tears, badges of either's woe.

43: 1 **I wink** I close my eyes, i.e., I sleep 2 **unrespected** unregarded
5 **shadow shadows** image darkness 6 **thy shadow's form** the body that
casts your shadow 13 **are night to see** look like nights

44: 1 **dull substance** i.e., earth and water (in contrast to air and fire)
2 **Injurious** malicious 4 **limits** districts 4 **where** to where 6 **farthest
earth removed** earth farthest removed 8 **he** it 11 **wrought**
compounded 12 **attend** await 14 **badges of either's woe** i.e., earth's
because heavy, water's because wet (and perhaps because salty)

45 The other two, slight air and purging fire,
  Are both with thee, wherever I abide;
  The first my thought, the other my desire,
4 These present-absent with swift motion slide.
  For when these quicker elements are gone
  In tender embassy of love to thee,
  My life, being made of four, with two alone
8 Sinks down to death, oppressed with melancholy;
  Until life's composition be recured
  By those swift messengers returned from thee,
  Who even but now come back again, assured
12 Of thy fair health, recounting it to me.
   This told, I joy, but then no longer glad,
   I send them back again, and straight grow sad.

46 Mine eye and heart are at a mortal war
  How to divide the conquest of thy sight;
  Mine eye my heart thy picture's sight would bar,
4 My heart mine eye the freedom of that right.
  My heart doth plead that thou in him dost lie—
  A closet never pierced with crystal eyes;
  But the defendant doth that plea deny,
8 And says in him thy fair appearance lies.
  To 'cide this title is impanelèd
  A quest of thoughts, all tenants to the heart;
  And by their verdict is determinèd
12 The clear eye's moiety, and the dear heart's part:
   As thus—mine eye's due is thy outward part,
   And my heart's right thy inward love of heart.

45: 1 two i.e., of the four elements (see note on the first line of the previous sonnet) 1 slight insubstantial 4 present-absent now here, now gone 7 two alone i.e., earth and water 9 recured restored to health 10 messengers i.e., fire and air

46: 2 conquest of thy sight i.e., the right to gaze on you 10 quest inquest, jury 12 moiety portion

47   Betwixt mine eye and heart a league is took,
     And each doth good turns now unto the other.
     When that mine eye is famished for a look,
4   Or heart in love with sighs himself doth smother,
     With my love's picture then my eye doth feast,
     And to the painted banquet bids my heart.
     Another time mine eye is my heart's guest
8   And in his thoughts of love doth share a part.
     So, either by thy picture or my love,
     Thyself away are present still with me;
     For thou not farther than my thoughts canst move,
12   And I am still with them, and they with thee;
       Or, if they sleep, thy picture in my sight
       Awakes my heart to heart's and eye's delight.

48   How careful was I, when I took my way,
     Each trifle under truest bars to thrust,
     That to my use it might unusèd stay
4   From hands of falsehood, in sure wards of trust!
     But thou, to whom my jewels trifles are,
     Most worthy comfort, now my greatest grief,
     Thou best of dearest, and mine only care,
8   Art left the prey of every vulgar thief.
     Thee have I not locked up in any chest,
     Save where thou art not, though I feel thou art,
     Within the gentle closure of my breast,
12   From whence at pleasure thou mayst come and part;
       And even thence thou wilt be stol'n, I fear,
       For truth proves thievish for a prize so dear.

47: 1 **a league is took** an agreement is made   8 **his** i.e., the heart's   12 **still** always

48: 2 **trifle** i.e., in comparison with the person addressed   2 **truest** most trusty   4 **wards** cells   5 **to** in comparison with   8 **vulgar** common 9 **chest** (1) coffer (2) breast   14 **truth** honesty

49 Against that time, if ever that time come,
    When I shall see thee frown on my defects,
    Whenas thy love hath cast his utmost sum,
4   Called to that audit by advised respects;
    Against that time when thou shalt strangely pass,
    And scarcely greet me with that sun, thine eye,
    When love, converted from the thing it was,
8   Shall reasons find of settled gravity.
    Against that time do I ensconce me here
    Within the knowledge of mine own desart,
    And this my hand against myself uprear,
12 To guard the lawful reasons on thy part.
        To leave poor me thou hast the strength of laws,
        Since why to love I can allege no cause.

50 How heavy do I journey on the way
    When what I seek, my weary travel's end,
    Doth teach that ease and that repose to say,
4   "Thus far the miles are measured from thy friend."
    The beast that bears me, tired with my woe,
    Plods dully on, to bear that weight in me,
    As if by some instinct the wretch did know
8   His rider loved not speed, being made from thee.
    The bloody spur cannot provoke him on,
    That sometimes anger thrusts into his hide,
    Which heavily he answers with a groan,
12 More sharp to me than spurring to his side;
        For that same groan doth put this in my mind:
        My grief lies onward and my joy behind.

49: 1 **Against** in preparation for   3 **cast his utmost sum** computed its
final reckoning   4 **advised respects** well-considered reasons   5 **strangely**
with a reserved manner (like a stranger)   9 **ensconce me** fortify myself
10 **desart** desert   11 **uprear** raise as a witness

50: 1 **heavy** sadly

51 Thus can my love excuse the slow offense
Of my dull bearer, when from thee I speed:
From where thou art why should I haste me thence?
4   Till I return, of posting is no need.
O, what excuse will my poor beast then find
When swift extremity can seem but slow?
Then should I spur, though mounted on the wind,
8   In wingèd speed no motion shall I know.
Then can no horse with my desire keep pace;
Therefore desire, of perfect'st love being made,
Shall neigh, no dull flesh in his fiery race;
12 But love, for love, thus shall excuse my jade:
   Since from thee going he went willful slow,
   Towards thee I'll run and give him leave to go.

52 So am I as the rich, whose blessèd key
Can bring him to his sweet up-lockèd treasure,
The which he will not ev'ry hour survey,
4   For blunting the fine point of seldom pleasure.
Therefore are feasts so solemn and so rare,
Since, seldom coming, in the long year set,
Like stones of worth they thinly placèd are,
8   Or captain jewels in the carcanet.
So is the time that keeps you as my chest,
Or as the wardrobe which the robe doth hide,
To make some special instant special blest,
12 By new unfolding his imprisoned pride.
   Blessèd are you whose worthiness gives scope,
   Being had, to triumph, being lacked, to hope.

51: 1 **slow offense** offense of slowness 4 **posting** riding hastily 6 **swift extremity** extreme swiftness 11 **neigh** i.e., in exultation in its ethereal speed (?) (some editors emend to "weigh" with the meaning that desire refuses to keep to the slow pace of the horse and will not weigh down the horse's "dull flesh") 12 **jade** nag 14 **go** walk

52: 1 **key** (rhymes with "survey") 4 **For** for fear of 4 **seldom pleasure** pleasure infrequently enjoyed 8 **captain** chief 8 **carcanet** collar of jewels 12 **his** its

53   What is your substance, whereof are you made,
     That millions of strange shadows on you tend?
     Since everyone hath, every one, one shade,
4   And you, but one, can every shadow lend.
     Describe Adonis, and the counterfeit
     Is poorly imitated after you;
     On Helen's cheek all art of beauty set,
8   And you in Grecian tires are painted new.
     Speak of the spring and foison of the year;
     The one doth shadow of your beauty show,
     The other as your bounty doth appear,
12   And you in every blessèd shape we know.
       In all external grace you have some part,
       But you like none, none you, for constant heart.

54   O, how much more doth beauty beauteous seem,
     By that sweet ornament which truth doth give!
     The rose looks fair, but fairer we it deem
4   For that sweet odor which doth in it live.
     The canker blooms have full as deep a dye,
     As the perfumèd tincture of the roses,
     Hang on such thorns, and play as wantonly,
8   When summmer's breath their maskèd buds discloses;
     But, for their virtue only is their show,
     They live unwooed and unrespected fade,
     Die to themselves. Sweet roses do not so;
12   Of their sweet deaths are sweetest odors made.
       And so of you, beauteous and lovely youth,
       When that shall vade, by verse distills your truth.

53: 2 **strange shadows** images not your own (the images of Adonis, Helen, spring, and autumn in the following lines) 2 **tend** wait on 3 **shade** shadow 4 **And you ... lend** i.e., and you, though one, can provide a variety of good traits (?) 5 **counterfeit** picture 8 **tires** attire 9 **foison** rich harvest

54: 2 **truth** fidelity 5 **canker blooms** dog roses (which lack the perfume of the damask rose) 6 **tincture** color 7 **wantonly** unrestrainedly 8 **maskèd** hidden 8 **discloses** opens 9 **for** because 9 **virtue only** only merit 10 **unrespected** unregarded 12 **are sweetest odors made** perfumes are made 14 **vade** depart, perish 14 **by verse distills your truth** by means of verse your essence is distilled ("by" is often emended to "my")

55 Not marble, nor the gilded monuments
Of princes, shall outlive this pow'rful rhyme,
But you shall shine more bright in these contents
4 Than unswept stone, besmeared with sluttish time.
When wasteful war shall statues overturn,
And broils root out the work of masonry,
Nor Mars his sword nor war's quick fire shall burn
8 The living record of your memory.
'Gainst death and all oblivious enmity
Shall you pace forth; your praise shall still find room
Even in the eyes of all posterity
12 That wear this world out to the ending doom.
    So, till the judgment that yourself arise,
    You live in this, and dwell in lovers' eyes.

56 Sweet love, renew thy force; be it not said
Thy edge should blunter be than appetite,
Which but today by feeding is allayed,
4 Tomorrow sharp'ned in his former might.
So, love, be thou; although today thou fill
Thy hungry eyes even till they wink with fullness,
Tomorrow see again, and do not kill
8 The spirit of love with a perpetual dullness.
Let this sad int'rim like the ocean be
Which parts the shore where two contracted new
Come daily to the banks, that, when they see
12 Return of love, more blest may be the view;
    Or call it winter, which being full of care,
    Makes summer's welcome thrice more wished, more rare.

55: 3 these contents i.e., the contents of this poem 4 Than than in
4 stone memorial tablet in the floor of a church 6 broils skirmishes
7 Nor ... nor neither ... nor 7 Mars his sword Mars' sword 7 burn
(either metaphorically governs "Mars his sword" as well as "war's quick
fire," or the verb governing "Mars his sword" is omitted) 9 all oblivious
enmity all enmity that brings oblivion (?) enmity that brings oblivion to all (?)
12 wear this world out outlasts this world 13 judgment that Judgment
Day when 14 lovers' admirers'

56: 1 love spirit of love, i.e., not the beloved 2 edge keenness 2 appetite
lust 6 wink shut in sleep 9 sad int'rim period of estrangement (?)
10 contracted new newly betrothed

57 Being your slave, what should I do but tend
    Upon the hours and times of your desire?
    I have no precious time at all to spend,
4   Nor services to do till you require.
    Nor dare I chide the world-without-end hour
    Whilst I, my sovereign, watch the clock for you,
    Nor think the bitterness of absence sour
8   When you have bid your servant once adieu.
    Nor dare I question with my jealous thought
    Where you may be, or your affairs suppose,
    But, like a sad slave, stay and think of naught
12 Save where you are how happy you make those.
        So true a fool is love that in your will,
        Though you do anything, he thinks no ill.

58 That god forbid that made me first your slave
    I should in thought control your times of pleasure,
    Or at your hand th' account of hours to crave,
4   Being your vassal bound to stay your leisure.
    O, let me suffer, being at your beck,
    Th' imprisoned absence of your liberty;
    And patience, tame to sufferance, bide each check.
8   Without accusing you of injury.
    Be where you list, your charter is so strong
    That you yourself may privilege your time
    To what you will; to you it doth belong
12 Yourself to pardon of self-doing crime.
        I am to wait, though waiting so be hell,
        Not blame your pleasure, be it ill or well.

57: 1 tend wait   5 world-without-end seemingly endless   7 Nor think
nor dare I think   9 question dispute   10 suppose guess at   13 will desire
(with a pun on Shakespeare's first name)

58: 4 stay your leisure wait until you are unoccupied   6 Th' imprisoned
... liberty the imprisonment brought to me by your freedom to absent
yourself   7 And patience ... check i.e., and patience, disciplined to
accept suffering, endures every rebuke   8 injury injustice   9 list wish
9 charter privilege   10 privilege authorize   12 self-doing (1) done by
one's self (2) done to one's self   13 am to must

59 If there be nothing new, but that which is
Hath been before, how are our brains beguiled,
Which, laboring for invention, bear amiss
4 The second burden of a former child!
O, that record could with a backward look,
Even of five hundred courses of the sun,
Show me your image in some antique book,
8 Since mind at first in character was done;
That I might see what the old world could say
To this composèd wonder of your frame;
Whether we are mended, or whe'r better they,
12 Or whether revolution be the same.
    O, sure I am the wits of former days
    To subjects worse have given admiring praise.

60 Like as the waves make towards the pebbled shore,
So do our minutes hasten to their end;
Each changing place with that which goes before,
4 In sequent toil all forwards do contend.
Nativity, once in the main of light,
Crawls to maturity, wherewith being crowned,
Crooked eclipses 'gainst his glory fight,
8 And Time that gave doth now his gift confound.
Time doth transfix the flourish set on youth,
And delves the parallels in beauty's brow,
Feeds on the rarities of nature's truth,
12 And nothing stands but for his scythe to mow:
    And yet to times in hope my verse shall stand,
    Praising thy worth, despite his cruel hand.

59: 3 **for invention** i.e., to create something new   3–4 **bear ... former child** futilely bring forth only a reproduction of what had already been created   5 **record** memory   6 **courses of the sun** years   8 **since mind ... done** since thought was first expressed in writing   10 **composèd wonder** wonderful composition   11 **mended** bettered   11 **whe'r** whether   12 **revolution be the same** i.e., cycles are repeated   13 **wits** men of intellect

60: 4 **sequent** successive   5 **Nativity ... light** i.e., the newborn, at first in the ocean (metaphorical for "great expanse" or "flood") of light   7 **Crooked** malignant   8 **confound** destroy   9 **transfix** destroy   10 **delves the parallels** i.e., digs wrinkles   13 **times in hope** future times

61 Is it thy will thy image should keep open
    My heavy eyelids to the weary night?
    Dost thou desire my slumbers should be broken
4   While shadows like to thee do mock my sight?
    Is it thy spirit that thou send'st from thee
    So far from home into my deeds to pry,
    To find out shames and idle hours in me,
8   The scope and tenure of thy jealousy?
    O no, thy love, though much, is not so great.
    It is my love that keeps mine eye awake,
    Mine own true love that doth my rest defeat,
12 To play the watchman ever for thy sake.
        For thee watch I, whilst thou dost wake elsewhere,
        From me far off, with others all too near.

62 Sin of self-love possesseth all mine eye
    And all my soul and all my every part;
    And for this sin there is no remedy,
4   It is so grounded inward in my heart.
    Methinks no face so gracious is as mine,
    No shape so true, no truth of such account,
    And for myself mine own worth do define,
8   As I all other in all worths surmount.
    But when my glass shows me myself indeed,
    Beated and chopped with tanned antiquity,
    Mine own self-love quite contrary I read;
12 Self so self-loving were iniquity.
        'Tis thee, myself, that for myself I praise,
        Painting my age with beauty of thy days.

61: 4 shadows images 8 The scope ... jealousy the aim and meaning of
your suspicion 11 defeat destroy 13 watch keep awake 13 wake revel at
night (with a pun on "wake up in bed")

62: 5 gracious attractive 8 As as though 8 other others 10 chopped
creased 10 antiquity old age 13 myself my alter ego 13 that for whom
as 14 days i.e., youth

63   Against my love shall be as I am now,
        With Time's injurious hand crushed and o'erworn;
        When hours have drained his blood and filled his brow
4   With lines and wrinkles, when his youthful morn
        Hath traveled on to Age's steepy night,
        And all those beauties whereof now he's king
        Are vanishing, or vanished out of sight,
8   Stealing away the treasure of his spring;
        For such a time do I now fortify
        Against confounding Age's cruel knife,
        That he shall never cut from memory
12   My sweet love's beauty, though my lover's life.
          His beauty shall in these black lines be seen,
          And they shall live, and he in them still green.

64   When I have seen by Time's fell hand defaced
        The rich proud cost of outward buried age,
        When sometime lofty towers I see down-razed,
4   And brass eternal slave to mortal rage;
        When I have seen the hungry ocean gain
        Advantage on the kingdom of the shore,
        And the firm soil win of the wat'ry main,
8   Increasing store with loss and loss with store;
        When I have seen such interchange of state,
        Or state itself confounded to decay,
        Ruin hath taught me thus to ruminate,
12   That Time will come and take my love away.
          This thought is as a death, which cannot choose
          But weep to have that which it fears to lose.

63: 1 **Against** in expectation of the time when   5 **Age's steepy night** i.e., old age, which precipitously leads to the darkness of death   9 **fortify** build defenses   10 **confounding** destructive   10 **knife** i.e., Time's scythe 12 **my lover's life** (1) the life of my lover (2) the life of me, the lover

64: 1 **fell** cruel 2 **cost** splendor 2 **age** past times 3 **sometime** once 4 **brass eternal** everlasting brass 4 **mortal rage** the rage of mortality 6 **Advantage** i.e., inroads 8 **Increasing store ... store** i.e., now one increases in abundance (**store**) with the other's loss, now one repairs its loss with abundance taken from the other 9 **state** condition (but in line 10 **state** = greatness) 10 **confounded** destroyed 14 **to have** because it has

65   Since brass, nor stone, nor earth, nor boundless sea,
       But sad mortality o'ersways their power,
       How with this rage shall beauty hold a plea,
4   Whose action is no stronger than a flower?
       O, how shall summer's honey breath hold out
       Against the wrackful siege of batt'ring days,
       When rocks impregnable are not so stout,
8   Nor gates of steel so strong but Time decays?
       O, fearful meditation, where, alack,
       Shall Time's best jewel from Time's chest lie hid?
       Or what strong hand can hold his swift foot back,
12   Or who his spoil of beauty can forbid?
          O, none, unless this miracle have might,
          That in black ink my love may still shine bright.

66   Tired with all these, for restful death I cry,
       As, to behold desert a beggar born,
       And needy nothing trimmed in jollity,
4   And purest faith unhappily forsworn,
       And gilded honor shamefully misplaced,
       And maiden virtue rudely strumpeted,
       And right perfection wrongfully disgraced,
8   And strength by limping sway disabled,
       And art made tongue-tied by authority,
       And folly (doctorlike) controlling skill,
       And simple truth miscalled simplicity,
12   And captive good attending captain ill.
          Tired with all these, from these would I be gone,
          Save that to die, I leave my love alone.

65: 1 Since since there is neither 3 rage fury 3 hold maintain 4 action case, suit 6 wrackful destructive 8 decays causes them to decay 10 from Time's chest lie hid i.e., conceal itself to avoid being enclosed in Time's coffer 12 spoil plundering 14 my love my beloved

66: 2 As for instance 2 desert a deserving person 3 needy ... jollity i.e., a nonentity, who is poor in virtues, festively attired 4 unhappily forsworn miserably perjured 5 gilded golden 7 disgraced disfigured 8 limping sway i.e., incompetent authority 10 doctorlike with the air of a learned man 11 simple pure 11 simplicity stupidity 12 attending subordinated to

67 Ah, wherefore with infection should he live,
    And with his presence grace impiety,
    That sin by him advantage should achieve
4   And lace itself with his society?
    Why should false painting imitate his cheek
    And steal dead seeing of his living hue?
    Why should poor beauty indirectly seek
8   Roses of shadow, since his rose is true?
    Why should he live, now Nature bankrout is,
    Beggared of blood to blush through lively veins,
    For she hath no exchequer now but his,
12 And, proud of many, lives upon his gains?
        O, him she stores, to show what wealth she had,
        In days long since, before these last so bad.

68 Thus is his cheek the map of days outworn,
    When beauty lived and died as flowers do now,
    Before these bastard signs of fair were born,
4   Or durst inhabit on a living brow;
    Before the golden tresses of the dead,
    The right of sepulchers, were shorn away
    To live a second life on second head,
8   Ere beauty's dead fleece made another gay.
    In him those holy antique hours are seen,
    Without all ornament, itself and true,
    Making no summer of another's green,
12 Robbing no old to dress his beauty new;
        And him as for a map doth Nature store,
        To show false Art what beauty was of yore.

67: 1 **infection** an age of corruption 4 **lace** adorn 5 **false painting** (possibly the reference is to the use of cosmetics or possibly to portraiture) 6 **dead seeing** the lifeless appearance (though perhaps **seeing** should be emended to "seeming") 7 **poor** second-rate 7 **indirectly** by imitation 8 **of shadow** painted (?) 9 **bankrout** bankrupt 10 **Beggared … veins** i.e., so impoverished that it can blush only with the aid of cosmetics 11 **exchequer** treasury (of natural beauty) 12 **proud** (perhaps "falsely proud," but possibly should be emended to "'prived," i.e., deprived)

68: 1 **map** representation, picture 1 **days outworn** past times 3 **bastard signs of fair** false appearances (cosmetics, wigs) of beauty 3 **born** (with pun on "borne") 9 **antique hours** ancient times 10 **all** any 13 **store** preserve

69 Those parts of thee that the world's eye doth view
Want nothing that the thought of hearts can mend;
All tongues, the voice of souls, give thee that due,
4 Utt'ring bare truth, even so as foes commend.
Thy outward thus with outward praise is crowned,
But those same tongues that give thee so thine own
In other accents do this praise confound
8 By seeing farther than the eye hath shown.
They look into the beauty of thy mind,
And that in guess they measure by thy deeds;
Then, churls, their thoughts, although their eyes were kind,
12 To thy fair flower add the rank smell of weeds;
But why thy odor matcheth not thy show,
The soil is this, that thou dost common grow.

70 That thou art blamed shall not be thy defect,
For slander's mark was ever yet the fair;
The ornament of beauty is suspect,
4 A crow that flies in heaven's sweetest air.
So thou be good, slander doth but approve
Thy worth the greater, being wooed of time;
For canker vice the sweetest buds doth love,
8 And thou present'st a pure unstainèd prime.
Thou hast passed by the ambush of young days,
Either not assailed, or victor being charged;
Yet this thy praise cannot be so thy praise
12 To tie up envy, evermore enlarged.
If some suspect of ill masked not thy show,
Then thou alone kingdoms of hearts shouldst owe.

69: 1 **parts** outward qualities 2 **Want** lack 4 **even so as foes commend**
i.e., without exaggeration 6 **so thine own** i.e., your due 7 **confound**
destroy 14 **soil** (1) ground (2) blemish

70: 3 **The ornament of beauty is suspect** suspicion (because it always seeks
out the beautiful) is an ornament of beauty 5 So provided that 5 **approve**
prove 6 **wooed of time** i.e., tempted to evil by the present times 7 **canker
vice** vice like a cankerworm (which preys on buds) 9 **ambush of young
days** snares of youth 10 **charged** attacked 12 **To tie up envy** to overcome
malice 12 **enlarged** at liberty 13 **If some ... show** i.e., if some suspicion
of evil did not surround you 14 **owe** own

71 No longer mourn for me when I am dead
    Than you shall hear the surly sullen bell
    Give warning to the world that I am fled
4   From this vile world with vilest worms to dwell.
    Nay, if you read this line, remember not
    The hand that writ it, for I love you so
    That I in your sweet thoughts would be forgot,
8   If thinking on me then should make you woe.
    O, if, I say, you look upon this verse,
    When I, perhaps, compounded am with clay,
    Do not so much as my poor name rehearse,
12 But let your love even with my life decay,
        Lest the wise world should look into your moan,
        And mock you with me after I am gone.

72 O, lest the world should task you to recite
    What merit lived in me that you should love
    After my death, dear love, forget me quite,
4   For you in me can nothing worthy prove;
    Unless you would devise some virtuous lie,
    To do more for me than mine own desert,
    And hang more praise upon deceasèd I
8   Than niggard truth would willingly impart.
    O, lest your true love may seem false in this,
    That you for love speak well of me untrue,
    My name be buried where my body is,
12 And live no more to shame nor me nor you;
        For I am shamed by that which I bring forth,
        And so should you, to love things nothing worth.

72: 1 recite tell 4 prove find 6 desert (rhymes with "impart") 8 niggard miserly 10 untrue untruly 11 My name be let my name be 12 nor ... nor neither ... nor

73   That time of year thou mayst in me behold
     When yellow leaves, or none, or few, do hang
     Upon those boughs which shake against the cold,
4   Bare ruined choirs where late the sweet birds sang.
     In me thou seest the twilight of such day
     As after sunset fadeth in the west,
     Which by and by black night doth take away,
8   Death's second self, that seals up all in rest.
     In me thou seest the glowing of such fire
     That on the ashes of his youth doth lie,
     As the deathbed whereon it must expire,
12   Consumed with that which it was nourished by.
         This thou perceiv'st, which makes thy love more strong,
         To love that well which thou must leave ere long.

74   But be contented. When that fell arrest
     Without all bail shall carry me away,
     My life hath in this line some interest
4   Which for memorial still with thee shall stay.
     When thou reviewest this, thou dost review
     The very part was consecrate to thee.
     The earth can have but earth, which is his due;
8   My spirit is thine, the better part of me.
     So then thou hast but lost the dregs of life,
     The prey of worms, my body being dead;
     The coward conquest of a wretch's knife,
12   Too base of thee to be rememberèd.
         The worth of that is that which it contains,
         And that is this, and this with thee remains.

73: 4 **choirs** the part of the chancel in which the service is performed   7 **by and by** shortly   8 **Death's second self** i.e., sleep   8 **seals up** encloses (with a suggestion of sealing a coffin)   10 **That** as   14 **that** i.e., that substance, the poet

74: 1 **fell** cruel   2 **Without all bail** i.e., without any possibility of release   3 **line** verse   3 **interest** part   4 **still** always   7 **his** its   11 **The coward conquest** i.e., conquest that even a coward can make   11 **wretch's** Death's (or possibly Time's)   13-14 **The worth ... remains** i.e., the value of the body is in the spirit it contains, and this spirit is in the poem and remains with you

75 So are you to my thoughts as food to life,
    Or as sweet-seasoned showers are to the ground;
    And for the peace of you I hold such strife
4   As 'twixt a miser and his wealth is found;
    Now proud as an enjoyer, and anon
    Doubting the filching age will steal his treasure;
    Now counting best to be with you alone,
8   Then bettered that the world may see my pleasure;
    Sometime all full with feasting on your sight,
    And by and by clean starvèd for a look;
    Possessing or pursuing no delight
12 Save what is had or must from you be took.
        Thus do I pine and surfeit day by day,
        Or gluttoning on all, or all away.

76 Why is my verse so barren of new pride,
    So far from variation or quick change?
    Why with the time do I not glance aside
4   To new-found methods and to compounds strange?
    Why write I still all one, ever the same,
    And keep invention in a noted weed,
    That every word doth almost tell my name,
8   Showing their birth, and where they did proceed?
    O, know, sweet love, I always write of you,
    And you and love are still my argument.
    So all my best is dressing all words new,
12 Spending again what is already spent:
        For as the sun is daily new and old,
        So is my love still telling what is told.

75: 2 **sweet-seasoned** of the sweet season, spring   3 **peace of you** i.e., the peace I find because of you   5 **enjoyer** possessor   5 **anon** soon   6 **Doubting** fearing   8 **bettered** made happier   10 **by and by** soon   10 **clean** wholly   14 **Or ... or** either ... or

76: 1 **pride** adornment   3 **with the time** (1) following the present fashion (2) with the passage of time   4 **compounds** (1) compositions (2) compound words   5 **still all one** always one way   6 **invention** imaginative creation   6 **noted weed** well-known dress   8 **where** whence   10 **argument** theme

77   Thy glass will show thee how thy beauties wear,
      Thy dial how thy precious minutes waste;
      The vacant leaves thy mind's imprint will bear,
4   And of this book this learning mayst thou taste.
      The wrinkles which thy glass will truly show,
      Of mouthèd graves, will give thee memory;
      Thou by thy dial's shady stealth mayst know
8   Time's thievish progress to eternity.
      Look what thy memory cannot contain,
      Commit to these waste blanks, and thou shalt find
      Those children nursed, delivered from thy brain,
12   To take a new acquaintance of thy mind.
        These offices, so oft as thou wilt look,
        Shall profit thee, and much enrich thy book.

78   So oft have I invoked thee for my Muse
      And found such fair assistance in my verse
      As every alien pen hath got my use
4   And under thee their poesy disperse.
      Thine eyes, that taught the dumb on high to sing
      And heavy ignorance aloft to fly,
      Have added feathers to the learnèd's wing,
8   And given grace a double majesty.
      Yet be most proud of that which I compile,
      Whose influence is thine, and born of thee.
      In others' works thou dost but mend the style,
12   And arts with thy sweet graces gracèd be;
        But thou art all my art and dost advance
        As high as learning my rude ignorance.

77: 2 **dial** sundial   3 **vacant leaves** i.e., the blank leaves (of a memorandum book, or "table" as in Sonnet 122)   6 **mouthèd** i.e., gaping, openmouthed 6 **give thee memory** remind you   7 **shady stealth** slowly moving shadow 3 **Look what** whatever   10 **waste blanks** blank plages   11 **children** i.e., your thoughts   13 **offices** duties (of looking at the mirror, the sundial, and the thoughts in the book)

78: 3 **As that**   3 **alien pen** pen belonging to others   3 **got my use** adopted my practice (either style or subject matter)   4 **under thee** i.e., with you as patron   5 **on high** (1) aloud (2) loftily   8 **grace** excellence   9 **compile** write   10 **influence** inspiration   14 **rude** unrefined

79   Whilst I alone did call upon thy aid,
     My verse alone had all thy gentle grace;
     But now my gracious numbers are decayed,
4   And my sick Muse doth give another place.
     I grant, sweet love, thy lovely argument
     Deserves the travail of a worthier pen,
     Yet what of thee thy poet doth invent
8   He robs thee of, and pays it thee again.
     He lends thee virtue, and he stole that word
     From thy behavior; beauty doth he give,
     And found it in thy cheek; he can afford
12   No praise to thee but what in thee doth live.
         Then thank him not for that which he doth say,
         Since what he owes thee thou thyself dost pay.

80   O, how I faint when I of you do write,
     Knowing a better spirit doth use your name,
     And in the praise thereof spends all his might,
4   To make me tongue-tied speaking of your fame.
     But since your worth, wide as the ocean is,
     The humble as the proudest sail doth bear,
     My saucy bark, inferior far to his,
8   On your broad main doth willfully appear.
     Your shallowest help will hold me up afloat
     Whilst he upon your soundless deep doth ride;
     Or, being wracked, I am a worthless boat,
12   He of tall building, and of goodly pride.
         Then if he thrive, and I be cast away,
         The worst was this: my love was my decay.

79: 3 gracious numbers pleasing verses   4 give another place yield to
another   5 thy lovely argument the theme of your loveliness   11 afford
offer   14 owes (poems are regarded as the poet's repayment of obligation; see
Sonnet 83, line 4)

80: 1 faint waver   2 better spirit greater genius   6 humble humblest
6 as as well as   8 willfully boldly   10 soundless bottomless   11 wracked
wrecked   11 boat small vessel (in contrast to a ship)   12 tall building
sturdy construction   12 pride magnificence   14 decay cause of ruin

81 Or I shall live your epitaph to make,
  Or you survive when I in earth am rotten.
  From hence your memory death cannot take,
4 Although in me each part will be forgotten.
  Your name from hence immortal life shall have,
  Though I, once gone, to all the world must die.
  The earth can yield me but a common grave,
8 When you entombèd in men's eyes shall lie.
  Your monument shall be my gentle verse,
  Which eyes not yet created shall o'erread,
  And tongues to be your being shall rehearse
12 When all the breathers of this world are dead.
   You still shall live—such virtue hath my pen—
   Where breath most breathes, even in the mouths of men.

82 I grant thou wert not married to my Muse,
  And therefore mayst without attaint o'erlook
  The dedicated words which writers use
4 Of their fair subject, blessing every book.
  Thou art as fair in knowledge as in hue,
  Finding thy worth a limit past my praise;
  And therefore art enforced to seek anew
8 Some fresher stamp of the time-bettering days.
  And do so, love; yet when they have devised
  What strainèd touches rhetoric can lend,
  Thou, truly fair, wert truly sympathized
12 In true plain words by thy true-telling friend:
   And their gross painting might be better used
   Where cheeks need blood; in thee it is abused.

81: 1 **Or** either 3 **From hence** from these poems (?) from the earth (?)
4 **in me each part** all of my qualities 5 **from hence** from these poems
11 **rehearse** repeat 13 **virtue** power 14 **breath** life

82: 1 **married to** closely joined to 2 **attaint** dishonor 2 **o'erlook** read
over 3 **dedicated** devoted (with a pun on dedications prefixed to books)
5 **hue** (1) complexion (2) figure 6 **limit** reach 8 **stamp** impression
8 **time-bettering** improving 11 **fair** beautiful 11 **truly sympathized**
represented to the life

83 I never saw that you did painting need,
    And therefore to your fair no painting set;
    I found, or thought I found, you did exceed
4   The barren tender of a poet's debt;
    And therefore have I slept in your report,
    That you yourself, being extant, well might show
    How far a modern quill doth come too short,
8   Speaking of worth, what worth in you doth grow.
    This silence for my sin you did impute,
    Which shall be most my glory, being dumb;
    For I impair not beauty, being mute,
12 When others would give life and bring a tomb.
        There lives more life in one of your fair eyes
        Than both your poets can in praise devise.

84 Who is it that says most, which can say more
    Than this rich praise, that you alone are you,
    In whose confine immurèd is the store
4   Which should example where your equal grew?
    Lean penury within that pen doth dwell,
    That to his subject lends not some small glory,
    But he that writes of you, if he can tell
8   That you are you, so dignifies his story.
    Let him but copy what in you is writ,
    Not making worse what nature made so clear,
    And such a counterpart shall frame his wit,
12 Making his style admirèd everywhere.
        You to your beauteous blessings add a curse,
        Being fond on praise, which makes your praises worse.

83: 2 **fair** beauty 4 **The barren ... debt** i.e., the worthless offer that the
poet is obliged to make 5 **slept in your report** refrained from praising
you 7 **modern** trivial

84: 1 **Who ... more** i.e., who, having said the utmost, can say more 3-4 **In
whose ... grew** in whom is stored all the abundance which would have to
serve as a model for any equal 6 **his** its 10 **clear** radiant 11 **fame his wit**
make famous his mind 14 **fond on** foolishly enamored of (but the sense
seemed called for here is that the patron's excellence is such that it wreaks
havoc with the poets who seek to praise him)

44

85 My tongue-tied Muse in manners holds her still
    While comments of your praise, richly compiled,
    Reserve their character with golden quill
4   And precious phrase by all the Muses filed.
    I think good thoughts whilst other write good words,
    And, like unlettered clerk, still cry "Amen"
    To every hymn that able spirit affords
8   In polished form of well-refinèd pen.
    Hearing you praised, I say, "'Tis so, 'tis true,"
    And to the most of praise add something more;
    But that is in my thought, whose love to you,
12 Though words come hindmost, holds his rank before.
        Then others for the breath of words respect,
        Me for my dumb thoughts, speaking in effect.

86 Was it the proud full sail of his great verse,
    Bound for the prize of all too precious you,
    That did my ripe thoughts in my brain inhearse,
4   Making their tomb the womb wherein they grew?
    Was it his spirit, by spirits taught to write
    Above a mortal pitch, that struck me dead?
    No, neither he, nor his compeers by night
8   Giving him aid, my verse astonishèd.
    He, nor that affable familiar ghost
    Which nightly gulls him with intelligence,
    As victors, of my silence cannot boast;
12 I was not sick of any fear from thence.
        But when your countenance filled up his line,
        Then lacked I matter, that enfeebled mine.

85: 1 **in manners holds her still** is politely silent 2-3 **While ... quill** while comments in your praise, richly composed with golden pen, preserve their features ("character" means both "writing" and "traits," "features") 4 **filed** polished 5 **other** others 6 **still** always 7 **able spirit affords** i.e., competent poets write 10 **most** utmost 13-14 **Then others ... effect** i.e., then take notice of other poets for their spoken words (but in "breath" there is a suggestion of their insubstantiality), and of me for my silent thoughts, which, by their silence, speak

86: 1 **his** i.e., a rival poet's 3 **inhearse** enclose as in a coffin 6 **dead** silent 8 **astonishèd** struck dumb 9 **familiar ghost** assisting spirit 10 **gulls him with intelligence** deceives him with rumors (?) 13 **countenance filled up his line** (1) beauty was the subject of his verse (2) approval polished his verse (if the quarto's "fild" is printed "filed" instead of "filled")

87   Farewell, thou art too dear for my possessing,
     And like enough thou know'st thy estimate.
     The charter of thy worth gives thee releasing;
4   My bonds in thee are all determinate.
     For how do I hold thee but by thy granting,
     And for that riches where is my deserving?
     The cause of this fair gift in me is wanting,
8   And so my patent back again is swerving.
     Thyself thou gav'st, thy own worth then not knowing
     Or me, to whom thou gav'st it, else mistaking;
     So thy great gift, upon misprision growing,
12 Comes home again, on better judgment making.
       Thus have I had thee as a dream doth flatter,
       In sleep a king, but waking no such matter.

88   When thou shalt be disposed to set me light
     And place my merit in the eye of scorn,
     Upon thy side against myself I'll fight
4   And prove thee virtuous, though thou art forsworn.
     With mine own weakness being best acquainted,
     Upon thy part I can set down a story
     Of faults concealed wherein I am attainted,
8   That thou in losing me shall win much glory.
     And I by this will be a gainer too,
     For, bending all my loving thoughts on thee,
     The injuries that to myself I do,
12 Doing thee vantage, double-vantage me.
       Such is my love, to thee I so belong,
       That for thy right myself will bear all wrong.

87: 2 **estimate** value 3 **charter** privilege 4 **bonds** in claims on
4 **determinate** expired 7 **wanting** lacking 8 **patent** privilege 8 **back
again is swerving** returns (to you) 11 **upon misprision growing** arising
from a mistake

88: 1 **set me light** value me little 8 **That** so that 12 **vantage**
advantage 14 **right** (1) good (2) privilege

46

89   Say that thou didst forsake me for some fault,
And I will comment upon that offense.
Speak of my lameness, and I straight will halt,
4   Against thy reasons making no defense.
Thou canst not, love, disgrace me half so ill,
To set a form upon desirèd change,
As I'll myself disgrace, knowing thy will.
8   I will acquaintance strangle and look strange;
Be absent from thy walks, and in my tongue
Thy sweet belovèd name no more shall dwell,
Lest I, too much profane, should do it wrong
12   And haply of our old acquaintance tell.
   For thee, against myself I'll vow debate,
   For I must ne'er love him whom thou dost hate.

90   Then hate me when thou wilt; if ever, now;
Now, while the world is bent my deeds to cross,
Join with the spite of fortune, make me bow,
4   And do not drop in for an after-loss.
Ah, do not, when my heart hath 'scaped this sorrow,
Come in the rearward of a conquered woe;
Give not a windy night a rainy morrow,
8   To linger out a purposed overthrow.
If thou wilt leave me, do not leave me last,
When other petty griefs have done their spite,
But in the onset come; so shall I taste
12   At first the very worst of fortune's might,
   And other strains of woe, which now seem woe,
   Compared with loss of thee will not seem so.

89: 1 **Say** i.e., assume   3 **halt** limp   4 **reasons** arguments   5 **disgrace** discredit   6 **To set ... change** to give a good appearance to the change you desire (?)   7 **disgrace** disfigure   8 **acquaintance** i.e., familiarity   12 **haply** by chance   13 **debate** contention

90: 4 **after-loss** later loss   6 **Come in ... woe** i.e., come belatedly when I have conquered my sorrow   8 **linger out** prolong   8 **purposed** intended   13 **strains** kinds

47

91   Some glory in their birth, some in their skill,
      Some in their wealth, some in their body's force,
      Some in their garments, though newfangled ill,
 4   Some in their hawks and hounds, some in their horse;
      And every humor hath his adjunct pleasure,
      Wherein it finds a joy above the rest,
      But these particulars are not my measure;
 8   All these I better in one general best.
      Thy love is better than high birth to me,
      Richer than wealth, prouder than garments' cost,
      Of more delight than hawks or horses be;
12   And having thee, of all men's pride I boast:
          Wretched in this alone, that thou mayst take
          All this away, and me most wretched make.

92   But do thy worst to steal thyself away,
      For term of life thou art assurèd mine,
      And life no longer than thy love will stay,
 4   For it depends upon that love of thine.
      Then need I not to fear the worst of wrongs,
      When in the least of them my life hath end.
      I see a better state to me belongs
 8   Than that which on thy humor doth depend.
      Thou canst not vex me with inconstant mind,
      Since that my life on thy revolt doth lie.
      O, what a happy title do I find,
12   Happy to have thy love, happy to die!
          But what's so blessèd-fair that fears no blot?
          Thou mayst be false, and yet I know it not.

91: 3 **newfangled ill** fashionably ugly 4 **horse** horses 5 **humor**
temperament 5 **his** its 7 **measure** standard (of happiness) 12 **all men's**
pride i.e., all that men take pride in

92: 6 **the least of them** i.e., any sign that the friend's love is cooling
8 **humor** caprice 10 **Since ... lie** since my life ends if you desert me
11 **happy title** title to happiness

48

93
So shall I live, supposing thou art true,
Like a deceivèd husband; so love's face
May still seem love to me, though altered new,
4 Thy looks with me, thy heart in other place.
For there can live no hatred in thine eye;
Therefore in that I cannot know thy change.
In many's looks, the false heart's history
8 Is writ in moods and frowns and wrinkles strange,
But heaven in thy creation did decree
That in thy face sweet love should ever dwell;
Whate'er thy thoughts or thy heart's workings be,
12 Thy looks should nothing thence but sweetness tell.
　How like Eve's apple doth thy beauty grow
　If thy sweet virtue answer not thy show.

94
They that have pow'r to hurt and will do none,
That do not do the thing they most do show,
Who, moving others, are themselves as stone,
4 Umovèd, cold, and to temptation slow;
They rightly do inherit heaven's graces
And husband nature's riches from expense;
They are the lords and owners of their faces,
8 Others but stewards of their excellence.
The summer's flow'r is to the summer sweet,
Though to itself it only live and die;
But if that flow'r with base infection meet,
12 The basest weed outbraves his dignity:
　For sweetest things turn sourest by their deeds;
　Lilies that fester smell far worse than weeds.

94: 2 do show (1) seem to do (?) (2) show they could do (?) 6 husband
manage prudently 6 expense loss 8 stewards custodians 12 outbraves
his surpasses its

95   How sweet and lovely dost thou make the shame
Which, like a canker in the fragrant rose,
Doth spot the beauty of thy budding name!
4   O, in what sweets dost thou thy sins enclose!
That tongue that tells the story of thy days,
Making lascivious comments on thy sport,
Cannot dispraise, but in a kind of praise;
8   Naming thy name blesses an ill report.
O, what a mansion have those vices got
Which for their habitation chose out thee,
Where beauty's veil doth cover every blot,
12   And all things turns to fair that eyes can see!
      Take heed, dear heart, of this large privilege;
      The hardest knife ill-used doth lose his edge.

96   Some say thy fault is youth, some wantonness,
Some say thy grace is youth and gentle sport;
Both grace and faults are loved of more and less;
4   Thou mak'st faults graces that to thee resort.
As on the finger of a thronèd queen
The basest jewel will be well esteemed,
So are those errors that in thee are seen
8   To truths translated and for true things deemed.
How many lambs might the stern wolf betray,
If like a lamb he could his looks translate;
How many gazers might'st thou lead away,
12   If thou wouldst use the strength of all thy state!
      But do not so; I love thee in such sort
      As, thou being mine, mine is thy good report.

95: 2 **canker** cankerworm (that feeds on blossoms) 6 **sport** amorous
dalliance 14 **his** its

96: 2 **gentle sport** amorous dalliance (a more favorable interpretation
of the "wantonness" of line 1) 3 **of more and less** by people high and
low 8 **translated** transformed 9 **stern** cruel 12 **state** eminent position
13-14 (this couplet ends Sonnet 36) 14 **report** reputation

97 How like a winter hath my absence been
    From thee, the pleasure of the fleeting year!
    What freezings have I felt, what dark days seen,
4   What old December's bareness everywhere!
    And yet this time removed was summer's time,
    The teeming autumn, big with rich increase,
    Bearing the wanton burden of the prime,
8   Like widowed wombs after their lords' decease.
    Yet this abundant issue seemed to me
    But hope of orphans and unfathered fruit;
    For summer and his pleasures wait on thee,
12 And, thou away, the very birds are mute;
        Or, if they sing, 'tis with so dull a cheer,
        That leaves look pale, dreading the winter's near.

98 From you have I been absent in the spring,
    When proud-pied April, dressed in all his trim,
    Hath put a spirit of youth in everything,
4   That heavy Saturn laughed and leaped with him,
    Yet nor the lays of birds, nor the sweet smell
    Of different flowers in odor and in hue,
    Could make me any summer's story tell,
8   Or from their proud lap pluck them where they grew.
    Nor did I wonder at the lily's white,
    Nor praise the deep vermilion in the rose;
    They were but sweet, but figures of delight,
12 Drawn after you, you pattern of all those.
        Yet seemed it winter still, and, you away,
        As with your shadow I with these did play.

97: 2 **pleasure of the fleeting year** i.e., the summer (normally the pleasant part of the year, but like a winter because of the friend's absence) **6 teeming** pregnant 7 **Bearing ... prime** i.e., bearing the load conceived in the wantonness of the spring (prime = spring) 9 **issue** offspring 11 **his** its

98: 2 **proud-pied** gorgeously variegated 2 **trim** ornamental dress 4 **That so that** 4 **heavy Saturn** (the planet Saturn was thought to cause gloominess) 5 **nor ... nor** neither ... nor 5 **lays** songs 7 **summer's story** i.e., pleasant stories suitable for summer ("a sad tale's best for winter") 14 **shadow** portrait

99 The forward violet thus did I chide:
Sweet thief, whence didst thou steal thy sweet that smells
If not from my love's breath? The purple pride
4 Which on thy soft cheek for complexion dwells
In my love's veins thou hast too grossly dyed.
The lily I condemnèd for thy hand,
And buds of marjoram had stol'n thy hair;
8 The roses fearfully on thorns did stand,
One blushing shame, another white despair;
A third, nor red nor white, had stol'n of both,
And to his robb'ry had annexed thy breath;
12 But for his theft, in pride of all his growth
A vengeful canker eat him up to death.
   More flowers I noted, yet I none could see,
   But sweet or color it had stol'n from thee.

100 Where art thou, Muse, that thou forget'st so long
To speak of that which gives thee all thy might?
Spend'st thou thy fury on some worthless song,
4 Dark'ning thy pow'r to lend base subjects light?
Return, forgetful Muse, and straight redeem
In gentle numbers time so idly spent,
Sing to the ear that doth thy lays esteem,
8 And gives thy pen both skill and argument.
Rise, resty Muse, my love's sweet face survey,
If Time have any wrinkle graven there;
If any, be a satire to decay
12 And make Time's spoils despisèd everywhere.
   Give my love fame faster than Time wastes life;
   So thou prevent'st his scythe and crooked knife.

99: 1 **forward** early   3 **purple** (Shakespeare often does not distinguish between purple and crimson)   3 **pride** splendor   6 **condemnèd for thy hand** condemned for stealing the whiteness of your hand   8 **fearfully** uneasily   13 **canker eat** cankerworm ate

100: 3 **fury** poetic enthusiasm   6 **numbers** verses   7 **lays** songs   8 **argument** subject   9 **resty** torpid   10 **If** to see if   11 **be a satire to decay** satirize decay

101   O truant Muse, what shall be thy amends
       For thy neglect of truth in beauty dyed?
       Both truth and beauty on my love depends;
4   So dost thou too, and therein dignified.
       Make answer, Muse, wilt thou not haply say,
       "Truth needs no color, with his color fixed,
       Beauty no pencil, beauty's truth to lay;
8   But best is best, if never intermixed?"
       Because he needs no praise, wilt thou be dumb?
       Excuse not silence so, for't lies in thee
       To make him much outlive a gilded tomb,
12   And to be praised of ages yet to be.
         Then do thy office, Muse; I teach thee how
         To make him seem, long hence, as he shows now.

102   My love is strength'ned, though more weak in seeming;
       I love not less, though less the show appear.
       That love is merchandized whose rich esteeming
4   The owner's tongue doth publish everywhere.
       Our love was new, and then but in the spring,
       When I was wont to greet it with my lays,
       As Philomel in summer's front doth sing
8   And stops her pipe in growth of riper days.
       Not that the summer is less pleasant now
       Than when her mournful hymns did hush the night,
       But that wild music burdens every bough,
12   And sweets grown common lose their dear delight.
         Therefore, like her, I sometime hold my tongue,
         Because I would not dull you with my song.

101: 3 **love** beloved 4 **dignified** you are dignified 5 **haply** perchance 6 **color** artificial color, disguise 6 **his color fixed** its unchangeable color 7 **to lay** i.e., to put on canvas 8 **intermixed** i.e., with the inadequate words of the Muse 13 **do thy office** perform your duty

102: 2 **show** outward manifestation 3 **merchandized** offered for sale, hawked 3 **esteeming** value 6 **lays** songs 7 **Philomel** the nightingale 7 **front** forefront 8 **riper** later 11 **But that** i.e., but it seems so because

103   Alack, what poverty my Muse brings forth,
That, having such a scope to show her pride,
The argument all bare is of more worth
4   Than when it hath my added praise beside.
O, blame me not if I no more can write!
Look in your glass, and there appears a face
That overgoes my blunt invention quite,
8   Dulling my lines and doing me disgrace.
Were it not sinful then, striving to mend,
To mar the subject that before was well?
For to no other pass my verses tend
12   Than of your graces and your gifts to tell;
    And more, much more, than in my verse can sit
    Your own glass shows you when you look in it.

104   To me, fair friend, you never can be old,
For as you were when first your eye I eyed,
Such seems your beauty still. Three winters cold
4   Have from the forests shook three summers' pride,
Three beauteous springs to yellow autumn turned
In process of the seasons have I seen,
Three April perfumes in three hot Junes burned,
8   Since first I saw you fresh, which yet are green.
Ah, yet doth beauty, like a dial hand,
Steal from his figure, and no pace perceived;
So your sweet hue, which methinks still doth stand,
12   Hath motion, and mine eye may be deceived;
    For fear of which, hear this, thou age unbred:
    Ere you were born was beauty's summer dead.

103: 1 **poverty** inferior matter 2 **pride** splendor 3 **argument** theme 3 **all bare** i.e., of itself 7 **overgoes my blunt invention** exceeds my awkward creation 8 **disgrace** discredit 9 **mend** improve 11 **pass** purpose

104: 4 **pride** splendor 10 **his figure** its numeral (with a pun on "figure," the friend's appearance) 11 **sweet hue** fair appearance 11 **still** (1) motionless (2) always, forever 13 **unbred** unborn

54

105   Let not my love be called idolatry,
      Nor my belovèd as an idol show,
      Since all alike my songs and praises be
4   To one, of one, still such, and ever so.
      Kind is my love today, tomorrow kind,
      Still constant in a wondrous excellence;
      Therefore my verse, to constancy confined,
8   One thing expressing, leaves out difference.
      Fair, kind, and true is all my argument,
      Fair, kind, and true, varying to other words;
      And in this change is my invention spent,
12 Three themes in one, which wondrous scope affords.
        Fair, kind, and true have often lived alone,
        Which three till now never kept seat in one.

106   When in the chronicle of wasted time
      I see descriptions of the fairest wights,
      And beauty making beautiful old rhyme
4   In praise of ladies dead and lovely knights;
      Then, in the blazon of sweet beauty's best,
      Of hand, of foot, of lip, of eye, of brow,
      I see their antique pen would have expressed
8   Even such a beauty as you master now.
      So all their praises are but prophecies
      Of this our time, all you prefiguring,
      And, for they looked but with divining eyes,
12 They had not still enough your worth to sing:
        For we, which now behold these present days,
        Have eyes to wonder, but lack tongues to praise.

105: 4 **still** always   5 **Kind** naturally benevolent   8 **difference** variety
9 **Fair** beautiful   9 **argument** theme   11 **And in ... spent** i.e., and in
variations on this theme I expend all my imagination

106: 1 **wasted** past   2 **wights** people   4 **lovely** attractive   5 **blazon**
commemorative description   11 **for** because   11 **divining** guessing
12 **still** yet (the common emendation to "skill" is unnecessary)   13 **For** for
even

107   Not mine own fears nor the prophetic soul
      Of the wide world dreaming on things to come
      Can yet the lease of my true love control,
4   Supposed as forfeit to a confined doom.
      The mortal moon hath her eclipse endured,
      And the sad augurs mock their own presage,
      Incertainties now crown themselves assured,
8   And peace proclaims olives of endless age.
      Now with the drops of this most balmy time
      My love looks fresh, and Death to me subscribes,
      Since, spite of him, I'll live in this poor rhyme,
12   While he insults o'er dull and speechless tribes:
        And thou in this shalt find thy monument,
        When tyrants' crests and tombs of brass are spent.

108   What's in the brain that ink may character
      Which hath not figured to thee my true spirit?
      What's new to speak, what now to register,
4   That may express my love or thy dear merit?
      Nothing, sweet boy, but yet, like prayers divine,
      I must each day say o'er the very same;
      Counting no old thing old, thou mine, I thine,
8   Even as when first I hallowed thy fair name.
      So that eternal love in love's fresh case
      Weighs not the dust and injury of age,
      Nor gives to necessary wrinkles place,
12   But makes antiquity for aye his page,
        Finding the first conceit of love there bred
        Where time and outward form would show it dead.

107: 3 **lease** allotted time 4 **Supposed ... doom** i.e., though it is thought doomed to expire after a limited time 5 **The mortal moon ... endured** (numerous commentators claim that this line dates the sonnet; among interpretations are: 1588, when the Spanish Armada, thought to have assumed a crescent formation, was destroyed; 1595, when the moon underwent a total eclipse; 1595, when Queen Elizabeth I survived a critical period in her horoscope; 1599, when Queen Elizabeth survived an illness) 6–7 **And the sad ... assured** and the prophets of gloom are mocked by their own predictions now that uncertainties yield to assurance (?) 10 **to me subscribes** acknowledges me as his superior 12 **insults** triumphs 14 **spent** consumed

108: 1 **character** write 2 **figured** shown 9 **fresh case** youthful appearance 10 **Weighs not** cares not for 12 **for aye his page** forever his servant 13 **conceit** conception

109   O, never say that I was false of heart,
      Though absence seemed my flame to qualify.
      As easy might I from myself depart
4   As from my soul, which in thy breast doth lie.
      That is my home of love; if I have ranged,
      Like him that travels, I return again,
      Just to the time, not with the time exchanged,
8   So that myself bring water for my stain.
      Never believe, though in my nature reigned
      All frailties that besiege all kinds of blood,
      That it could so preposterously be stained
12   To leave for nothing all thy sum of good;
        For nothing this wide universe I call
        Save thou, my Rose; in it thou art my all.

110   Alas, 'tis true I have gone here and there
      And made myself a motley to the view,
      Gored mine own thoughts, sold cheap what is most dear,
4   Made old offenses of affections new.
      Most true it is that I have looked on truth
      Askance and strangely; but, by all above,
      These blenches gave my heart another youth,
8   And worse essays proved thee my best of love.
      Now all is done, have what shall have no end.
      Mine appetite I never more will grind
      On newer proof, to try an older friend,
12   A god in love, to whom I am confined.
        Then give me welcome, next my heaven the best,
        Even to thy pure and most most loving breast.

109: 2 **qualify** moderate   5 **ranged** wandered   7 **Just** punctual   7 **exchanged** changed   10 **blood** flesh, temperament

110: 2 **motley** jester   3 **Gored** wounded   4 **affections** passions   5 **truth** fidelity   6 **strangely** in a reserved manner   7 **blenches** side glances (?)   8 **worse essays** trials of worse friendships (?)   9 **have what shall have no end** take what shall be eternal   11 **proof** experiment   11 **try** test   13 **next** next to

111 O, for my sake do you with Fortune chide,
The guilty goddess of my harmful deeds,
That did not better for my life provide
4 Than public means which public manners breeds.
Thence comes it that my name receives a brand,
And almost thence my nature is subdued
To what it works in, like the dyer's hand.
8 Pity me then, and wish I were renewed,
Whilst, like a willing patient, I will drink
Potions of eisel 'gainst my strong infection;
No bitterness that I will bitter think,
12 Nor double penance, to correct correction.
Pity me then, dear friend, and I assure ye
Even that your pity is enough to cure me.

112 Your love and pity doth th' impression fill,
Which vulgar scandal stamped upon my brow;
For what care I who calls me well or ill,
4 So you o'er-green my bad, my good allow?
You are my all the world, and I must strive
To know my shames and praises from your tongue;
None else to me, nor I to none alive,
8 That my steeled sense or changes right or wrong.
In so profound abysm I throw all care
Of others' voices, that my adder's sense
To critic and to flatter stoppèd are.
12 Mark how with my neglect I do dispense:
You are so strongly in my purpose bred,
That all the world besides methinks are dead.

111: 3 **That** who 3 **life** livelihood 4 **Than ... breeds** than earning a livelihood by satisfying the public, which engenders vulgar manners 5 **brand** stimga 6-7 **subdued/To** subjected to 10 **eisel** vinegar (used as a preventative against the plague)

112: 1 **doth th' impression fill** effaces the scar 2 **stamped** (allusion to branding felons) 4 **allow** approve 6 **shames** faults 7-8 **None else ... wrong** only you can change my sense of what is right and wrong (?) 9 **profound** deep 10 **adder's sense** i.e., deaf ears (adders were thought to be deaf) 12 **Mark how ... dispense** listen to how I excuse ("dispense with") my neglect (i.e., of others) 13 **in my purpose bred** grown in my mind 14 **That all ... dead** that I think only you have life

113 Since I left you, mine eye is in my mind,
    And that which governs me to go about
    Doth part his function and is partly blind,
4   Seems seeing, but effectually is out;
    For it no form delivers to the heart
    Of bird, of flow'r, or shape, which it doth latch.
    Of his quick objects hath the mind no part,
8   Nor his own vision holds what it doth catch;
    For if it see the rud'st or gentlest sight,
    The most sweet favor or deformèd'st creature,
    The mountain, or the sea, the day, or night,
12 The crow, or dove, it shapes them to your feature.
        Incapable of more, replete with you,
        My most true mind thus maketh mine eye untrue.

114 Or whether doth my mind, being crowned with you,
    Drink up the monarch's plague, this flattery?
    Or whether shall I say mine eye saith true,
4   And that your love taught it this alchemy,
    To make of monsters, and things indigest,
    Such cherubins as your sweet self resemble,
    Creating every bad a perfect best
8   As fast as objects to his beams assemble?
    O, 'tis the first, 'tis flatt'ry in my seeing,
    And my great mind most kingly drinks it up.
    Mine eye well knows what with his gust is 'greeing,
12 And to his palate doth prepare the cup.
        If it be poisoned, 'tis the lesser sin
        That mine eye loves it and doth first begin.

113: 3 **Doth part ... blind** i.e., performs only part of its function, receiving images but not conveying them to the mind or "heart" 3, 7, 8 **his** its 4 **effectually** in reality 6 **latch** catch sight of 7 **quick** fleeting 10 **favor** face 13 **Incapable of** unable to take in 14 **true** faithful

114: 1, 3 **Or whether** (indicates alternative questions) 1 **being crowned with you** made a king by possessing you 2 **this flattery** i.e., false appearances (such as surround a monarch) as specified in the previous sonnet 5 **indigest** formless 6 **cherubins** angelic creatures 8 **to his beams assemble** appear to his eye (the eye was thought to cast beams; see Sonnet 20, line 6) 11 **with his gust is 'greeing** agrees with the mind's taste 14 **That** since

115

Those lines that I before have writ do lie,
Even those that said I could not love you dearer.
Yet then my judgment knew no reason why
4   My most full flame should afterwards burn clearer.
But reckoning Time, whose millioned accidents
Creep in 'twixt vows and change decrees of kings,
Tan sacred beauty, blunt the sharp'st intents,
8   Divert strong minds to th' course of alt'ring things.
Alas, why, fearing of Time's tyranny,
Might I not then say, "Now I love you best,"
When I was certain o'er incertainty,
12   Crowning the present, doubting of the rest?
      Love is a babe; then might I not say so,
      To give full growth to that which still doth grow.

116

Let me not to the marriage of true minds
Admit impediments; love is not love
Which alters when it alteration finds,
4   Or bends with the remover to remove.
O, no, it is an ever-fixèd mark
That looks on tempests and is never shaken;
It is the star to every wand'ring bark,
8   Whose worth's unknown, although his height be taken.
Love's not Time's fool, though rosy lips and cheeks
Within his bending sickle's compass come;
Love alters not with his brief hours and weeks,
12   But bears it out even to the edge of doom.
      If this be error and upon me proved,
      I never writ, nor no man ever loved.

115: 5 **millioned accidents** innumerable happenings 7 **Tan** i.e., darken, coarsen 8 **Divert** alter 12 **Crowning** glorifying 13 **then** therefore 13 **so** i.e., "Now I love you best" (line 10)

116: 2 **impediments** (an echo of the marriage service in the Book of Common Prayer: "If any of you know cause or just impediment ...") 5 **mark** seamark 7 **the star** the North Star 8 **Whose worth's ... taken** whose value (e.g., to mariners) is inestimable although the star's altitude has been determined 9 **fool** plaything 10 **compass** range, circle 11 **his** Time's 12 **bears it out** survives 12 **edge of doom** Judgment Day 13 **upon** against

117 Accuse me thus: that I have scanted all
    Wherein I should your great deserts repay,
    Forgot upon your dearest love to call,
4   Whereto all bonds do tie me day by day;
    That I have frequent been with unknown minds,
    And given to time your own dear-purchased right;
    That I have hoisted sail to all the winds
8   Which should transport me farthest from your sight.
    Book both my willfulness and errors down,
    And on just proof surmise accumulate;
    Bring me within the level of your frown,
12 But shoot not at me in your wakened hate;
      Since my appeal says I did strive to prove
      The constancy and virtue of your love.

118 Like as to make our appetites more keen
    With eager compounds we our palate urge,
    As to prevent our maladies unseen,
4   We sicken to shun sickness when we purge;
    Even so, being full of your ne'er-cloying sweetness,
    To bitter sauces did I frame my feeding;
    And, sick of welfare, found a kind of meetness
8   To be diseased ere that there was true needing.
    Thus policy in love, t' anticipate
    The ills that were not, grew to faults assured,
    And brought to medicine a healthful state,
12 Which, rank of goodness, would by ill be cured.
      But thence I learn, and find the lesson true,
      Drugs poison him that so fell sick of you.

117: 1 **scanted all** given only grudgingly 5 **frequent** intimate 5 **unknown minds** i.e., nonentities 6 **given to time** squandered on other people of the time 9 **Book** write down in a book 10 **surmise accumulate** add suspicions 11 **level** range, aim 13 **appeal** plea 13 **prove** test

118: 2 **eager compounds** tart sauces 2 **urge** stimulate 3 **prevent** forestall 6 **bitter sauces** i.e., undesirable people 6 **frame** direct 7 **sick of welfare** gorged with well-being 7 **meetness** fitness 9 **policy** prudence 11 **medicine** i.e., the need of medicine 12 **rank of** gorged with

119 What potions have I drunk of Siren tears
  Distilled from limbecks foul as hell within,
  Applying fears to hopes and hopes to fears,
4 Still losing when I saw myself to win!
  What wretched errors hath my heart committed,
  Whilst it hath thought itself so blessèd never!
  How have mine eyes out of their spheres been fitted
8 In the distraction of this madding fever!
  O, benefit of ill: now I find true
  That better is by evil still made better;
  And ruined love, when it is built anew,
12 Grows fairer than at first, more strong, far greater.
   So I return rebuked to my content,
   And gain by ills thrice more than I have spent.

120 That you were once unkind befriends me now,
  And for that sorrow which I then did feel
  Needs must I under my transgression bow,
4 Unless my nerves were brass or hammered steel.
  For if you were by my unkindness shaken,
  As I by yours, y'have passed a hell of time,
  And I, a tyrant, have no leisure taken
8 To weigh how once I suffered in your crime.
  O, that our night of woe might have rememb'red
  My deepest sense how hard true sorrow hits,
  And soon to you, as you to me then, tend'red
12 The humble salve which wounded bosoms fits!
   But that your trespass now becomes a fee;
   Mine ransoms yours, and yours must ransom me.

119: 2 **limbecks** alembics 3 **Applying** i.e., as an ointment 4 **Still**
always 6 **so blessèd never** never so blessed 7 **spheres** sockets 7 **fitted**
forced by fits

120: 2 **for** because of 4 **nerves** sinews 7–8 **no leisure ... weigh** not taken
the time to consider 9 **night of woe** i.e., estrangement 9 **rememb'red**
reminded 11 **soon** as soon 11 **tend'red** offered 12 **humble salve**
balm of humility 12 **fits** suits 13 **that your trespass** that trespass of yours
13 **fee** compensation 14 **ransoms** atones for

121　'Tis better to be vile than vile esteemed
　　　When not to be receives reproach of being,
　　　And the just pleasure lost, which is so deemed
4　　Not by our feeling, but by others' seeing.
　　　For why should others' false adulterate eyes
　　　Give salutation to my sportive blood?
　　　Or on my frailties why are frailer spies,
8　　Which in their wills count bad what I think good?
　　　No, I am that I am, and they that level
　　　At my abuses reckon up their own;
　　　I may be straight though they themselves be bevel.
12　By their rank thoughts my deeds must not be shown,
　　　　　Unless this general evil they maintain:
　　　　　All men are bad and in their badness reign.

122　Thy gift, thy tables, are within my brain
　　　Full charactered with lasting memory,
　　　Which shall above that idle rank remain
4　　Beyond all date, even to eternity;
　　　Or, at the least, so long as brain and heart
　　　Have faculty by nature to subsist,
　　　Till each to rased oblivion yield his part
8　　Of thee, thy record never can be missed.
　　　That poor retention could not so much hold,
　　　Nor need I tallies thy dear love to score.
　　　Therefore to give them from me was I bold,
12　To trust those tables that receive thee more.
　　　　　To keep an adjunct to remember thee
　　　　　Were to import forgetfulness in me.

121: 2 **being** i.e., being vile　3 **just** legitimate　3 **so** i.e., vile　6 **Give salutation to** act on　6 **sportive** wanton　8 **in their wills** i.e., willfully (?)　9 **that** who (an echo of Exodus 3:14)　9 **level** aim　10 **abuses** transgressions　11 **bevel** i.e., crooked　12 **rank** corrupt

122: 1 **tables** memorandum books　2 **charactered** written　3 **that idle rank** that useless series of leaves　7 **rased oblivion** oblivion which erases　7 **his** its　9 **That poor retention** i.e., the memorandum books　10 **tallies** accounting devices　12 **those tables** i.e., the mind　14 **import** imply

123 No, Time, thou shalt not boast that I do change.
   Thy pyramids built up with newer might
   To me are nothing novel, nothing strange;
4 They are but dressings of a former sight.
   Our dates are brief, and therefore we admire
   What thou dost foist upon us that is old,
   And rather make them born to our desire
8 Than think that we before have heard them told.
   Thy registers and thee I both defy,
   Not wond'ring at the present, nor the past;
   For thy records and what we see doth lie,
12 Made more or less by thy continual haste.
    This I do vow, and this shall ever be:
    I will be true despite thy scythe and thee.

124 If my dear love were but the child of state,
   It might for Fortune's bastard be unfathered,
   As subject to Time's love, or to Time's hate,
4 Weeds among weeds, or flowers with flowers gathered.
   No, it was builded far from accident;
   It suffers not in smiling pomp, nor falls
   Under the blow of thrallèd discontent,
8 Whereto th' inviting time our fashion calls.
   It fears not Policy, that heretic,
   Which works on leases of short-numb'red hours,
   But all alone stands hugely politic,
12 That it nor grows with heat, nor drowns with showers.
    To this I witness call the fools of Time,
    Which die for goodness, who have lived for crime.

123: 2 **pyramids** (possibly an allusion to Egyptian obelisks erected in Rome by Pope Sextus 1586–89; more likely an allusion to triumphal structures erected in London to welcome James I in 1603; most likely a reference to all monuments) 5 **dates** allotted times 5 **admire** regard with wonder 7 **born to our desire** turn them into the new things we wish to see 9 **registers** records

124: 1 **love** i.e., the emotion, not the person 1 **but** only 1 **child of state** i.e., product of externals such as wealth and power 2 **for Fortune's bastard be unfathered** i.e., be marked as the bastard son of Fortune 5 **accident** chance 7 **thrallèd discontent** discontent of persons oppressed 9 **Policy, that heretic** i.e., unprincipled self-interest which is faithless 11 **all alone stands hugely politic** i.e., only love is infinitely prudent 12 **That it nor ... nor** since it neither ... nor 13 **fools of Time** playthings of Time (?) time-servers (?) 14 **Which ... crime** i.e., who at the last minute repent their criminal lives

125   Were't aught to me I bore the canopy,
      With my extern the outward honoring,
      Or laid great bases for eternity,
4   Which proves more short than waste or ruining?
      Have I not seen dwellers on form and favor
      Lose all and more by paying too much rent,
      For compound sweet forgoing simple savor,
8   Pitiful thrivers, in their gazing spent?
      No, let me be obsequious in thy heart,
      And take thou my oblation, poor but free,
      Which is not mixed with seconds, knows no art,
12   But mutual render, only me for thee.
         Hence, thou suborned informer! A true soul
         When most impeached stands least in thy control.

126   O thou, my lovely boy, who in thy power
      Dost hold Time's fickle glass, his sickle hour,
      Who hast by waning grown, and therein show'st
4   Thy lovers withering, as thy sweet self grow'st;
      If Nature, sovereign mistress over wrack,
      As thou goest onwards, still will pluck thee back,
      She keeps thee to this purpose, that her skill
8   May Time disgrace and wretched minutes kill.
      Yet fear her, O thou minion of her pleasure;
      She may detain, but not still keep her treasure.
         Her audit, though delayed, answered must be,
12   And her quietus is to render thee.

125: 1 **Were't aught** would it be anything 1 **canopy** (borne over an eminent person) 2 **extern** outward action 5 **dwellers on form and favor** i.e., those who make much of appearance and external beauty 6 **paying too much rent** i.e., obsequiousness 7 **simple** pure 8 **Pitiful ... spent** pitiable creatures who use themselves up in looking at outward honor 9 **obsequious** devoted 11 **seconds** i.e., baser matter 11 **art** artifice 12 **render** surrender 13 **suborned informer** perjured witness 14 **impeached** accused

126: 2 **glass** mirror 2 **hour** hourglass 3 **by waning grown** i.e., by growing older growing more beautiful 5 **wrack** destruction 6, 10 **still** always 9 **minion** favorite 11 **audit** final account 11 **answered** paid 12 **quietus** final settlement 12 **render** surrender

127   In the old age black was not counted fair,
     Or, if it were, it bore not beauty's name.
     But now is black beauty's successive heir,
4   And beauty slandered with a bastard shame;
     For since each hand hath put on nature's power,
     Fairing the foul with art's false borrowed face,
     Sweet beauty hath no name, no holy bower,
8   But is profaned, if not lives in disgrace.
     Therefore my mistress' eyes are raven black,
     Her eyes so suited, and they mourners seem,
     At such who, not born fair, no beauty lack,
12   Sland'ring creation with a false esteem:
       Yet so they mourn, becoming of their woe,
       That every tongue says beauty should look so.

127: 1 **old age** i.e., age of chivalry   1 **black** i.e., brunette   1 **fair** beautiful (with a pun on the obvious meaning)   3 **successive heir** legitimate heir 4 **And beauty ... shame** i.e., blond beauty is defamed as illegitimate   5 **put on** taken over 6 **art's false borrowed face** i.e., cosmetics 7 **Sweet** natural, i.e., blond 11 **At** for 13 **becoming of** gracing

128   How oft, when thou, my music, music play'st
Upon that blessèd wood whose motion sounds
With thy sweet fingers when thou gently sway'st
4   The wiry concord that mine ear confounds,
Do I envy those jacks that nimble leap
To kiss the tender inward of thy hand,
Whilst my poor lips, which should that harvest reap,
8   At the wood's boldness by thee blushing stand.
To be so tickled, they would change their state
And situation with those dancing chips
O'er whom thy fingers walk with gentle gait,
12   Making dead wood more blest than living lips.
     Since saucy jacks so happy are in this,
     Give them thy fingers, me thy lips to kiss.

128: 2 **wood** keys (of the spinet or virginal)   2 **motion** movement   3 **thou gently sway'st** you gently direct   4 **wiry concord** harmony of the strings   4 **confounds** delightfully overcomes   5 **jacks** (devices which pluck the strings, but here probably misused for keys; in line 13, there is a pun on the meaning "fellows")   9 **they** i.e., the poet's lips

5-6 There are always some who cannot bear to think that the Swan of Avon could ever make a mistake about anything. A certain E. W. Naylor explains these lines as follows. "The lady, having removed the rail which ordinarily stops the 'jacks' from jumping right out of the instrument when the keys are struck, was leaning over her work, testing it by striking the defective note, and holding the 'tender inward' of her hand over the 'jack' to prevent it from flying to the other end of the room."

                                                   W.H.A.

129   Th' expense of spirit in a waste of shame
       Is lust in action; and, till action, lust
       Is perjured, murd'rous, bloody, full of blame,
4   Savage, extreme, rude, cruel, not to trust;
       Enjoyed no sooner but despisèd straight;
       Past reason hunted, and no sooner had,
       Past reason hated as a swallowed bait
8   On purpose laid to make the taker mad;
       Made in pursuit, and in possession so;
       Had, having, and in quest to have, extreme;
       A bliss in proof, and proved, a very woe,
12   Before, a joy proposed; behind, a dream.
           All this the world well knows, yet none knows well
           To shun the heaven that leads men to this hell.

130   My mistress' eyes are nothing like the sun;
       Coral is far more red than her lips' red;
       If snow be white, why then her breasts are dun;
4   If hairs be wires, black wires grown on her head.
       I have seen roses damasked, red and white,
       But no such roses see I in her cheeks,
       And in some perfumes is there more delight
8   Than in the breath that from my mistress reeks.
       I love to hear her speak, yet well I know
       That music hath a far more pleasing sound.
       I grant I never saw a goddess go;
12   My mistress when she walks treads on the ground.
           And yet, by heaven, I think my love as rare
           As any she belied with false compare.

129: 1 **expense** expenditure   1 **spirit** vital power, semen   6, 7 **Past** beyond
9 **Made** i.e., made mad (most editors emend to "Mad")   11 **in proof** while
being experienced   11 **proved** i.e., when experienced   12 **dream** night-
mare (?)   14 **heaven** the sensation (or place?) of bliss

130: 5 **damasked** mingled red and white   8 **reeks** emanates   11 **go**
walk   14 **she** woman   14 **compare** comparison

131   Thou art as tyrannous, so as thou art,
As those whose beauties proudly make them cruel;
For well thou know'st to my dear doting heart
4   Thou art the fairest and most precious jewel.
Yet, in good faith, some say that thee behold,
Thy face hath not the power to make love groan;
To say they err I dare not be so bold,
8   Although I swear it to myself alone.
And, to be sure that is not false I swear,
A thousand groans, but thinking on thy face,
One on another's neck, do witness bear
12   Thy black is fairest in my judgment's place.
   In nothing art thou black save in thy deeds,
   And thence this slander, as I think, proceeds.

132   Thine eyes I love, and they, as pitying me,
Knowing thy heart torment me with disdain,
Have put on black and loving mourners be,
4   Looking with pretty ruth upon my pain.
And truly not the morning sun of heaven
Better becomes the gray cheeks of the east,
Nor that full star that ushers in the even
8   Doth half that glory to the sober west
As those two mourning eyes become thy face.
O, let it then as well beseem thy heart
To mourn for me, since mourning doth thee grace,
12   And suit thy pity like in every part.
   Then will I swear beauty herself is black,
   And all they foul that thy complexion lack.

131: 1 so as thou art i.e., even though you are black and not beautiful
3 dear loving   10 but thinking on when I but think of   11 One on
another's neck i.e., in quick succession   12 in my judgment's place in the
place assigned it by my judgment   13 black foul

132: 2 torment to torment   4 ruth pity   7 even evening   9 mourning
(with a pun on "morning")   12 suit thy pity like clothe thy pity alike
14 foul ugly

133   Beshrew that heart that makes my heart to groan
      For that deep wound it gives my friend and me.
      Is't not enough to torture me alone,
4   But slave to slavery my sweet'st friend must be?
      Me from myself thy cruel eye hath taken,
      And my next self thou harder hast engrossed.
      Of him, myself, and thee, I am forsaken;
8   A torment thrice threefold thus to be crossed.
      Prison my heart in thy steel bosom's ward,
      But then my friend's heart let my poor heart bail;
      Whoe'er keeps me, let my heart be his guard;
12   Thou canst not then use rigor in my jail.
        And yet thou wilt, for I, being pent in thee,
        Perforce am thine, and all that is in me.

134   So, now I have confessed that he is thine
      And I myself am mortgaged to thy will,
      Myself I'll forfeit, so that other mine
4   Thou wilt restore to be my comfort still.
      But thou wilt not, nor he will not be free,
      For thou art covetous, and he is kind;
      He learned but surety-like to write for me
8   Under that bond that him as fast doth bind.
      The statute of thy beauty thou wilt take,
      Thou usurer that put'st forth all to use,
      And sue a friend came debtor for my sake;
12   So him I lose through my unkind abuse.
        Him have I lost, thou hast both him and me;
        He pays the whole, and yet am I not free.

133: 1 **Beshrew** curse (mild imprecation) 2 **For** because of 6 **my next self** i.e., my friend 6 **engrossed** captured 8 **crossed** thwarted 9 **ward** cell 10 **bail** go bail for, i.e., free 11 **keeps** guards 11 **guard** guardhouse 12 **rigor** cruelty 12 **my jail** i.e., my heart

134: 2 **will** (1) purpose (2) carnal desire (perhaps with puns on Shakespeare's name and the name of the friend) 3 **so** provided that 3 **other mine** i.e., my friend 4 **still** always 7-8 **He learned ... bind** (perhaps the idea is that the friend, as proxy, wooed the woman for the poet but is now in her bondage) 9 **statute** security 10 **use** usury 11 **came** who became (?) 12 **my unkind abuse** unkind deception of me

135 Whoever hath her wish, thou hast thy *Will*,
     And *Will* to boot, and *Will* in overplus;
     More than enough am I that vex thee still,
4   To thy sweet will making addition thus.
     Wilt thou, whose will is large and spacious,
     Not once vouchsafe to hide my will in thine?
     Shall will in others seem right gracious,
8   And in my will no fair acceptance shine?
     The sea, all water, yet receives rain still
     And in abundance addeth to his store;
     So thou being rich in *Will* add to thy *Will*
12   One will of mine, to make thy large *Will* more.
        Let no unkind, no fair beseechers kill;
        Think all but one, and me in that one *Will*.

135: 1 Will (1) person named Will (perhaps the poet, perhaps the friend, perhaps the woman's husband, perhaps all; Will is capitalized and italicized in this and in the next sonnet wherever it so appears in the quarto) (2) desire, volition 3, 9 still always 4 making addition thus i.e., by adding myself 5, 7 (rhyming words are trisyllabic) 6 vouchsafe consent 10 his its 13 no unkind no unkind act, word, or person 13 no fair beseechers i.e., any applicants for your favors (?) 14 Think all ... Will think all Wills as one and include me in that one

13 So in Q and a perfectly possible reading. Personally, however, I am inclined to accept Malone's emendation, Let no unkind No fair beseechers kill, which makes No a noun and fair beseechers the object of the verb kill.

                                                                    W.H.A.

136   If thy soul check thee that I come so near,
Swear to thy blind soul that I was thy *Will*,
And will, thy soul knows, is admitted there;
4   Thus far for love my love-suit, sweet, fulfill.
Will will fulfill the treasure of thy love,
Ay, fill it full with wills, and my will one.
In things of great receipt with ease we prove
8   Among a number one is reckoned none.
Then in the number let me pass untold,
Though in thy store's account I one must be;
For nothing hold me, so it please thee hold
12   That nothing me, a something, sweet, to thee.
    Make but my name thy love, and love that still,
    And then thou lovest me for my name is *Will*.

137   Thou blind fool, Love, what dost thou to mine eyes
That they behold and see not what they see?
They know what beauty is, see where it lies,
4   Yet what the best is take the worst to be.
If eyes, corrupt by overpartial looks,
Be anchored in the bay where all men ride,
Why of eyes' falsehood hast thou forgèd hooks,
8   Whereto the judgment of my heart is tied?
Why should my heart think that a several plot,
Which my heart knows the wide world's common place?
Or mine eyes seeing this, say this is not,
12   To put fair truth upon so foul a face?
    In things right true my heart and eyes have erred,
    And to this false plague are they now transferred.

136: 1 **check** rebuke 1 **come so near** (1) touch to the quick (2) come so near to your bed 5 **fulfill the treasure** fill the treasury 6 **one** one of them 7 **things of great receipt** i.e., large matters 8 **Among ... none** ("one is no number" was an Elizabethan saying) 9 **untold** uncounted 10 **thy store's account** i.e., the inventory of your supply (of lovers) 13 **my name** i.e., will, carnal desire (?) 13 **still** always

137: 3 **lies** inhabits 5 **corrupt** corrupted 6 **ride** (pun on the sense "to mount sexually") 9 **that a several plot** that place a private field 10 **common place** open field (with a pun on **common** = promiscuous) 12 **To** so as to 14 **plague** (1) plague of falseness (2) mistress

138   When my love swears that she is made of truth,
       I do believe her though I know she lies,
       That she might think me some untutored youth,
  4   Unlearnèd in the world's false subtleties.
       Thus vainly thinking that she thinks me young,
       Although she knows my days are past the best,
       Simply I credit her false-speaking tongue;
  8   On both sides thus is simple truth suppressed.
       But wherefore says she not she is unjust?
       And wherefore say not I that I am old?
       O, love's best habit is in seeming trust,
 12   And age in love loves not to have years told.
         Therefore I lie with her, and she with me,
         And in our faults by lies we flattered be.

139   O, call not me to justify the wrong
       That thy unkindness lays upon my heart;
       Wound me not with thine eye but with thy tongue;
  4   Use power with power and slay me not by art.
       Tell me thou lov'st elsewhere; but in my sight,
       Dear heart, forbear to glance thine eye aside;
       What need'st thou wound with cunning when thy might
  8   Is more than my o'erpressed defense can bide?
       Let me excuse thee; ah, my love well knows
       Her pretty looks have been mine enemies,
       And therefore from my face she turns my foes,
 12   That they elsewhere might dart their injuries.
         Yet do not so; but since I am near slain,
         Kill me outright with looks and rid my pain.

138: 1 truth fidelity   3 That so that   7 Simply (1) foolishly (2) pretending to be simple   7 credit believe   9 unjust unfaithful   11 habit appearance   11 seeming trust the appearance of truth   12 told counted   13 lie with (1) lie to (2) sleep with

139: 4 with power i.e., openly, directly   4 art artful means   8 o'erpressed overpowered   11 my foes i.e., her looks

140 Be wise as thou art cruel; do not press
   My tongue-tied patience with too much disdain,
   Lest sorrow lend me words, and words express
4 The manner of my pity-wanting pain.
   If I might teach thee wit, better it were,
   Though not to love, yet love, to tell me so;
   As testy sick men, when their deaths be near,
8 No news but health from their physicians know.
   For if I should despair, I should grow mad,
   And in my madness might speak ill of thee.
   Now this ill-wresting world is grown so bad
12 Mad slanderers by mad ears believèd be.
    That I may not be so, nor thou belied,
    Bear thine eyes straight, though thy proud heart go wide.

141 In faith I do not love thee with mine eyes,
   For they in thee a thousand errors note;
   But 'tis my heart that loves what they despise,
4 Who in despite of view is pleased to dote.
   Nor are mine ears with thy tongue's tune delighted,
   Nor tender feeling to base touches prone,
   Nor taste, nor smell, desire to be invited
8 To any sensual feast with thee alone.
   But my five wits nor my five senses can
   Dissuade one foolish heart from serving thee,
   Who leaves unswayed the likeness of a man,
12 Thy proud heart's slave and vassal wretch to be.
    Only my plague thus far I count my gain,
    That she that makes me sin awards me pain.

140: 1 **press** oppress 4 **manner** nature 4 **pity-wanting** unpitied 5 **wit** wisdom 6 **so** i.e., that you love me 7 **testy** fretful 11 **ill-wresting** i.e., misinterpreting everything for the worse 13 **so** (1) a "mad slanderer" (2) so believed 14 **wide** wide of the mark

141: 4 **Who in despite of view** which in spite of what they see 6 **base touches** sexual contact 9 **But** but neither 9 **five wits** common wit, imagination, fantasy, estimation, memory 10 **serving** loving 11 **Who ... man** i.e., which ceases to rule and so leaves me what is only the semblance of a man

142   Love is my sin, and thy dear virtue hate,
        Hate of my sin, grounded on sinful loving.
        O, but with mine compare thou thine own state,
4   And thou shalt find it merits not reproving,
        Of if it do, not from those lips of thine,
        That have profaned their scarlet ornaments
        And sealed false bonds of love as oft as mine,
8   Robbed others' beds' revenues of their rents.
        Be it lawful I love thee as thou lov'st those
        Whom thine eyes woo as mine importune thee.
        Root pity in thy heart, that, when it grows,
12   Thy pity may deserve to pitied be.
           If thou dost seek to have what thou dost hide,
           By self-example mayst thou be denied.

143   Lo, as a careful housewife runs to catch
        One of her feathered creatures broke away,
        Sets down her babe, and makes all swift dispatch
4   In pursuit of the thing she would have stay;
        Whilst her neglected child holds her in chase,
        Cries to catch her whose busy care is bent
        To follow that which flies before her face,
8   Not prizing her poor infant's discontent:
        So run'st thou after that which flies from thee,
        Whilst I, thy babe, chase thee afar behind;
        But if thou catch thy hope, turn back to me
12   And play the mother's part, kiss me, be kind.
           So will I pray that thou mayst have thy *Will*,
           If thou turn back and my loud crying still.

142: 1 **dear** inmost   4 **it** i.e., my state   6 **scarlet ornaments** i.e., lips
(compared to scarlet wax that seals documents) 8 **Robbed ... rents** i.e., has
robbed wives of what their husbands owed them 9 **Be** it let it be 13 **what**
that which, i.e., pity

143: 5 **holds her in chase** chases her 8 **prizing** regarding
13–14 Some scholarly follies are so extraordinary that they deserve to be
immortalized. Gregor Sarrazin, a German-Swiss, emended these lines as
follows:
So will I pray that thou may'est have thy *Hen*, (short for Henry)
If thou turn back and my loud crying pen.
                                            W.H.A.

144   Two loves I have, of comfort and despair,
       Which like two spirits do suggest me still;
       The better angel is a man right fair,
4   The worser spirit a woman colored ill.
       To win me soon to hell, my female evil
       Tempteth my better angel from my side,
       And would corrupt my saint to be a devil,
8   Wooing his purity with her foul pride.
       And whether that my angel be turned fiend
       Suspect I may, yet not directly tell;
       But being both from me, both to each friend,
12   I guess one angel in another's hell.
         Yet this shall I ne'er know, but live in doubt,
         Till my bad angel fire my good one out.

145   Those lips that Love's own hand did make
       Breathed forth the sound that said, "I hate"
       To me that languished for her sake.
4   But when she saw my woeful state,
       Straight in her heart did mercy come,
       Chiding that tongue that ever sweet
       Was used in giving gentle doom,
8   And taught it thus anew to greet:
       "I hate," she altered with an end
       That followed it as gentle day
       Doth follow night, who, like a fiend,
12   From heaven to hell is flown away.
         "I hate" from hate away she threw,
         And saved my life, saying, "not you."

144: 1 **of comfort and despair** i.e., one offering heavenly mercy, the other offering hellish despair   2 **suggest me still** always urge me   4 **colored ill** i.e., dark   10 **directly** precisely   11 **from** away from   11 **each** each other   12 **in another's hell** (with an allusion to the female sexual organ) 14 **fire my good one out** i.e., communicate venereal disease

145: 7 **doom** judgment   9 **end** ending

146   Poor soul, the center of my sinful earth,
       My sinful earth these rebel pow'rs that thee array,
       Why dost thou pine within and suffer dearth,
   4   Painting thy outward walls so costly gay?
       Why so large cost, having so short a lease,
       Dost thou upon thy fading mansion spend?
       Shall worms, inheritors of this excess,
   8   Eat up thy charge? Is this thy body's end?
       Then, soul, live thou upon thy servant's loss,
       And let that pine to aggravate thy store;
       Buy terms divine in selling hours of dross;
   12 Within be fed, without be rich no more:
           So shalt thou feed on Death, that feeds on men,
           And Death once dead, there's no more dying then.

147   My love is as a fever, longing still
       For that which longer nurseth the disease,
       Feeding on that which doth preserve the ill,
   4   Th' uncertain sickly appetite to please.
       My reason, the physician to my love,
       Angry that his prescriptions are not kept,
       Hath left me, and I desperate now approve
   8   Desire is death, which physic did except.
       Past cure I am, now reason is past care,
       And frantic-mad with evermore unrest;
       My thoughts and my discourse as madmen's are,
   12 At random from the truth vainly expressed:
           For I have sworn thee fair, and thought thee bright,
           Who art as black as hell, as dark as night.

146: 1 **sinful earth** i.e., body   2 **My sinful earth** (obviously the printer mistakenly repeated here words of the previous line. Among suggested emendations are: "Thrall to," "Fooled by," "Rebuke," and "Leagued with")   4 **Painting** i.e., adorning   5 **cost** expense   7 **excess** extravagant expenditure   8 **charge** (1) expense (2) burden, i.e., the body   10 **that** i.e., the body   10 **aggravate** increase   11 **terms divine** ages of immortality

147: 1 **still** always   3 **preserve the ill** prolong the illness   7-8 **approve ... except** find by experience that Desire, which refused medicine, is death (?)

148   O me, what eyes hath Love put in my head,
Which have no correspondence with true sight!
Or, if they have, where is my judgment fled,
4   That censures falsely what they see aright?
If that be fair whereon my false eyes dote,
What means the world to say it is not so?
If it be not, then love doth well denote
8   Love's eye is not so true as all men's no.
How can it? O, how can Love's eye be true,
That is so vexed with watching and with tears?
No marvel then though I mistake my view;
12   The sun itself sees not till heaven clears.
        O cunning Love, with tears thou keep'st me blind,
        Lest eyes well-seeing thy foul faults should find.

149   Canst thou, O cruel, say I love thee not,
When I against myself with thee partake?
Do I not think on thee when I forgot
4   Am of myself, all tyrant for thy sake?
Who hateth thee that I do call my friend?
On whom frown'st thou that I do fawn upon?
Nay, if thou lour'st on me, do I not spend
8   Revenge upon myself with present moan?
What merit do I in myself respect
That is so proud thy service to despise,
When all my best doth worship thy defect,
12   Commanded by the motion of thine eyes?
        But, love, hate on, for now I know thy mind;
        Those that can see thou lov'st, and I am blind.

148: 4 censures judges **8 eye** (with a pun on "aye" in contrast with **all men's no**) 10 **watching** wakefulness 11 **mistake my view** err in what I see

149: 2 partake unite 3–4 **forgot/Am of** forget **4 all tyrant** i.e., having become altogether a tyrant 8 **present moan** immediate grief 11 **defect** lack of good qualities

150   O, from what pow'r hast thou this pow'rful might
      With insufficiency my heart to sway?
      To make me give the lie to my true sight
4   And swear that brightness doth not grace the day?
      Whence hast thou this becoming of things ill
      That in the very refuse of thy deeds
      There is such strength and warrantize of skill
8   That in my mind thy worst all best exceeds?
      Who taught thee how to make me love thee more,
      The more I hear and see just cause of hate?
      O, though I love what others do abhor,
12   With others thou shouldst not abhor my state:
        If thy unworthiness raised love in me,
        More worthy I to be beloved of thee.

151   Love is too young to know what conscience is,
      Yet who knows not conscience is born of love?
      Then, gentle cheater, urge not my amiss,
4   Lest guilty of my faults thy sweet self prove.
      For, thou betraying me, I do betray
      My nobler part to my gross body's treason;
      My soul doth tell my body that he may
8   Triumph in love; flesh stays no farther reason,
      But, rising at thy name, doth point out thee,
      As his triumphant prize. Proud of this pride,
      He is contented thy poor drudge to be,
12   To stand in thy affairs, fall by thy side.
        No want of conscience hold it that I call
        Her "love" for whose dear love I rise and fall.

150: 2 insufficiency unworthiness   2 sway rule   3 give the lie to my true sight accuse my true sight of lying   5 becoming of things ill i.e., power to make evil look attractive   7 warrantize of skill guarantee of mental power   13 raised (sexual innuendo?)

151: 3 urge not my amiss stress not my sinfulness   8 flesh the penis 8 stays awaits   8 reason talk   9 rising rebelling (with a sexual pun, as in "point," line 9; "stand" and "fall," line 12; and "rise and fall," line 14) 10 Proud of swelling with

152   In loving thee thou know'st I am forsworn,
But thou art twice forsworn, to me love swearing;
In act thy bed-vow broke, and new faith torn
4   In vowing new hate after new love bearing.
But why of two oaths' breach do I accuse thee,
When I break twenty? I am perjured most,
For all my vows are oaths but to misuse thee,
8   And all my honest faith in thee is lost;
For I have sworn deep oaths of thy deep kindness,
Oaths of thy love, thy truth, thy constancy;
And, to enlighten thee, gave eyes to blindness,
12   Or made them swear against the thing they see;
    For I have sworn thee fair; more perjured eye,
    To swear against the truth so foul a lie.

153   Cupid laid by his brand and fell asleep.
A maid of Dian's this advantage found,
And his love-kindling fire did quickly steep
4   In a cold valley-fountain of that ground;
Which borrowed from this holy fire of Love
A dateless lively heat, still to endure,
And grew a seething bath, which yet men prove
8   Against strange maladies a sovereign cure.
But at my mistress' eye Love's brand new-fired,
The boy for trial needs would touch my breast;
I, sick withal, the help of bath desired,
12   And thither hied, a sad distempered guest,
    But found no cure; the bath for my help lies
    Where Cupid got new fire—my mistress' eyes.

152: 1 **am forsworn** i.e., have broken (my marriage) vows   7 **but to misuse** merely to misrepresent   11 **enlighten thee** make you shine   11 **gave eyes to blindness** i.e., caused my eyes not to see the truth   13 **eye** eyes (with a pun on "I")

153: 1 **brand** torch   2 **Dian** Diana, goddess of chastity   2 **advantage** opportunity   6 **dateless lively** eternal living   6 **still** always   7 **seething** boiling   7 **prove** find by experience   8 **sovereign** potent   10 **for trial needs would** as a test had to   11 **withal** with it   11 **bath** (possibly an allusion to the city of Bath, famous for its curative waters)   12 **distempered** diseased

154   The little Love-god lying once asleep
       Laid by his side his heart-inflaming brand,
       Whilst many nymphs that vowed chaste life to keep
4   Came tripping by, but in her maiden hand
       The fairest votary took up that fire,
       Which many legions of true hearts had warmed;
       And so the general of hot desire
8   Was, sleeping, by a virgin hand disarmed.
       This brand she quenchèd in a cool well by,
       Which from Love's fire took heart perpetual,
       Growing a bath and healthful remedy
12   For men diseased; but I, my mistress' thrall,
         Came there for cure, and this by that I prove:
         Love's fire heats water, water cools not love.

FINIS

154: 1 **Love-god** Cupid   2 **brand** torch   5 **votary** one vowed to chastity
7 **general** leader, i.e., Cupid   12 **thrall** slave

Textual Note

The present text of the sonnets is based on the quarto of 1609, the only edition of any authority; all subsequent editions of the sonnets derive from that of 1609. Two of the sonnets (138 and 144) had been published, in slightly different versions, in a volume of poems entitled *The Passionate Pilgrim* (1599); quite possibly all or almost all of the sonnets were written in the middle '90s, though it is equally possible that some were written only shortly before Thorpe issued his quarto with 154 sonnets. There is no evidence that Shakespeare oversaw the publication; probably the order in which the sonnets are presented is the publisher's rather than the author's. In 1640 John Benson issued a second edition. He dropped Thorpe's dedication and eight sonnets, rearranged the order of the remaining ones, made numerous verbal changes to suggest that the sonnets were written to a woman and not to a man, and implied in a preface that the sonnets had never before been published.

The present edition keeps the arrangement of the 1609 quarto, but corrects obvious typographical errors and modernizes spelling and punctuation. Other departures from the quarto are listed below, the present reading first, in bold, and then the reading of the quarto, in roman.

The Textual Editor wishes to acknowledge his indebtedness, especially in the glosses, to his late teacher, Hyder Edward Rollins, whose indispensable *New Variorum Edition* is as likely as any scholarly book to bear it out to the edge of doom.

W.B.

12.4 **are** or   13.7 **Yourself** You selfe   19.3 **jaws** yawes   19.5 **fleets** fleet'st   25.9 **might** worth   26.12 **thy** their   27.10 **thy** their   34.12 **cross** losse   35.8 **thy ... thy** their ... their   41.8 **she** he   43.11 **thy** their   44.13 **naught** naughts   45.12 **thy** their   46.3 **thy** their   46.8 **thy** their   46.9 **'cide** side   46.14 **thy** their   47.11 **not** nor   50.6 **dully** duly   51.10 **perfect'st** perfects   55.1 **monuments** monument   56.13 **Or** As   65.12 **of** or   69.3 **due** end   69.5 **Thy** Their   70.1 **art** are   70.6 **Thy** Their   74.12 **rememberèd** remembred   76.7 **tell** fel   77.10 **blanks** blacks   90.11 **shall** stall   91.8 **better** bitter   99.9 **One** Our   102.8 **her** his   111.1 **with** wish   112.14 **are** y'are   113.6 **latch** lack   113.14 **mine eye** mine   126.8 **minutes** mynuit   128.11 **thy** their   128.14 **thy** their   129.11 **proved, a** proud and   132.6 **of the** of th'   132.9 **mourning** morning   138.12 **to have t'** haue   144.6 **side** sight   144.9 **fiend** finde   153.14 **eyes** eye

Index of First Lines

Accuse me thus: that I have scanted all (117)
Against my love shall be as I am now (63)
Against that time, if ever that time come (49)
Ah, wherefore with infection should he live (67)
Alack, what poverty my Muse brings forth (103)
Alas, 'tis true I have gone here and there (110)
As a decrepit father takes delight (37)
As an unperfect actor on the stage (23)
As fast as thou shalt wane, so fast thou grow'st (11)
A woman's face, with Nature's own hand painted (20)

Being your slave, what should I do but tend (57)
Beshrew that heart that make my heart to groan (133)
Betwixt mine eye and heart a league is took (47)
Be wise as thou art cruel; do not press (140)
But be contented. When that fell arrest (74)
But do thy worst to steal thyself away (92)
But wherefore do not you a mightier way (16)

Canst thou, O cruel, say I love thee not (149)
Cupid laid by his brand and fell asleep (153)

Devouring Time, blunt thou the lion's paws (19)

Farewell, thou art too dear for my possessing (87)
For shame, deny that thou bear'st love to any (10)
From fairest creatures we desire increase (1)
From you have I been absent in the spring (98)
Full many a glorious morning have I seen (33)

How can I then return in happy plight (28)
How can my Muse want subject to invent (38)
How careful was I, when I took my way (48)
How heavy do I journey on the way (50)
How like a winter hath my absence been (97)
How oft, when thou, my music, music play'st (128)
How sweet and lovely dost thou make the shame (95)

If my dear love were but the child of state (124)
If the dull substance of my flesh were thought (44)
If there be nothing new, but that which is (59)
If thou survive my well-contented day (32)

If thy soul check thee that I come so near (136)
I grant thou wert not married to my Muse (82)
I never saw that you did painting need (83)
In faith I do not love thee with mine eyes (141)
In loving thee thou know'st I am forsworn (152)
In the old age black was not counted fair (127)
Is it for fear to wet a widow's eye (9)
Is it thy will thy image should keep open (61)

Let me confess that we two must be twain (36)
Let me not to the marriage of true minds (116)
Let not my love be called idolatry (105)
Let those who are in favor with their stars (25)
Like as the waves make towards the pebbled shore (60)
Like as to make our appetites more keen (118)
Lo, as a careful housewife runs to catch (143)
Lo, in the orient when the gracious light (7)
Look in thy glass and tell the face thou viewest (3)
Lord of my love, to whom in vassalage (26)
Love is my sin, and thy dear virtue hate (142)
Love is too young to know what conscience is (151)

Mine eye and heart are at a mortal war (46)
Mine eye hath played the painter and hath steeled (24)
Music to hear, why hear'st thou music sadly (8)
My glass shall not persuade me I am old (22)
My love is as a fever, longing still (147)
My love is strength'ned, though more weak in seeming (102)
My mistress' eyes are nothing like the sun (130)
My tongue-tied Muse in manners holds her still (85)

No longer mourn for me when I am dead (71)
No more be grieved at that which thou hast done (35)
Not from the stars do I my judgment pluck (14)
No, Time, thou shalt not boast that I do change (123)
Not marble, nor the gilded monuments (55)
Not mine own fears nor the prophetic soul (107)

O, call not me to justify the wrong (139)
O, for my sake do you with Fortune chide (111)
O, from what pow'r hast thou this pow'rful might (150)
O, how I faint when I of you do write (80)
O, how much more doth beauty beauteous seem (54)
O, how thy worth with manners may I sing (39)
O, lest the world should task you to recite (72)

O me, what eyes hath Love put in my head (148)
O, never say that was I false of heart (109)
Or I shall live your epitaph to make (81)
Or whether doth my mind, being crowned with you (114)
O, that you were yourself, but, love, you are (13)
O thou, my lovely boy, who in thy power (126)
O truant Muse, what shall be thy amends (101)

Poor soul, the center of my sinful earth (146)

Say that thou didst forsake me for some fault (89)
Shall I compare thee to a summer's day (18)
Since brass, nor stone, nor earth, nor boundless sea (65)
Since I left you, mine eye is in my mind (113)
Sin of self-love possesseth all mine eye (62)
So am I as the rich, whose blessèd key (52)
So are you to my thoughts as food to life (75)
So is it not with me as with that Muse (21)
Some glory in their birth, some in their skill (91)
Some say thy fault is youth, some wantonness (96)
So, now I have confessed that he is thine (134)
So oft have I invoked thee for my Muse (78)
So shall I live, supposing thou art true (93)
Sweet love, renew thy force; be it not said (56)

Take all my loves, my love, yea take them all (40)
That god forbid that made me first your slave (58)
That thou art blamed shall not be thy defect (70)
That thou hast her, it is not all my grief (42)
That time of year thou mayst in me behold (73)
That you were once unkind befriends me now (120)
The forward violet thus did I chide (99)
The little Love-god lying once asleep (154)
Then hate me when thou wilt; if ever, now (90)
Then let not winter's ragged hand deface (6)
The other two, slight air and purging fire (45)
Th' expense of spirit in a waste of shame (129)
They that have pow'r to hurt and will do none (94)
Thine eyes I love, and they, as pitying me (132)
Those hours that with gentle work did frame (5)
Those lines that I before have writ do lie (115)
Those lips that Love's own hand did make (145)
Those parts of thee that the world's eye doth view (69)
Those pretty wrongs that liberty commits (41)
Thou art as tyrannous, so as thou art (131)

Thou blind fool, Love, what dost thou to mine eyes (137)
Thus can my love excuse the slow offense (51)
Thus is his cheek the map of days outworn (68)
Thy bosom is endearèd with all hearts (31)
Thy gift, thy tables, are within my brain (122)
Thy glass will show thee how thy beauties wear (77)
Tired with all these, for restful death I cry (66)
'Tis better to be vile than vile esteemed (121)
To me, fair friend, you never can be old (104)
Two loves I have, of comfort and despair (144)

Unthrifty loveliness, why dost thou spend (4)

Was it the proud full sail of his great verse (86)
Weary with toil, I haste me to my bed (27)
Were't aught to me I bore the canopy (125)
What is your substance, whereof are you made (53)
What potions have I drunk of Siren tears (119)
What's in the brain that ink may character (108)
When forty winters shall besiege thy brow (2)
When I consider everything that grows (15)
When I do count the clock that tells the time (12)
When I have seen by Time's fell hand defaced (64)
When, in disgrace with Fortune and men's eyes (29)
When in the chronicle of wasted time (106)
When most I wink, then do mine eyes best see (43)
When my love swears that she is made of truth (138)
When thou shalt be disposed to set me light (88)
When to the sessions of sweet silent thought (30)
Where art thou, Muse, that thou forget'st so long (100)
Whilst I alone did call upon thy aid (79)
Whoever hath her wish, thou hast thy *Will* (135)
Who is it that says most, which can say more (84)
Who will believe my verse in time to come (17)
Why didst thou promise such a beauteous day (34)
Why is my verse so barren of new pride (76)

Your love and pity doth th' impression fill (112)

WILLIAM SHAKESPEARE

NARRATIVE POEMS

Edited by William Burto

VENUS AND ADONIS

Vilia miretur vulgus: mihi flavus Apollo
Pocula Castalia plena ministret aqua.

To the Right Honorable
Henry Wriothesley
Earl of Southampton and Baron of Titchfield

Right Honorable,

5   I know not how I shall offend in dedicating my unpolished
lines to your Lordship, nor how the world will censure me for
choosing so strong a prop to support so weak a burden; only, if
your Honor seem but pleased, I account myself highly praised,
and vow to take advantage of all idle hours, till I have honored
10   you with some graver labor. But if the first heir of my invention
prove deformed, I shall be sorry it had so noble a godfather, and
never after ear so barren a land, for fear it yield me still so bad a
harvest. I leave it to your honorable survey, and your Honor to
your heart's content; which I wish may always answer
15   your own wish and the world's hopeful expectation.

Your Honor's in all duty,

William Shakespeare.

Vilia ... aqua (from Ovid, *Amores*, I.xv.35–36: Let the mob admire base
things; may golden Apollo serve me full cups from the Castalian spring)
2 Henry Wriothesley third Earl of Southampton, 1573–1624, thought to be
Shakespeare's patron   11–12 the first heir of my invention my first work
brought to publication (a number of plays had already been written and
produced but were unpublished; and plays were usually considered not worth
publishing)   13 ear plow, till

VENUS AND ADONIS

Even as the sun with purple-colored face
Had ta'en his last leave of the weeping morn,
Rose-cheeked Adonis hied him to the chase;
Hunting he loved, but love he laughed to scorn.
5   Sick-thoughted Venus makes amain unto him,
    And like a bold-faced suitor 'gins to woo him.

"Thrice fairer than myself," thus she began,
"The field's chief flower, sweet above compare,
Stain to all nymphs, more lovely than a man,
10 More white and red than doves or roses are,
    Nature that made thee, with herself at strife,
    Saith that the world hath ending with thy life.

"Vouchsafe, thou wonder, to alight thy steed,
And rein his proud head to the saddlebow.
15 If thou wilt deign this favor, for thy meed
A thousand honey secrets shalt thou know.
    Here come and sit, where never serpent hisses,
    And being set, I'll smother thee with kisses.

"And yet not cloy thy lips with loathed satiety,
20 But rather famish them amid their plenty,
Making them red and pale with fresh variety:
Ten kisses short as one, one long as twenty.
    A summer's day will seem an hour but short,
    Being wasted in such time-beguiling sport."

---

1 **purple-colored** crimson 5 **Sick-thoughted** love-sick 5 **amain** swiftly,
strongly 9 **Stain to all nymphs** i.e., by his surpassing beauty he eclipses
them 15 **meed** reward 16 **honey** sweet 24 **wasted** spent

25 With this she seizeth on his sweating palm,
The precedent of pith and livelihood,
And trembling in her passion, calls it balm,
Earth's sovereign salve to do a goddess good:
    Being so enraged, desire doth lend her force
30   Courageously to pluck him from his horse.

Over one arm the lusty courser's rein,
Under her other was the tender boy,
Who blushed and pouted in a dull disdain,
With leaden appetite, unapt to toy;
35   She red and hot as coals of glowing fire,
    He red for shame, but frosty in desire.

The studded bridle on a ragged bough
Nimbly she fastens. O, how quick is love!
The steed is stallèd up, and even now
40 To tie the rider she begins to prove.
    Backward she pushed him, as she would be thrust,
    And governed him in strength, though not in lust.

So soon was she along as he was down,
Each leaning on their elbows and their hips.
45 Now doth she stroke his cheek, now doth he frown
And 'gins to chide, but soon she stops his lips,
    And kissing speaks, with lustful language broken,
    "If thou wilt chide, thy lips shall never open."

He burns with bashful shame; she with her tears
50 Doth quench the maiden burning of his cheeks;
Then with her windy sighs and golden hairs
To fan and blow them dry again she seeks.
    He saith she is immodest, blames her miss;
    What follows more, she murders with a kiss.

---

26 **precedent ... livelihood** sign of strength and energy   29 **enraged** aroused   34 **unapt to toy** not ready for love's play   40 **prove** try   43 **along** stretched out   53 **miss** misbehavior

55   Even as an empty eagle, sharp by fast,
      Tires with her beak on feathers, flesh, and bone,
      Shaking her wings, devouring all in haste,
      Till either gorge be stuffed or prey be gone—
         Even so she kissed his brow, his cheek, his chin,
60   And where she ends she doth anew begin.

      Forced to content, but never to obey,
      Panting he lies and breatheth in her face.
      She feedeth on the steam as on a prey
      And calls it heavenly moisture, air of grace,
65   Wishing her cheeks were gardens full of flowers,
         So they were dewed with such distilling showers.

      Look how a bird lies tangled in a net,
      So fastened in her arms Adonis lies.
      Pure shame and awed resistance made him fret,
70   Which bred more beauty in his angry eyes:
       Rain added to a river that is rank
         Perforce will force it overflow the bank.

      Still she entreats, and prettily entreats,
      For to a pretty ear she tunes her tale.
75   Still is he sullen, still he low'rs and frets,
      'Twixt crimson shame and anger ashy-pale.
       Being red, she loves him best; and being white,
         Her best is bettered with a more delight.

      Look how he can, she cannot choose but love;
80   And by her fair immortal hand she swears
      From his soft bosom never to remove
      Till he take truce with her contending tears,
       Which long have rained, making her cheeks all wet;
         And one sweet kiss shall pay this comptless debt.

---

55 **sharp by fast** hungry from fasting   56 **Tires** tears   61 **content** endure   67 **Look how** just as   69 **awed** intimidated   71 **rank** full   74 **ear** (pun on "air")   78 **more** greater   84 **comptless** countless

85 Upon this promise did he raise his chin,
    Like a divedapper peering through a wave,
    Who, being looked on, ducks as quickly in:
    So offers he to give what she did crave,
        But when her lips were ready for his pay,
90   He winks, and turns his lips another way.

    Never did passenger in summer's heat
    More thirst for drink than she for this good turn.
    Her help she sees, but help she cannot get;
    She bathes in water, yet her fire must burn.
95   "O, pity," 'gan she cry, "flint-hearted boy!
        'Tis but a kiss I beg—why art thou coy?

    "I have been wooed as I entreat thee now,
    Even by the stern and direful god of war,
    Whose sinewy neck in battle ne'er did bow,
100 Who conquers where he comes in every jar;
        Yet hath he been my captive and my slave,
        And begged for that which thou unasked shalt have.

    "Over my altars hath he hung his lance,
    His batt'red shield, his uncontrollèd crest,
105 And for my sake hath learned to sport and dance,
    To toy, to wanton, dally, smile, and jest.
        Scorning his churlish drum and ensign red,
        Making my arms his field, his tent my bed.

    "Thus he that overruled I overswayèd,
110 Leading him prisoner in a red-rose chain.
    Strong-tempered steel his stronger strength obeyèd;
    Yet was he servile to my coy disdain.
        O, be not proud, nor brag not of thy might,
        For mast'ring her that foiled the god of fight!

---

86 **divedapper** small waterbird   90 **winks** (1) winces (2) shuts his eyes
91 **passenger** traveler   100 **jar** fight   104 **uncontrollèd crest** unbowed
helmet

115 "Touch but my lips with those fair lips of thine—
Though mine be not so fair, yet are they red—
The kiss shall be thine own as well as mine.
What seest thou in the ground? Hold up thy head,
    Look in mine eyeballs, there thy beauty lies,
120   Then why not lips on lips, since eyes in eyes?

"Art thou ashamed to kiss? Then wink again,
And I will wink; so shall the day seem night.
Love keeps his revels where there are but twain.
Be bold to play; our sport is not in sight.
125   These blue-veined violets whereon we lean
    Never can blab, nor know not what we mean.

"The tender spring upon thy tempting lip
Shows thee unripe; yet mayst thou well be tasted.
Make use of time, let not advantage slip;
130 Beauty within itself should not be wasted.
    Fair flowers that are not gath'red in their prime
    Rot and consume themselves in little time.

"Were I hard-favored, foul, or wrinkled old,
Ill-nurtured, crooked, churlish, harsh in voice,
135 O'erworn, despisèd, rheumatic, and cold,
Thick-sighted, barren, lean, and lacking juice,
    Then mightst thou pause, for then I were not for thee;
    But having no defects, why dost abhor me?

"Thou canst not see one wrinkle in my brow;
140 Mine eyes are gray and bright and quick in turning.
My beauty as the spring doth yearly grow,
My flesh is soft and plump, my marrow burning;
    My smooth moist hand, were it with thy hand felt,
    Would in thy palm dissolve, or seem to melt.

121 **wink** close your eyes   127 **tender spring** young growth (that will become a beard)   136 **Thick-sighted** with poor eyesight

145 "Bid me discourse, I will enchant thine ear,
Or like a fairy trip upon the green,
Or like a nymph with long dishevelled hair,
Dance on the sands, and yet no footing seen.
    Love is a spirit all compact of fire,
150   Not gross to sink, but light, and will aspire.

"Witness this primrose bank whereon I lie;
These forceless flowers like sturdy trees support me.
Two strengthless doves will draw me through the sky
From morn till night, even where I list to sport me.
155   Is love so light, sweet boy, and may it be
    That thou should think it heavy unto thee?

"Is thine own heart to thine own face affected?
Can thy right hand seize love upon thy left?
Then woo thyself, be of thyself rejected;
160 Steal thine own freedom, and complain on theft.
    Narcissus so himself himself forsook,
    And died to kiss his shadow in the brook.

"Torches are made to light, jewels to wear,
Dainties to taste, fresh beauty for the use,
165 Herbs for their smell, and sappy plants to bear.
Things growing to themselves are growth's abuse.
    Seeds spring from seeds, and beauty breedeth beauty.
    Thou wast begot; to get it is thy duty.

"Upon the earth's increase why shouldst thou feed
170 Unless the earth with thy increase be fed?
By law of nature thou art bound to breed,
That thine may live when thou thyself art dead;
    And so in spite of death thou dost survive,
    In that thy likeness still is left alive."

149 **compact** composed   150 **aspire** rise up, float   151 **Witness ...lie** let
this bank whereon I lie bear witness   152 **forceless** frail, without
strength   157 **to ... affected** in love with thine own face   161 **Narcissus** a
beautiful youth who fell in love with his own reflection   169 **increase**
produce

175 By this the lovesick queen began to sweat,
For where they lay the shadow had forsook them,
And Titan, tirèd in the midday heat,
With burning eye did hotly overlook them,
    Wishing Adonis had his team to guide,
180 So he were like him, and by Venus' side.

And now Adonis, with a lazy sprite,
And with a heavy, dark, disliking eye,
His low'ring brows o'erwhelming his fair sight,
Like misty vapors when they blot the sky,
185   Souring his cheeks, cries, "Fie, no more of love!
    The sun doth burn my face—I must remove."

"Ay me," quoth Venus, "young, and so unkind?
What bare excuses mak'st thou to be gone!
I'll sigh celestial breath, whose gentle wind
190 Shall cool the heat of this descending sun.
    I'll make a shadow for thee of my hairs;
    If they burn too, I'll quench them with my tears.

"The sun that shines from heaven shines but warm,
And, lo, I lie between that sun and thee:
195 The heat I have from thence doth little harm,
Thine eye darts forth the fire that burneth me;
    And were I not immortal, life were done
    Between this heavenly and earthly sun.

"Art thou obdurate, flinty, hard as steel?
200 Nay, more than flint, for stone at rain relenteth.
Art thou a woman's son, and canst not feel
What 'tis to love? how want of love tormenteth?
    O, had thy mother borne so hard a mind,
    She had not brought forth thee, but died unkind.

175 **By this** by this time, now   177 **Titan** the sun-god   181 **lazy sprite** dull spirit   188 **bare** inadequate   200 **relenteth** i.e., is worn away

205 "What am I that thou shouldst contemn me this?
Or what great danger dwells upon my suit?
What were thy lips the worse for one poor kiss?
Speak, fair, but speak fair words or else be mute.
    Give me one kiss, I'll give it thee again,
210   And one for int'rest, if thou wilt have twain.

"Fie, lifeless picture, cold and senseless stone,
Well-painted idol, image dull and dead,
Statue contenting but the eye alone,
Thing like a man, but of no woman bred!
210   Thou art no man, though of a man's complexion,
    For men will kiss even by their own direction."

This said, impatience chokes her pleading tongue,
And swelling passion doth provoke a pause.
Red cheeks and fiery eyes blaze forth her wrong;
220 Being judge in love, she cannot right her cause.
    And now she weeps, and now she fain would speak,
    And now her sobs do her intendments break.

Sometime she shakes her head, and then his hand,
Now gazeth she on him, now on the ground.
225 Sometime her arms infold him like a band:
She would, he will not in her arms be bound.
    And when from thence he struggles to be gone,
    She locks her lily fingers one in one.

"Fondling," she saith, "since I have hemmed thee here
230 Within the circuit of this ivory pale,
I'll be a park, and thou shalt be my deer:
Feed where thou wilt, on mountain or in dale;
    Graze on my lips; and if those hills be dry,
    Stray lower, where the pleasant fountains lie.

205 **this** thus   208 **fair** fair one   215 **complexion** external appearance
216 **direction** volition   220 **Being judge ... cause** i.e., though Venus is the
judge in all disputes of love, she cannot obtain justice for herself   221 **fain**
gladly   222 **intendments break** intentions (i.e., what she was going to say)
interrupt   229 **Fondling** little fool (affectionate)   230 **pale** fence (here, her
arms)

235 "Within this limit is relief enough,
Sweet bottom-grass, and high delightful plain,
Round rising hillocks, brakes obscure and rough,
To shelter thee from tempest and from rain.
    Then be my deer since I am such a park;
240   No dog shall rouse thee though a thousand bark."

At this Adonis smiles as in disdain,
That in each cheek appears a pretty dimple;
Love made those hollows, if himself were slain,
He might be buried in a tomb so simple,
245   Foreknowing well, if there he came to lie,
    Why, there Love lived, and there he could not die.

These lovely caves, these round enchanting pits,
Opened their mouths to swallow Venus' liking.
Being mad before, how doth she now for wits?
250 Struck dead at first, what needs a second striking?
    Poor queen of love, in thine own law forlorn,
    To love a cheek that smiles at thee in scorn!

Now which way shall she turn? What shall she say?
Her words are done, her woes the more increasing;
255 The time is spent, her object will away,
And from her twining arms doth urge releasing.
    "Pity!" she cries, "some favor, some remorse!"
    Away he springs and hasteth to his horse.

But, lo, from forth a copse that neighbors by
260 A breeding jennet, lusty, young, and proud,
Adonis' trampling courser doth espy,
And forth she rushes, snorts, and neighs aloud.
    The strong-necked steed, being tied unto a tree,
    Breaketh his rein, and to her straight goes he.

235 **relief** (1) topography, as on a relief-map (2) (sexual) **satisfaction**
236 **bottom-grass** valley-grass 237 **brakes** thickets 240 **rouse** drive
from cover 242 **That** so that 243 **if** so that if he 248 **liking** desire
257 **remorse** mercy 260 **jennet** small Spanish horse

265 Imperiously he leaps, he neighs, he bounds,
And now his woven girths he breaks asunder;
The bearing earth with his hard hoof he wounds,
Whose hollow womb resounds like heaven's thunder;
    The iron bit he crusheth 'tween his teeth,
270   Controlling what he was controllèd with.

His ears up-pricked, his braided hanging mane
Upon his compassed crest now stand on end;
His nostrils drink the air, and forth again,
As from a furnace, vapors doth he send;
275   His eye, which scornfully glisters like fire,
    Shows his hot courage and his high desire.

Sometime he trots, as if he told the steps,
With gentle majesty and modest pride;
Anon he rears upright, curvets, and leaps,
280 As who should say, "Lo, thus my strength is tried,
    And this I do to captivate the eye
    Of the fair breeder that is standing by."

What recketh he his rider's angry stir,
His flattering "Holla" or his "Stand, I say"?
285 What cares he now for curb or pricking spur,
For rich caparisons or trappings gay?
    He sees his love, and nothing else he sees,
    For nothing else with his proud sight agrees.

Look when a painter would surpass the life
290 In limning out a well-proportioned steed,
His art with nature's workmanship at strife,
As if the dead the living should exceed—
    So did this horse excel a common one
    In shape, in courage, color, pace, and bone.

---

267 **bearing** receiving   272 **compassed** arched   276 **courage** lust
277 **told** counted   279 **curvets** hops   283 **stir** excitement   284 **flattering**
calming   289 **Look when** just as   290 **limning out** drawing   294 **bone**
frame

295 Round-hoofed, short-jointed, fetlocks shag and long,
Broad breast, full eye, small head, and nostril wide,
High crest, short ears, straight legs and passing strong,
Thin mane, thick tail, broad buttock, tender hide:
    Look what a horse should have he did not lack,
300   Save a proud rider on so proud a back.

Sometime he scuds far off, and there he stares;
Anon he starts at stirring of a feather.
To bid the wind a base he now prepares,
And whe'r he run or fly they know not whether,
305   For through his mane and tail the high wind sings,
    Fanning the hairs, who wave like feath'red wings.

He looks upon his love and neighs unto her;
She answers him, as if she knew his mind.
Being proud, as females are, to see him woo her,
310 She puts on outward strangeness, seems unkind,
    Spurns at his love and scorns the heat he feels,
    Beating his kind embracements with her heels.

Then, like a melancholy malcontent,
He vails his tail, that, like a falling plume,
315 Cool shadow to his melting buttock lent;
He stamps, and bites the poor flies in his fume.
    His love, perceiving how he was enraged,
    Grew kinder, and his fury was assuaged.

His testy master goeth about to take him,
320 When, lo, the unbacked breeder, full of fear,
Jealous of catching, swiftly doth forsake him,
With her the horse, and left Adonis there.
    As they were mad unto the wood they hie them,
    Outstripping crows that strive to overfly them.

---

297 **crest** ridge of the neck   299 **Look what** whatever   303 **bid the wind a base** challenge the wind to a chase   304 **whe'r** whether   310 **outward strangeness** show of indifference   314 **vails** lowers   316 **fume** rage 320 **unbacked** unbroken   321 **Jealous of catching** afraid of being caught 322 **horse** i.e., stallion

325 All swol'n with chafing, down Adonis sits,
Banning his boist'rous and unruly beast;
And now the happy season once more fits
That lovesick Love by pleading may be blest;
   For lovers say the heart hath treble wrong
330   When it is barred the aidance of the tongue.

An oven that is stopped, or river stayed,
Burneth more hotly, swelleth with more rage;
So of concealèd sorrow may be said
Free vent of words love's fire doth assuage;
335   But when the heart's attorney once is mute,
   The client breaks, as desperate in his suit.

He sees her coming and begins to glow,
Even as a dying coal revives with wind,
And with his bonnet hides his angry brow,
340 Looks on the dull earth with disturbèd mind,
   Taking no notice that she is so nigh,
   For all askance he holds her in his eye.

O, what a sight it was, wistly to view
How she came stealing to the wayward boy!
345 To note the fighting conflict of her hue,
How white and red each other did destroy!
   But now her cheek was pale, and by and by
   It flashed forth fire, as lightning from the sky.

Now was she just before him as he sat,
350 And like a lowly lover down she kneels;
With one fair hand she heaveth up his hat,
Her other tender hand his fair cheek feels.
   His tend'rer cheek receives her soft hand's print
   As apt as new-fall'n snow takes any dint.

326 **Banning** cursing   328 **Love** i.e., Venus   335 **the heart's attorney** i.e.,
the tongue   366 **breaks** goes bankrupt   343 **wistly** attentively   344 **way-**
ward willful   347 **by and by** quickly   354 **dint** impression

355 O, what a war of looks was then between them,
Her eyes petitioners to his eyes suing!
His eyes saw her eyes as they had not seen them;
Her eyes wooed still, his eyes disdained the wooing;
    And all this dumb play had his acts made plain
360   With tears which chorus-like her eyes did rain.

Full gently now she takes him by the hand,
A lily prisoned in a jail of snow,
Or ivory in an alablaster band:
So white a friend engirts so white a foe.
365   This beauteous combat, willful and unwilling,
    Showed like two silver doves that sit a-billing.

Once more the engine of her thoughts began:
"O fairest mover on this mortal round,
Would thou wert as I am, and I a man,
370 My heart all whole as thine, thy heart my wound!
    For one sweet look thy help I would assure thee,
    Though nothing but my body's bane would cure thee."

"Give me my hand," saith he. "Why dost thou feel it?"
"Give me my heart," saith she, "and thou shalt have it.
375 O, give it me lest thy hard heart do steel it,
And being steeled, soft sighs can never grave it.
    Then love's deep groans I never shall regard,
    Because Adonis' heart hath made mine hard."

"For shame!" he cries. "Let go, and let me go:
380 My day's delight is past, my horse is gone,
And 'tis your fault I am bereft him so.
I pray you hence, and leave me here alone;
    For all my mind, my thought, my busy care
    Is how to get my palfrey from the mare."

---

357 **as** as if   359 **dumb play** dumb-show, pantomime   359 **his** its
360 **chorus-like** i.e., served as a commentator   367 **engine of her thoughts**
i.e., her tongue   368 **mover ... mortal round** living creature on earth
370 **my wound** i.e., wounded like mine   372 **bane** ruin   375 **steel** turn to
steel   376 **grave** engrave

385 Thus she replies: "Thy palfrey, as he should,
Welcomes the warm approach of sweet desire.
Affection is a coal that must be cooled;
Else, suffered, it will set the heart on fire.
  The sea hath bounds, but deep desire hath none;
390   Therefore no marvel though thy horse be gone.

"How like a jade he stood, tied to the tree,
Servilely mastered with a leathern rein;
But when he saw his love, his youth's fair fee,
He held such petty bondage in disdain,
395   Throwing the base thong from his bending crest,
  Enfranchising his mouth, his back, his breast.

"Who sees his true-love in her naked bed,
Teaching the sheets a whiter hue than white,
But, when his glutton eye so full hath fed,
400 His other agents aim at like delight?
  Who is so faint that dares not be so bold
  To touch the fire, the weather being cold?

"Let me excuse thy courser, gentle boy;
And learn of him, I heartily beseech thee,
405 To take advantage on presented joy.
Though I were dumb, yet his proceedings teach thee.
  O, learn to love! The lesson is but plain,
  And once made perfect, never lost again."

"I know not love," quoth he, "nor will not know it,
410 Unless it be a boar, and then I chase it.
'Tis much to borrow, and I will not owe it:
My love to love is love but to disgrace it;
  For I have heard it is a life in death,
  That laughs and weeps, and all but with a breath.

387 **Affection** passion 388 **suffered** tolerated 391 **jade** contemptuous
term for horse 393 **fair fee** due reward 396 **Enfranchising** setting
free 397 **naked** (modifies "true-love," not "bed") 400 **agents** organs
405 **on** of 411 **owe** own 412 **My love ... disgrace it** my only attitude
toward love is a desire to discredit it 414 **but with a** in the same

415 "Who wears a garment shapeless and unfinished?
Who plucks the bud before one leaf put forth?
If springing things be any jot diminished,
They wither in their prime, prove nothing worth.
    The colt that's backed and burdened being young
420   Loseth his pride, and never waxeth strong.

"You hurt my hand with wringing; let us part,
And leave this idle theme, this bootless chat;
Remove your siege from my unyielding heart;
To love's alarms it will not ope the gate.
425   Dismiss your vows, your feignèd tears, your flatt'ry;
    For where a heart is hard they make no batt'ry."

"What! canst thou talk?" quoth she. "Hast thou a tongue?
O, would thou hadst not, or I had no hearing!
Thy mermaid's voice hath done me double wrong;
430 I had my load before, now pressed with bearing:
    Melodious discord, heavenly tune harsh sounding,
    Ear's deep-sweet music, and heart's deep-sore wounding.

"Had I no eyes but ears, my ears would love
That inward beauty and invisible;
435 Or were I deaf, thy outward parts would move
Each part in me that were but sensible.
    Though neither eyes nor ears, to hear nor see,
    Yet should I be in love by touching thee.

"Say that the sense of feeling were bereft me,
440 And that I could not see, nor hear, nor touch,
And nothing but the very smell were left me,
Yet would my love to thee be still as much;
    For from the stillitory of thy face excelling
    Comes breath perfumed that breedeth love by smelling.

---

419   backed broken in   422 bootless useless   424 alarms attacks   426
batt'ry successful entry   429 mermaid's siren's   430 pressed oppressed
436 sensible able to receive any other sensations   443 stillitory distilling
plant

445 "But, O, what banquet wert thou to the taste,
Being nurse and feeder of the other four!
Would they not wish the feast might ever last
And bid Suspicion double-lock the door,
    Lest Jealousy, that sour unwelcome guest,
450   Should by his stealing in disturb the feast?"

Once more the ruby-colored portal opened
Which to his speech did honey passage yield;
Like a red morn that ever yet betokened
Wrack to the seaman, tempest to the field,
455   Sorrow to shepherds, woe unto the birds,
    Gusts and foul flaws to herdmen and to herds.

This ill presage advisedly she marketh.
Even as the wind is hushed before it raineth,
Or as the wolf doth grin before he barketh,
460 Or as the berry breaks before it staineth,
    Or like the deadly bullet of a gun,
    His meaning struck her ere his words begun.

And at his look she flatly falleth down,
For looks kill love, and love by looks reviveth;
465 A smile recures the wounding of a frown.
But blessèd bankrout that by love so thriveth!
    The silly boy, believing she is dead,
    Claps her pale cheek, till clapping makes it red,

And all amazed brake off his late intent,
470 For sharply he did think to reprehend her,
Which cunning love did wittily prevent.
Fair fall the wit that can so well defend her!
    For on the grass she lies as she were slain
    Till his breath breatheth life in her again.

454 **Wrack** wreck   456 **flaws** blasts of wind   459 **grin** bare its fangs   465
recures heals   466 **bankrout** bankrupt   467 **silly** innocent   471 **wittily**
cleverly   472 **Fair fall** prosperity befall

475 He wrings her nose, he strikes her on the cheeks,
He bends her fingers, holds her pulses hard,
He chafes her lips; a thousand ways he seeks
To mend the hurt that his unkindness marred.
    He kisses her; and she, by her good will,
480   Will never rise, so he will kiss her still.

The night of sorrow now is turned to day:
Her two blue windows faintly she upheaveth,
Like the fair sun when in his fresh array
He cheers the morn and all the earth relieveth;
485   And as the bright sun glorifies the sky,
    So is her face illumined with her eye;

Whose beams upon his hairless face are fixed,
As if from thence they borrowed all their shine.
Were never four such lamps together mixed,
490 Had not his clouded with his brow's repine;
    But hers, which through the crystal tears gave light,
    Shine like the moon in water seen by night.

"O, where am I?" quoth she, "in earth or heaven,
Or in the ocean drenched, or in the fire?
495 What hour is this? or morn or weary even?
Do I delight to die, or life desire?
    But now I lived, and life was death's annoy;
    But now I died, and death was lively joy.

"O, thou didst kill me, kill me once again!
500 Thy eyes' shrewd tutor, that hard heart of thine,
Hath taught them scornful tricks, and such disdain
That they have murd'red this poor heart of mine;
    And these mine eyes, true leaders to their queen,
    But for thy piteous lips no more had seen.

478 **marred** inflicted   479 **by her good will** willingly   482 **blue windows**
i.e., her eyelids   490 **repine** vexation   495 **or ... or** either ... or   497
annoy torment   500 **shrewd** harsh   503 **their queen** i.e., the heart

505 "Long may they kiss each other, for this cure!
O, never let their crimson liveries wear;
And as they last, their verdure still endure,
To drive infection from the dangerous year;
    That the stargazers, having writ on death,
510 May say the plague is banished by thy breath.

"Pure lips, sweet seals in my soft lips imprinted,
What bargains may I make, still to be sealing?
To sell myself I can be well contented,
So thou wilt buy, and pay, and use good dealing;
515 Which purchase if thou make, for fear of slips
    Set thy seal manual on my wax-red lips.

"A thousand kisses buys my heart from me;
And pay them at thy leisure, one by one.
What is ten hundred touches unto thee?
520 Are they not quickly told and quickly gone?
    Say for nonpayment that the debt should double,
    Is twenty hundred kisses such a trouble?"

"Fair queen," quoth he, "if any love you owe me,
Measure my strangeness with my unripe years.
525 Before I know myself, seek not to know me:
No fisher but the ungrown fry forbears;
    The mellow plum doth fall, the green sticks fast,
    Or being early plucked is sour to taste.

"Look, the world's comforter, with weary gait,
530 His day's hot task hath ended in the west;
The owl, night's herald, shrieks; 'tis very late;
The sheep are gone to fold, birds to their nest,
    And coal-black clouds that shadow heaven's light
    Do summon us to part, and bid good night.

506 crimson liveries wear red colors wear out 507 verdure freshness
509 stargazers ... death astrologers, who have predicted an epidemic 512
still always 512 sealing i.e., kissing 515 slips errors 516 seal manual
signet ring (i.e., lips) 519 touches i.e., kisses 520 told counted 523
owe bear 524 Measure ... unripe years account for my shyness by my
youth 526 fry young fish

535 "Now let me say good night, and so say you.
If you will say so, you shall have a kiss."
"Good night," quoth she; and, ere he says "Adieu,"
The honey fee of parting tend'red is:
 Her arms do lend his neck a sweet embrace;
540 Incorporate then they seem; face grows to face;

Till breathless he disjoined, and backward drew
The heavenly moisture, that sweet coral mouth,
Whose precious taste her thirsty lips well knew,
Whereon they surfeit, yet complain on drouth.
545 He with her plenty pressed, she faint with dearth,
 Their lips together glued, fall to the earth.

Now quick desire hath caught the yielding prey,
And glutton-like she feeds, yet never filleth.
Her lips are conquerors, his lips obey,
550 Paying what ransom the insulter willeth;
 Whose vulture thought doth pitch the price so high
 That she will draw his lips' rich treasure dry.

And having felt the sweetness of the spoil,
With blindfold fury she begins to forage;
555 Her face doth reek and smoke, her blood doth boil,
And careless lust stirs up a desperate courage,
 Planting oblivion, beating reason back,
 Forgetting shame's pure blush and honor's wrack.

Hot, faint, and weary with her hard embracing,
560 Like a wild bird being tamed with too much handling,
Or as the fleet-foot roe that's tired with chasing,
Or like the froward infant stilled with dandling,
 He now obeys and now no more resisteth,
 While she takes all she can, not all she listeth.

---

540 **Incorporate** joined into one body 545 **pressed** oppressed
550 **insulter** exultant winner 555 **reek** i.e., steam 562 **froward** fretful
564 **listeth** wants

565 What wax so frozen but dissolves with temp'ring
And yields at last to every light impression?
Things out of hope are compassed oft with vent'ring,
Chiefly in love, whose leave exceeds commission.
    Affection faints not like a pale-faced coward,
570   But then woos best when most his choice is froward.

When he did frown, O, had she then gave over,
Such nectar from his lips she had not sucked.
Foul words and frowns must not repel a lover.
What though the rose have prickles, yet 'tis plucked.
575   Were beauty under twenty locks kept fast,
    Yet love breaks through and picks them all at last.

For pity now she can no more detain him;
The poor fool prays her that he may depart.
She is resolved no longer to restrain him;
580 Bids him farewell, and look well to her heart,
    The which, by Cupid's bow she doth protest,
    He carries thence incagèd in his breast.

"Sweet boy," she says, "this night I'll waste in sorrow,
For my sick heart commands mine eyes to watch.
585 Tell me, love's master, shall we meet tomorrow?
Say, shall we? shall we? wilt thou make the match?"
    He tells her no; tomorrow he intends
    To hunt the boar with certain of his friends.

"The boar!" quoth she; whereat a sudden pale,
590 Like lawn being spread upon the blushing rose,
Usurps her cheek; she trembles at his tale,
And on his neck her yoking arms she throws.
    She sinketh down, still hanging by his neck,
    He on her belly falls, she on her back.

567 out of beyond   567 compassed ... vent'ring achieved often by venturing   568 leave exceeds commission liberty goes beyond what was permitted   569 Affection passion, desire   570 when most his choice is froward when the object of his passion is most obstinate   573 Foul unpleasant   578 poor fool (expression of tenderness)   583 waste spend   584 watch stay open   589 pale pallor   590 lawn a fine linen

595 Now is she in the very lists of love,
  Her champion mounted for the hot encounter.
  All is imaginary she doth prove,
  He will not manage her, although he mount her;
   That worse than Tantalus' is her annoy,
600 To clip Elysium and to lack her joy.

  Even so poor birds, deceived with painted grapes,
  Do surfeit by the eye and pine the maw;
  Even so she languisheth in her mishaps
  As those poor birds that helpless berries saw.
605   The warm effects which she in him finds missing
   She seeks to kindle with continual kissing.

  But all in vain; good queen, it will not be!
  She hath assayed as much as may be proved:
  Her pleading hath deserved a greater fee;
610 She's Love, she loves, and yet she is not loved.
   "Fie, fie!" he says. "You crush me; let me go!
   You have no reason to withhold me so."

  "Thou hadst been gone," quoth she, "sweet boy, ere this,
  But that thou told'st me thou wouldst hunt the boar.
615 O, be advised, thou know'st not what it is
  With javelin's point a churlish swine to gore,
   Whose tushes never sheathed he whetteth still,
   Like to a mortal butcher bent to kill.

  "On his bow-back he hath a battle set
620 Of bristly pikes that ever threat his foes;
  His eyes like glowworms shine when he doth fret;
  His snout digs sepulchers where'er he goes;
   Being moved, he strikes whate'er is in his way,
   And whom he strikes his crooked tushes slay.

---

595 **lists** field of combat 597 **prove** experience (i.e., all that she experiences is in her imagination) 598 **manage** ride 599 **That worse ... annoy** so that her torment is worse than that of Tantalus (in Hades, Tantalus was surrounded by food and drink that he could never touch) 600 **clip** embrace 602 **pine the maw** starve the stomach 605 **effects** consequences 608 **assayed** tried 608 **proved** tried 617 **tushes** tusks 618 **mortal** deadly 621 **fret** rage 623 **moved** angered

625 "His brawny sides, with hairy bristles armèd,
Are better proof than thy spear's point can enter;
His short thick neck cannot be easily harmèd;
Being ireful, on the lion he will venter.
 The thorny brambles and embracing bushes,
630 As fearful of him, part; through whom he rushes.

"Alas, he naught esteems that face of thine,
To which Love's eyes pay tributary gazes;
Nor thy soft hands, sweet lips, and crystal eyne,
Whose full perfection all the world amazes;
635 But having thee at vantage (wondrous dread!)
 Would root these beauties as he roots the mead.

"O, let him keep his loathsome cabin still:
Beauty hath naught to do with such foul fiends.
Come not within his danger by thy will.
640 They that thrive well take counsel of their friends.
 When thou didst name the boar, not to dissemble,
 I feared thy fortune, and my joints did tremble.

"Didst thou not mark my face? Was it not white?
Saw'st thou not signs of fear lurk in mine eye?
645 Grew I not faint? and fell I not downright?
Within my bosom, whereon thou dost lie,
 My boding heart pants, beats, and takes no rest,
 But, like an earthquake, shakes thee on my breast.

"For where Love reigns, disturbing Jealousy
650 Doth call himself Affection's sentinel,
Gives false alarms, suggesteth mutiny,
And in a peaceful hour doth cry 'Kill, kill!'
 Distemp'ring gentle Love in his desire,
 As air and water do abate the fire.

---

626 **better proof** stronger armor   628 **venter** venture   633 **eyne** eyes
636 **root** uproot   637 **cabin** i.e., sty   639 **within his danger** within
distance of his power to harm   641 **not to dissemble** to tell the truth   645
downright directly   649 **Jealousy** anxiety   651 **suggesteth** incites   653
Distemp'ring decreasing

655 "This sour informer, this bate-breeding spy,
This canker that eats up Love's tender spring,
This carry-tale, dissentious Jealousy,
That sometime true news, sometime false doth bring,
Knocks at my heart, and whispers in mine ear
660 That if I love thee, I thy death should fear.

"And more than so, presenteth to mine eye
The picture of an angry-chafing boar,
Under whose sharp fangs on his back doth lie
An image like thyself, all stained with gore;
665 Whose blood upon the fresh flowers being shed
Doth make them droop with grief and hang the head.

"What should I do, seeing thee so indeed,
That tremble at th' imagination?
The thought of it doth make my faint heart bleed,
670 And fear doth teach it divination.
I prophesy thy death, my living sorrow,
If thou encounter with the boar tomorrow.

"But if thou needs wilt hunt, be ruled by me:
Uncouple at the timorous flying hare,
675 Or at the fox which lives by subtlety,
Or at the roe which no encounter dare.
Pursue these fearful creatures o'er the downs,
And on thy well-breathed horse keep with thy hounds.

"And when thou hast on foot the purblind hare,
680 Mark the poor wretch, to overshoot his troubles,
How he outruns the wind, and with what care
He cranks and crosses with a thousand doubles.
The many musits through the which he goes
Are like a labyrinth to amaze his foes.

655 **bate-breeding** strife-creating 656 **canker** worm (that preys on blossoms) 656 **spring** bud 674 **Uncouple at** loose your hounds upon 677 **fearful** timid 678 **well-breathed** well-conditioned 679 **on foot** in chase 679 **purblind** weak-sighted 680 **overshoot** run beyond 682 **cranks** turns 683 **musits** gaps in a hedge or fence 684 **amaze** confuse

685 "Sometime he runs among a flock of sheep,
To make the cunning hounds mistake their smell,
And sometime where earth-delving conies keep,
To stop the loud pursuers in their yell;
    And sometime sorteth with a herd of deer.
690   Danger deviseth shifts, wit waits on fear;

"For there his smell with others being mingled,
The hot scent-snuffing hounds are driven to doubt,
Ceasing their clamorous cry, till they have singled
With much ado the cold fault cleanly out.
695   Then do they spend their mouths; echo replies,
    As if another chase were in the skies.

"By this, poor Wat, far off upon a hill,
Stands on his hinder legs with list'ning ear,
To hearken if his foes pursue him still.
700 Anon their loud alarums he doth hear,
    And now his grief may be comparèd well
    To one sore sick that hears the passing bell.

"Then shalt thou see the dew-bedabbled wretch
Turn, and return, indenting with the way.
705 Each envious brier his weary legs do scratch;
Each shadow makes him stop, each murmur stay;
    For misery is trodden on by many
    And, being low, never relieved by any.

"Lie quietly and hear a little more.
710 Nay, do not struggle, for thou shalt not rise.
To make thee hate the hunting of the boar,
Unlike myself thou hear'st me moralize,
    Applying this to that, and so to so,
    For love can comment upon every woe.

---

687 **earth-delving conies keep** rabbits that dig burrows dwell   688 **in their yell** i.e., in full cry   689 **sorteth** mingles   690 **shifts** tricks   690 **waits on** goes with   694 **cold fault** lost scent   695 **spend their mouths** yelp   697 **Wat** (traditional name for a hare)   702 **passing** funeral   704 **indenting** zigzagging   705 **envious** malicious

715 "Where did I leave?" "No matter where," quoth he;
"Leave me, and then the story aptly ends.
The night is spent." "Why, what of that?" quoth she.
"I am," quoth he, "expected of my friends;
     And now 'tis dark, and going I shall fall."
720   "In night," quoth she, "desire sees best of all.

"But if thou fall, O, then imagine this:
The earth, in love, with thee, thy footing trips,
And all is but to rob thee of a kiss.
Rich preys make true men thieves. So do thy lips
725   Make modest Dian cloudy and forlorn,
     Lest she should steal a kiss and die forsworn.

"Now of this dark night I perceive the reason:
Cynthia for shame obscures her silver shine,
Till forging Nature be condemned of treason
730 For stealing molds from heaven that were divine;
     Wherein she framed thee, in high heaven's despite,
     To shame the sun by day, and her by night.

"And therefore hath she bribed the Destinies
To cross the curious workmanship of Nature,
735 To mingle beauty with infirmities
And pure perfection with impure defeature,
     Making it subject to the tyranny
     Of mad mischances and much misery;

"As burning fevers, agues pale and faint,
740 Life-poisoning pestilence, and frenzies wood,
The marrow-eating sickness whose attaint
Disorder breeds by heating of the blood,
     Surfeits, imposthumes, grief, and damned despair
     Swear Nature's death for framing thee so fair.

724 preys booty   724 true honest   725 Dian Diana (goddess of chastity
and of the hunt)   725 cloudy gloomy   726 forsworn i.e., having broken
her vow of chastity   728 Cynthia the moon, i.e., Diana   729 forging
counterfeiting   723 her i.e., the moon   734 cross thwart   734 curious
elaborate   736 defeature disfigurement   740 wood mad   741 marrow-
eating sickness syphilis (?)   741 attaint infection   743 imposthumes
abscesses

745 "And not the least of all these maladies
But in one minute's fight brings beauty under;
Both favor, savor, hue, and qualities,
Whereat th' impartial gazer late did wonder,
    Are on the sudden wasted, thawed, and done,
750   As mountain snow melts with the midday sun.

"Therefore, despite of fruitless chastity,
Love-lacking vestals, and self-loving nuns,
That on the earth would breed a scarcity
And barren dearth of daughters and of sons,
755   Be prodigal; the lamp that burns by night
    Dries up his oil to lend the world his light.

"What is thy body but a swallowing grave,
Seeming to bury that posterity
Which by the rights of time thou needs must have
760 If thou destroy them not in dark obscurity?
    If so, the world will hold thee in disdain,
    Sith in thy pride so fair a hope is slain.

"So in thyself thyself art made away,
A mischief worse than civil home-bred strife,
765 Or theirs whose desperate hands themselves do slay,
Or butcher sire that reaves his son of life.
    Foul cank'ring rust the hidden treasure frets,
    But gold that's put to use more gold begets."

"Nay, then," quoth Adon, "you will fall again
770 Into your idle over-handled theme.
The kiss I gave you is bestowed in vain,
And all in vain you strive against the stream;
    For by this black-faced night, desire's foul nurse,
    Your treatise makes me like you worse and worse.

745-46 And ... under i.e., even the least of these maladies in one minute can
destroy beauty   747 favor features   747 hue complexion   762 Sith since
766 reaves deprives   767 frets erodes   774 treatise discourse

775 "If love have lent you twenty thousand tongues,
And every tongue more moving than your own,
Bewitching like the wanton mermaid's songs,
Yet from mine ear the tempting tune is blown;
      For know, my heart stands armèd in mine ear
780 And will not let a false sound enter there,

"Lest the deceiving harmony should run
Into the quiet closure of my breast;
And then my little heart were quite undone,
In his bedchamber to be barred of rest.
785   No, lady, no; my heart longs not to groan,
But soundly sleeps while now it sleeps alone.

"What have you urged that I cannot reprove?
The path is smooth that leadeth on to danger.
I hate not love, but your device in love,
790 That lends embracements unto every stranger.
      You do it for increase. O strange excuse,
      When reason is the bawd to lust's abuse!

"Call it not love, for Love to heaven is fled
Since sweating Lust on earth usurped his name;
795 Under whose simple semblance he hath fed
Upon fresh beauty, blotting it with blame;
      Which the hot tyrant stains and soon bereaves,
      As caterpillars do the tender leaves.

"Love comforteth like sunshine after rain,
800 But Lust's effect is tempest after sun.
Love's gentle spring doth always fresh remain;
Lust's winter comes ere summer half be done.
      Love surfeits not, Lust like a glutton dies;
      Love is all truth, Lust full of forgèd lies.

782 **closure** enclosure   787 **reprove** refute   789 **device** cunning   797 **hot
tyrant** i.e., lust   797 **bereaves** spoils

805   "More I could tell, but more I dare not say:
The text is old, the orator too green.
Therefore in sadness now I will away.
My face is full of shame, my heart of teen;
     Mine ears, that to your wanton talk attended,
810   Do burn themselves for having so offended."

With this he breaketh from the sweet embrace
Of those fair arms which bound him to her breast
And homeward through the dark laund runs apace;
Leaves Love upon her back, deeply distressed.
815   Look how a bright star shooteth from the sky,
     So glides he in the night from Venus' eye;

Which after him she darts, as one on shore
Gazing upon a late-embarkèd friend
Till the wild waves will have him seen no more,
820   Whose ridges with the meeting clouds contend.
     So did the merciless and pitchy night
     Fold in the object that did feed her sight.

Whereat amazed, as one that unaware
Hath dropped a precious jewel in the flood,
825   Or 'stonished as night-wand'rers often are,
Their light blown out in some mistrustful wood,
     Even so confounded in the dark she lay,
     Having lost the fair discovery of her way.

And now she beats her heart, whereat it groans,
830   That all the neighbor caves, as seeming troubled,
Make verbal repetition of her moans.
Passion on passion deeply is redoubled;
     "Ay me!" she cries, and twenty times, "Woe, woe!"
     And twenty echoes twenty times cry so.

---

806 **green** young   807 **in sadness** in all seriousness   808 **teen** sorrow   813
laund open space in a forest   815 **Look how** just as   825 **'stonished**
bewildered   826 **mistrustful** feared   832 **Passion** lamentation

835 She, marking them, begins a wailing note
    And sings extemporally a woeful ditty:
    How love makes young men thrall, and old men dote;
    How love is wise in folly, foolish-witty.
        Her heavy anthem still concludes in woe,
840   And still the choir of echoes answer so.

    Her song was tedious and outwore the night,
    For lovers' hours are long, though seeming short.
    If pleased themselves, others, they think, delight
    In such-like circumstance, with such-like sport.
845   Their copious stories, oftentimes begun,
        End without audience, and are never done.

    For who hath she to spend the night withal
    But idle sounds resembling parasits,
    Like shrill-tongued tapsters answering every call,
850 Soothing the humor of fantastic wits?
        She says " 'Tis so." They answer all, " 'Tis so,"
        And would say after her if she said "No."

    Lo, here the gentle lark, weary of rest,
    From his moist cabinet mounts up on high
855 And wakes the morning, from whose silver breast
    The sun ariseth in his majesty;
        Who doth the world so gloriously behold
        That cedar tops and hills seem burnished gold.

    Venus salutes him with this fair good-morrow:
860 "O thou clear god, and patron of all light,
    From whom each lamp and shining star doth borrow
    The beauteous influence that makes him bright;
        There lives a son that sucked an earthly mother
        May lend thee light, as thou dost lend to other."

865 This said, she hasteth to a myrtle grove,
    Musing the morning is so much o'erworn
    And yet she hears no tidings of her love.
    She hearkens for his hounds and for his horn.
        Anon she hears them chant it lustily,
870   And all in haste she coasteth to the cry.

837 **thrall** captive 848 **parasits** i.e., flatterers 854 **cabinet** i.e., nest 870 **coasteth** approaches

And as she runs, the bushes in the way
Some catch her by the neck, some kiss her face,
Some twine about her thigh to make her stay.
She wildly breaketh from their strict embrace,
875 Like a milch doe, whose swelling dugs do ache,
  Hasting to feed her fawn, hid in some brake.

By this she hears the hounds are at a bay;
Whereat she starts, like one that spies an adder
Wreathed up in fatal folds just in his way,
880 The fear whereof doth make him shake and shudder.
  Even so the timorous yelping of the hounds
  Appals her senses and her spirit confounds.

For now she knows it is no gentle chase,
But the blunt boar, rough bear, or lion proud,
885 Because the cry remaineth in one place,
Where fearfully the dogs exclaim aloud;
  Finding their enemy to be so curst,
  They all strain court'sy who shall cope him first.

This dismal cry rings sadly in her ear,
890 Through which it enters to surprise her heart,
Who, overcome by doubt and bloodless fear,
With cold-pale weakness numbs each feeling part:
  Like soldiers when their captain once doth yield,
  They basely fly, and dare not stay the field.

895 Thus stands she in a trembling ecstasy,
Till cheering up her senses all dismayed,
She tells them 'tis a causeless fantasy,
And childish error that they are afraid;
  Bids them leave quaking, bids them fear no more;
900 And with that word she spied the hunted boar,

874 **strict** tight 876 **brake** thicket 877 **at a bay** (the moment during a hunt when an animal is forced to turn against its pursuers) 884 **blunt** rough 887 **curst** savage 888 **They all strain court'sy** i.e., each holds back to allow the other to go first 895 **ecstasy** fit

Whose frothy mouth, bepainted all with red,
Like milk and blood being mingled both togither,
A second fear through all her sinews spread,
Which madly hurries her she knows not whither.
905   This way she runs, and now she will no further,
    But back retires, to rate the boar for murther.

A thousand spleens bear her a thousand ways;
She treads the path that she untreads again;
Her more than haste is mated with delays,
910 Like the proceedings of a drunken brain,
    Full of respects, yet naught at all respecting,
    In hand with all things, naught at all effecting.

Here kennelled in a brake she finds a hound
And asks the weary caitiff for his master;
915 And there another licking of his wound,
    'Gainst venomed sores the only sovereign plaster;
    And here she meets another sadly scowling,
    To whom she speaks, and he replies with howling.

When he hath ceased his ill-resounding noise,
920 Another flap-mouthed mourner, black and grim,
Against the welkin volleys out his voice;
Another and another answer him,
    Clapping their proud tails to the ground below,
    Shaking their scratched ears, bleeding as they go.

925 Look how the world's poor people are amazèd
At apparitions, signs, and prodigies,
Whereon with fearful eyes they long have gazèd,
Infusing them with dreadful prophecies:
    So she at these sad signs draws up her breath
930   And sighing it again, exclaims on Death.

907 **spleens** impulses   909 **mated with** checked by   911 **respects** considerations   912 **In hand** occupied   914 **caitiff** wretch   920 **flap-mouthed** loose-lipped   921 **welkin** sky   925 **amazèd** perplexed   930 **exclaims on** denounces

"Hard-favored tyrant, ugly, meager, lean,
Hateful divorce of love!" (thus chides she Death)
"Grim-grinning ghost, earth's worm, what dost thou mean,
To stifle beauty and to steal his breath
935　　Who, when he lived, his breath and beauty set
　　　　Gloss on the rose, smell to the violet?

"If he be dead—O no, it cannot be,
Seeing his beauty, thou shouldst strike at it!
O yes, it may; thou hast no eyes to see,
940　But hatefully at randon dost thou hit;
　　　　Thy mark is feeble age, but thy false dart
　　　　Mistakes that aim, and cleaves an infant's heart.

"Hadst thou but bid beware, then he had spoke,
And hearing him, thy power had lost his power.
945　The Destinies will curse thee for this stroke:
They bid thee crop a weed; thou pluck'st a flower.
　　　　Love's golden arrow at him should have fled,
　　　　And not Death's ebon dart to strike him dead.

"Dost thou drink tears, that thou provok'st such weeping?
950　What may a heavy groan advantage thee?
Why hast thou cast into eternal sleeping
Those eyes that taught all other eyes to see?
　　　　Now Nature cares not for thy mortal vigor,
　　　　Since her best work is ruined with thy rigor."

955　Here overcome, as one full of despair,
She vailed her eyelids, who like sluices stopped
The crystal tide that from her two cheeks fair
In the sweet channel of her bosom dropped;
　　　　But through the floodgates breaks the silver rain
960　　And with his strong course opens them again.

---

940 **randon** random　944 **his** its　948 **ebon** black　950 **advantage** profit　953 **mortal vigor** deadly power　956 **vailed** lowered　956 **who like sluices stopped** which, like floodgates, dammed

O, how her eyes and tears did lend and borrow,
Her eye seen in the tears, tears in her eye,
Both crystals, where they viewed each other's sorrow—
Sorrow that friendly sighs sought still to dry;
965   But like a stormy day, now wind, now rain,
    Sighs dry her cheeks, tears make them wet again.

Variable passions throng her constant woe,
As striving who should best become her grief.
All entertained, each passion labors so
970 That every present sorrow seemeth chief,
    But none is best; then join they all together
    Like many clouds consulting for foul weather.

By this far off she hears some huntsman halloa.
A nurse's song ne'er pleased her babe so well.
975 The dire imagination she did follow
This sound of hope doth labor to expel;
    For now reviving joy bids her rejoice
    And flatters her it is Adonis' voice.

Whereat her tears began to turn their tide,
980 Being prisoned in her eye like pearls in glass;
Yet sometimes falls an orient drop beside,
Which her cheek melts, as scorning it should pass
    To wash the foul face of the sluttish ground,
    Who is but drunken when she seemeth drowned.

985 O hard-believing love, how strange it seems
Not to believe, and yet too credulous!
Thy weal and woe are both of them extremes;
Despair and hope makes thee ridiculous:
    The one doth flatter thee in thoughts unlikely,
990   In likely thoughts the other kills thee quickly.

963 **crystals** i.e., mirrors   968 **striving who** competing which   969 **entertained** admitted   972 **consulting** plotting   979 **turn their tide** ebb   981 **orient** bright   985 **hard-believing** i.e., skeptical

Now she unweaves the web that she hath wrought:
Adonis lives, and Death is not to blame;
It was not she that called him all to naught.
Now she adds honors to his hateful name:
995   She clepes him king of graves, and grave for kings,
Imperious supreme of all mortal things.

"No, no," quoth she, "sweet Death, I did but jest;
Yet pardon me I felt a kind of fear
When as I met the boar, that bloody beast
1000 Which knows no pity but is still severe.
Then, gentle shadow (truth I must confess),
I railed on thee, fearing my love's decesse.

" 'Tis not my fault the boar provoked my tongue;
Be wreaked on him, invisible commander.
1005 'Tis he, foul creature, that hath done thee wrong;
I did but act; he's author of thy slander.
Grief hath two tongues, and never woman yet
Could rule them both, without ten women's wit."

Thus hoping that Adonis is alive,
1010 Her rash suspect she doth extenuate;
And that his beauty may the better thrive,
With Death she humbly doth insinuate;
Tells him of trophies, statues, tombs; and stories
His victories, his triumphs, and his glories.

1015 "O Jove," quoth she, "how much a fool was I
To be of such a weak and silly mind
To wail his death who lives, and must not die
Till mutual overthrow of mortal kind!
For he being dead, with him is beauty slain,
1020 And, beauty dead, black chaos comes again.

---

993 **all to naught** worthless   995 **clepes** names   996 **Imperious supreme**
imperial ruler 1001 **shadow** specter 1002 **decesse** decease 1004
wreaked revenged 1010 **suspect** suspicion 1012 **insinuate** ingratiate
herself 1013 **stories** relates

"Fie, fie, found love, thou art as full of fear
As one with treasure laden, hemmed with thieves.
Trifles, unwitnessèd with eye, or ear,
Thy coward heart with false bethinking grieves."
1025   Even at this word she hears a merry horn,
   Whereat she leaps that was but late forlorn.

As falcons to the lure, away she flies;
The grass stoops not, she treads on it so light,
And in her haste unfortunately spies
1030 The foul boar's conquest on her fair delight;
   Which seen, her eyes, as murd'red with the view,
   Like stars ashamed of day, themselves withdrew;

Or as the snail, whose tender horns being hit,
Shrinks backward in his shelly cave with pain,
1035 And there, all smoth'red up, in shade doth sit,
Long after fearing to creep forth again;
   So at his bloody view her eyes are fled
   Into the deep-dark cabins of her head;

Where they resign their office and their light
1040 To the disposing of her troubled brain,
Who bids them still consort with ugly night
And never wound the heart with looks again;
   Who, like a king perplexèd in his throne,
   By their suggestion gives a deadly groan,

1045 Whereat each tributary subject quakes,
As when the wind, imprisoned in the ground,
Struggling for passage, earth's foundation shakes,
Which with cold terror doth men's minds confound.
   This mutiny each part doth so surprise
1050   That from their dark beds once more leap her eyes,

1023 **unwitnessèd with** unperceived by   1032 **ashamed of** put to shame
by   1041 **still consort** always keep company   1043 **Who** which

And, being opened, threw unwilling light
Upon the wide wound that the boar had trenched
In his soft flank, whose wonted lily white
With purple tears that his wound wept was drenched.
1055   No flow'r was nigh, no grass, herb, leaf, or weed,
    But stole his blood and seemed with him to bleed.

This solemn sympathy poor Venus noteth.
Over one shoulder doth she hang her head.
Dumbly she passions, franticly she doteth:
1060 She thinks he could not die, he is not dead;
    Her voice is stopped, her joints forget to bow;
    Her eyes are mad that they have wept till now.

Upon his hurt she looks so steadfastly
That her sight dazzling makes the wound seem three;
1065 And then she reprehends her mangling eye,
    That makes more gashes where no breach should be.
    His face seems twain, each several limb is doubled;
    For oft the eye mistakes, the brain being troubled.

"My tongue cannot express my grief for one,
1070 And yet," quoth she, "behold two Adons dead!
My sighs are blown away, my salt tears gone,
Mine eyes are turned to fire, my heart to lead.
    Heavy heart's lead, melt at mine eyes' red fire!
    So shall I die by drops of hot desire.

1075 "Alas, poor world, what treasure hast thou lost!
What face remains alive that's worth the viewing?
Whose tongue is music now? What canst thou boast
Of things long since, or any thing ensuing?
    The flowers are sweet, their colors fresh and trim,
1080   But true sweet beauty lived and died with him.

1052 **trenched** cut   1059 **passions** grieves   1062 **mad** distracted 1062 **till**
i.e., before

"Bonnet nor veil henceforth no creature wear;
Nor sun nor wind will ever strive to kiss you.
Having no fair to lose, you need not fear:
The sun doth scorn you, and the wind doth hiss you.
1085   But when Adonis lived, sun and sharp air
      Lurked like two thieves, to rob him of his fair;

"And therefore would he put his bonnet on,
Under whose brim the gaudy sun would peep;
The wind would blow it off, and being gone,
1090   Play with his locks; then would Adonis weep;
      And straight, in pity of his tender years,
      They both would strive who first should dry his tears.

"To see his face the lion walked along,
Behind some hedge, because he would not fear him.
1095   To recreate himself when he hath song,
The tiger would be tame, and gently hear him.
      If he had spoke, the wolf would leave his prey
      And never fright the silly lamb that day.

"When he beheld his shadow in the brook,
1100   The fishes spread on it their golden gills;
When he was by, the birds such pleasure took
That some would sing, some other in their bills
      Would bring him mulberries and ripe-red cherries:
      He fed them with his sight, they him with berries.

1105   "But this foul, grim, and urchin-snouted boar,
Whose downward eye still looketh for a grave,
Ne'er saw the beauteous livery that he wore;
Witness the entertainment that he gave.
      If he did see his face, why then I know
1110   He thought to kiss him, and hath killed him so.

1083 **fair** beauty   1088 **gaudy** bright   1094 **fear** frighten   1098 **silly** innocent   1105 **urchin-snouted** hedgehog-snouted   1108 **entertainment** reception

" 'Tis true, 'tis true! thus was Adonis slain:
He ran upon the boar with his sharp spear,
Who did not whet his teeth at him again,
But by a kiss thought to persuade him there;
1115   And nuzzling in his flank, the loving swine
      Sheathed unaware the tusk in his soft groin.

"Had I been toothed like him, I must confess,
With kissing him I should have killed him first;
But he is dead, and never did he bless
1120   My youth with his; the more am I accurst."
      With this she falleth in the place she stood
      And stains her face with his congealèd blood.

She looks upon his lips, and they are pale;
She takes him by the hand, and that is cold;
1125   She whispers in his ears a heavy tale,
As if they heard the woeful words she told.
      She lifts the coffer-lids that close his eyes,
      Where lo, two lamps burnt out in darkness lies;

Two glasses, where herself herself beheld
1130   A thousand times, and now no more reflect;
Their virtue lost wherein they late excelled,
And every beauty robbed of his effect.
      "Wonder of time," quoth she, "this is my spite,
      That thou being dead, the day should yet be light.

1135   "Since thou art dead, lo here I prophesy,
Sorrow on love hereafter shall attend.
It shall be waited on with jealousy,
Find sweet beginning, but unsavory end,
      Ne'er settled equally, but high or low,
1140   That all love's pleasure shall not match his woe.

1127 **coffer-lids** lids to treasure-chests   1133 **spite** grief

127

"It shall be fickle, false, and full of fraud;
Bud, and be blasted, in a breathing while;
The bottom poison, and the top o'erstrawed
With sweets that shall the truest sight beguile.
1145   The strongest body shall it make most weak,
    Strike the wise dumb, and teach the fool to speak.

"It shall be sparing, and too full of riot,
Teaching decrepit age to tread the measures;
The staring ruffian shall it keep in quiet,
1150 Pluck down the rich, enrich the poor with treasures;
    It shall be raging mad, and silly mild,
    Make the young old, the old become a child.

"It shall suspect where is no cause of fear;
It shall not fear where it should most mistrust;
1155 It shall be merciful, and too severe,
And most deceiving when it seems most just;
    Perverse it shall be where it shows most toward;
    Put fear to valor, courage to the coward.

"It shall be cause of war and dire events
1160 And set dissension 'twixt the son and sire,
Subject and servile to all discontents,
As dry combustious matter is to fire.
    Sith in his prime death doth my love destroy,
    They that love best their loves shall not enjoy."

1165 By this the boy that by her side lay killed
Was melted like a vapor from her sight,
And in his blood, that on the ground lay spilled,
A purple flower sprung up, check'red with white,
    Resembling well his pale cheeks and the blood
1170   Which in round drops upon their whiteness stood.

1142 **in a breathing while** in one breath   1143 **o'erstrawed** strewn
docile 1168 **purple flower** i.e., the anemone

She bows her head the new-sprung flower to smell,
Comparing it to her Adonis' breath,
And says within her bosom it shall dwell,
Since he himself is reft from her by death;
1175   She crops the stalk, and in the breach appears
     Green-dropping sap, which she compares to tears.

"Poor flow'r," quoth she, "this was thy father's guise—
Sweet issue of a more sweet-smelling sire—
For every little grief to wet his eyes;
1180   To grow unto himself was his desire,
     And so 'tis thine; but know, it is as good
     To wither in my breast as in his blood.

"Here was thy father's bed, here in my breast;
Thou art the next of blood, and 'tis thy right.
1185   Lo in this hollow cradle take thy rest;
     My throbbing heart shall rock thee day and night:
     There shall not be one minute in an hour
     Wherein I will not kiss my sweet love's flow'r."

Thus weary of the world, away she hies,
1190   And yokes her silver doves, by whose swift aid
Their mistress, mounted, though the empty skies
In her light chariot quickly is conveyed,
     Holding their course to Paphos, where their queen
     Means to immure herself and not be seen.

FINIS

1175 **breach** break (in the stalk)   1177 **guise** custom   1193 **Paphos** (where
Venus dwells in Cyprus)

THE RAPE OF LUCRECE

To the Right Honorable
Henry Wriothesley

Earl of Southampton, and Baron of Titchfield

The love I dedicate to your Lordship is without end; whereof
this pamphlet without beginning is but a superfluous moiety.
The warrant I have of your honorable disposition, not the
worth of my untutored lines, makes it assured of acceptance.
What I have done is yours; what I have to do is yours; being part
in all I have, devoted yours. Were my worth greater, my duty
would show greater; meantime, as it is, it is bound to your
Lordship, to whom I wish long life still lengthened with all
happiness.

Your Lordship's in all duty,

William Shakespeare

THE ARGUMENT

Lucius Tarquinius (for his excessive pride surnamed Super-
bus), after he had caused his own father-in-law Servius Tullius
to be cruelly murdered, and, contrary to the Roman laws and
customs, not requiring or staying for the people's suffrages, had
possessed himself of the kingdom, went, accompanied with his
sons and other noblemen of Rome, to besiege Ardea; during

---

5 **without beginning** i.e., the narrative begins *in medias res*   5 **moiety** small
part

which siege the principal men of the army meeting one evening
at the tent of Sextus Tarquinius, the King's son, in their
discourses after supper every one commended the virtues of his
10 own wife; among whom Collatinus extolled the incomparable
chastity of his wife Lucretia. In that pleasant humor they all
posted to Rome; and intending by their secret and sudden
arrival to make trial of that which every one had before
avouched, only Collatinus finds his wife (though it were late in
15 the night) spinning amongst her maids; the other ladies were all
found dancing and reveling, or in several disports. Whereupon
the noblemen yielded Collatinus the victory, and his wife the
fame. At that time Sextus Tarquinius being inflamed with
Lucrece' beauty, yet smothering his passions for the present,
20 departed with the rest back to the camp; from whence he
shortly after privily withdrew himself, and was (according to
his estate) royally entertained and lodged by Lucrece at
Collatium. The same night he treacherously stealeth into her
chamber, violently ravished her, and early in the morning
25 speedeth away. Lucrece, in this lamentable plight, hastily
dispatcheth messengers, one to Rome for her father, another to
the camp for Collatine. They came, the one accompanied with
Junius Brutus, the other with Publius Valerius; and finding
Lucrece attired in mourning habit, demanded the cause of her
30 sorrow. She, first taking an oath of them for her revenge,
revealed the actor and whole manner of his dealing, and withal
suddenly stabbed herself. Which done, with one consent they
all vowed to root out the whole hated family of the Tarquins;
and bearing the dead body to Rome, Brutus acquainted the
35 people with the doer and manner of the vile deed, with a bitter
invective against the tyranny of the King; wherewith the people
were so moved that with one consent and a general acclamation
the Tarquins were all exiled, and the state government changed
from kings to consuls.

THE RAPE OF LUCRECE

From the besiegèd Ardea all in post,
Borne by the trustless wings of false desire,
Lust-breathèd Tarquin leaves the Roman host
And to Collatium bears the lightless fire
5   Which, in pale embers hid, lurks to aspire
     And girdle with embracing flames the waist
     Of Collatine's fair love, Lucrece the chaste.

Haply that name of "chaste" unhap'ly set
This bateless edge on his keen appetite;
10 When Collatine unwisely did not let
To praise the clear unmatchèd red and white
Which triumphed in that sky of his delight,
     Where mortal stars, as bright as heaven's beauties,
     With pure aspects did him peculiar duties.

15 For he the night before, in Tarquin's tent,
Unlocked the treasure of his happy state:
What priceless wealth the heavens had him lent
In the possession of his beauteous mate;
Reck'ning his fortune at such high proud rate
20   That kings might be espousèd to more fame,
     But king nor peer to such a peerless dame.

O happiness enjoyed but of a few,
And if possessed, as soon decayed and done
As is the morning's silver-melting dew
25 Against the golden splendor of the sun!
An expired date, canceled ere well begun.
     Honor and beauty, in the owner's arms,
     Are weakly fortressed from a world of harms.

---

1 **all in post** in great haste   2 **trustless** treacherous   3 **Lust-breathèd** inspired by lust   4 **lightless** smoldering   5 **aspire** ascend   8 **Haply** perhaps   9 **bateless** unbated   9 **appetite** lust   10 **let** forbear   12 **that sky of his delight** i.e., Lucrece's face   13 **mortal stars** i.e., Lucrece's eyes   14 **aspects** (1) looks (2) astrological influences   14 **peculiar** private   22 **of** by   23 **done** consumed   26 **date** lease

Beauty itself doth of itself persuade
30 The eyes of men without an orator.
What needeth then apologies be made
To set forth that which is so singular?
Or why is Collatine the publisher
 Of that rich jewel he should keep unknown
35 From thievish ears, because it is his own?

Perchance his boast of Lucrece' sov'reignty
Suggested this proud issue of a king;
For by our ears our hearts oft tainted be.
Perchance that envy of so rich a thing,
40 Braving compare, disdainfully did sting
 His high-pitched thoughts, that meaner men should vaunt
 That golden hap which their superiors want.

But some untimely thought did instigate
His all too timeless speed, if none of those.
45 His honor, his affairs, his friends, his state,
Neglected all, with swift intent he goes
To quench the coal which in his liver glows.
 O rash false heat, wrapped in repentant cold,
 Thy hasty spring still blasts and ne'er grows old!

50 When at Collatium this false lord arrivèd,
Well was he welcomed by the Roman dame,
Within whose face Beauty and Virtue strivèd
Which of them both should underprop her fame.
When Virtue bragged, Beauty would blush for shame;
55 When Beauty boasted blushes, in despite
 Virtue would stain that o'er with silver white.

31 **apologies** i.e., vindications 33 **publisher** proclaimer 37 **Suggested** prompted 37 **issue** i.e., son 40 **Braving compare** challenging comparison 42 **hap** luck 42 **want** lack 44 **timeless** untimely 45 **state** status, estate 47 **liver** (thought to have been the seat of sexual desire) 49 **still blasts** always is blasted

But Beauty in that white entitulèd
From Venus' doves, doth challenge that fair field;
Then Virtue claims from Beauty Beauty's red,
60 Which Virtue gave the Golden Age to gild
Their silver cheeks, and called it then their shield,
    Teaching them thus to use it in the fight,
    When shame assailed, the red should fence the white.

This heraldry in Lucrece' face was seen,
65 Argued by Beauty's red and Virtue's white;
Of either's color was the other queen,
Proving from world's minority their right.
Yet their ambition makes them still to fight,
    The sovereignty of either being so great
70   That oft they interchange each other's seat.

This silent war of lilies and of roses,
Which Tarquin viewed in her fair face's field,
In their pure ranks his traitor eye encloses;
Where, lest between them both it should be killed,
75 The coward captive vanquishèd doth yield
    To those two armies that would let him go
    Rather than triumph in so false a foe.

Now thinks he that her husband's shallow tongue,
The niggard prodigal that praised her so,
80 In that high task hath done her beauty wrong,
Which far exceeds his barren skill to show.
Therefore that praise which Collatine doth owe
    Enchanted Tarquin answers with surmise,
    In silent wonder of still-gazing eyes.

---

57 **entitulèd** having a claim 58 **field** (1) field of battle (2) ground of a
shield 60 **gild** color (with a blush) 63 **fence** defend 65 **Argued**
expressed 67 **minority** youth (i.e., the Golden Age of line 60) 83
answers pays 83 **surmise** amazement

85 This earthly saint, adorèd by this devil,
 Little suspecteth the false worshipper;
 For unstained thoughts do seldom dream on evil;
 Birds never limed no secret bushes fear.
 So guiltless she securely gives good cheer
90   And reverend welcome to her princely guest,
   Whose inward ill no outward harm expressed;

 For that he colored with his high estate,
 Hiding base sin in pleats of majesty;
 That nothing in him seemed inordinate,
95 Save sometime too much wonder of his eye,
 Which, having all, all could not satisfy;
   But poorly rich, so wanteth in his store
   That, cloyed with much, he pineth still for more.

 But she, that never coped with stranger eyes,
100 Could pick no meaning from their parling looks,
 Nor read the subtle shining secrecies
 Writ in the glassy margents of such books.
 She touched no unknown baits, nor feared no hooks;
   Nor could she moralize his wanton sight,
105   More than his eyes were opened to the light.

 He stories to her ears her husband's fame,
 Won in the fields of fruitful Italy;
 And decks with praises Collatine's high name,
 Made glorious by his manly chivalry,
110 With bruisèd arms and wreaths of victory.
   Her joy with heaved-up hand she doth express,
   And wordless so greets heaven for his success.

---

88 **limed** caught by bird-lime (a sticky substance smeared upon branches) 89 **securely** unsuspectingly 90 **reverend** reverent 92 **colored** cloaked 94 **That** so that 97 **store** wealth 99 **coped with** encountered 99 **stranger** i.e., strangers' 100 **parling** speaking 102 **glassy margents** margins (of his eyes) 104 **moralize** interpret 104 **sight** glance 110 **bruisèd arms** battered armor 111 **heaved-up** uplifted

Far from the purpose of his coming thither
He makes excuses for his being there.
115 No cloudy show of stormy blust'ring weather
Doth yet in his fair welkin once appear,
Till sable Night, mother of dread and fear,
　　Upon the world dim darkness doth display
　　And in her vaulty prison stows the day.

120 For then is Tarquin brought unto his bed,
Intending weariness with heavy sprite;
For, after supper, long he questionèd
With modest Lucrece, and wore out the night.
Now leaden slumber with life's strength doth fight,
125 　　And everyone to rest themselves betake,
　　Save thieves, and cares, and troubled minds that wake.

As one of which doth Tarquin lie revolving
The sundry dangers of his will's obtaining;
Yet ever to obtain his will resolving,
130 Though weak-built hopes persuade him to abstaining.
Despair to gain doth traffic oft for gaining;
　　And when great treasure is the meed proposèd,
　　Though death be adjunct, there's no death supposèd.

Those that much covet are with gain so fond
135 That what they have not, that which they possess
They scatter and unloose it from their bond,
And so by hoping more they have but less;
Or, gaining more, the profit of excess
　　Is but to surfeit, and such griefs sustain
140 　　That they prove bankrout in this poor rich gain.

116 welkin sky　121 Intending pretending　121 sprite spirit　122 questionèd talked　131 traffic trade　132 meed reward　133 adjunct i.e., the consequence　134 fond infatuated　140 bankrout bankrupt

The aim of all is but to nurse the life
With honor, wealth, and ease in waning age;
And in this aim there is such thwarting strife
That one for all, or all for one we gage:
₁₄₅ As life for honor in fell battle's rage;
   Honor for wealth; and oft that wealth doth cost
   The death of all, and all together lost;

So that in vent'ring ill we leave to be
The things we are for that which we expect;
₁₅₀ And this ambitious foul infirmity,
In having much, torments us with defect
Of that we have: so then we do neglect
   The thing we have, and all for want of wit,
   Make something nothing by augmenting it.

₁₅₅ Such hazard now must doting Tarquin make,
Pawning his honor to obtain his lust;
And for himself himself he must forsake.
Then where is truth, if there be no self-trust?
When shall he think to find a stranger just,
₁₆₀   When he himself himself confounds, betrays
   To sland'rous tongues and wretched hateful days?

Now stole upon the time the dead of night,
When heavy sleep had closed up mortal eyes.
No comfortable star did lend his light,
₁₆₅ No noise but owls, and wolves' death-boding cries;
Now serves the season that they may surprise
   The silly lambs: pure thoughts are dead and still,
   While lust and murder wake to stain and kill.

---

144 **gage** pledge 145 **As** for example 145 **fell** fierce 148 **vent'ring**
risking 148 **leave** cease 151 **defect** the insufficiency 160 **confounds**
destroys 164 **comfortable** comforting 167 **silly** innocent

And now this lustful lord leapt from his bed,
170 Throwing his mantle rudely o'er his arm;
Is madly tossed between desire and dread:
Th' one sweetly flatters, th' other feareth harm;
But honest fear, bewitched with lust's foul charm,
    Doth too too oft betake him to retire,
175   Beaten away by brainsick rude desire.

His falchion on a flint he softly smiteth,
That from the cold stone sparks of fire do fly;
Whereat a waxen torch forthwith he lighteth,
Which must be lodestar to his lustful eye;
180 And to the flame thus speaks advisedly:
    "As from this cold flint I enforced this fire,
    So Lucrece must I force to my desire."

Here pale with fear he doth premeditate
The dangers of his loathsome enterprise,
185 And in his inward mind he doth debate
What following sorrow may on this arise;
Then looking scornfully, he doth despise
    His naked armor of still-slaught'red lust
    And justly thus controls his thoughts unjust:

190 "Fair torch, burn out thy light, and lend it not
To darken her whose light excelleth thine;
And die, unhallowed thoughts, before you blot
With your uncleanness that which is divine.
Offer pure incense to so pure a shrine.
195   Let fair humanity abhor the deed
    That spots and stains love's modest snow-white weed.

175 brainsick mad   176 falchion curved sword   176 softly silently   179
lodestar guiding star   180 advisedly deliberately   188 His naked ... lust
i.e., his armor, lust, is no armor, for when lust is fulfilled it is killed   196
weed garment, i.e., chastity

"O shame to knighthood and to shining arms!
O foul dishonor to my household's grave!
O impious act including all foul harms!
200   A martial man to be soft fancy's slave!
True valor still a true respect should have;
   Then my digression is so vile, so base,
   That it will live engraven in my face.

"Yea, though I die, the scandal will survive
205   And be an eyesore in my golden coat.
Some loathsome dash the herald will contrive
To cipher me how fondly I did dote;
That my posterity, shamed with the note,
   Shall curse my bones, and hold it for no sin
210   To wish that I their father had not been.

"What win I if I gain the thing I seek?
A dream, a breath, a froth of fleeting joy.
Who buys a minute's mirth to wail a week?
Or sells eternity to get a toy?
215   For one sweet grape who will the vine destroy?
   Or what fond beggar, but to touch the crown,
   Would with the scepter straight be stroken down?

"If Collatinus dream of my intent,
Will he not wake, and in a desp'rate rage
220   Post hither this vile purpose to prevent?
This siege that hath engirt his marriage,
This blur to youth, this sorrow to the sage,
   This dying virtue, this surviving shame,
   Whose crime will bear an ever-during blame?

198 **my household's grave** the tomb of my ancestors   200 **soft fancy's** i.e., love's   201 **still** always   201 **respect** regard   205 **coat** coat of arms   206 **loathsome dash** i.e., a mark of disgrace   207 **cipher** show   207 **fondly** foolishly   221 **engirt** surrounded to attack   224 **ever-during** ever-enduring

225 "O, what excuse can my invention make
When thou shalt charge me with so black a deed?
Will not my tongue be mute, my frail joints shake,
Mine eyes forgo their light, my false heart bleed?
The guilt being great, the fear doth still exceed;
230 　And extreme fear can neither fight nor fly,
　　But coward-like with trembling terror die.

"Had Collatinus killed my son or sire,
Or lain in ambush to betray my life,
Or were he not my dear friend, this desire
235 Might have excuse to work upon his wife,
As in revenge or quittal of such strife;
　But as he is my kinsman, my dear friend,
　　The shame and fault finds no excuse nor end.

"Shameful it is—ay, if the fact be known.
240 Hateful it is—there is no hate in loving.
I'll beg her love—but she is not her own.
The worst is but denial and reproving.
My will is strong, past reason's weak removing.
　Who fears a sentence or an old man's saw
245 　Shall by a painted cloth be kept in awe."

Thus graceless holds he disputation
'Tween frozen conscience and hot-burning will,
And with good thoughts makes dispensation,
Urging the worser sense for vantage still;
250 Which in a moment doth confound and kill
　All pure effects, and doth so far proceed
　　That what is vile shows like a virtuous deed.

236 quittal requital　243 will desire　243 removing dissuasion　244
sentence moral judgment　244 saw moral saying　245 painted cloth wall
hanging on which were painted moral texts and illustrative Biblical and
classical subjects　248 makes dispensation dispenses　249 vantage
advantage　251 effects emotions

Quoth he, "She took me kindly by the hand
And gazed for tidings in my eager eyes,
255 Fearing some hard news from the warlike band
Where her belovèd Collatinus lies.
O, how her fear did make her color rise!
    First red as roses that on lawn we lay,
    Then white as lawn, the roses took away.

260 "And how her hand, in my hand being locked,
Forced it to tremble with her loyal fear!
Which strook her sad, and then it faster rocked
Until her husband's welfare she did hear;
Whereat she smilèd with so sweet a cheer
265   That, had Narcissus seen her as she stood,
    Self-love had never drowned him in the flood.

"Why hunt I then for color or excuses?
All orators are dumb when beauty pleadeth;
Poor wretches have remorse in poor abuses;
270 Love thrives not in the heart that shadows dreadeth.
Affection is my captain, and he leadeth;
    And when his gaudy banner is displayed,
    The coward fights and will not be dismayed.

"Then childish fear avaunt, debating die!
275 Respect and reason wait on wrinkled age!
My heart shall never countermand mine eye.
Sad pause and deep regard beseems the sage;
My part is youth, and beats these from the stage.
    Desire my pilot is, beauty my prize;
280   Then who fears sinking where such treasure lies?"

258 **lawn** (fine) linen   262 **Which** i.e., the fact that his hand trembled   262
it i.e., her heart   265 **Narcissus** a beautiful youth who fell in love with his
own reflection   267 **color** pretext   269 **Poor wretches ... abuses** remorse
is felt only by lesser men in their petty transgressions   270 **shadows
dreadeth** i.e., has scruples   271 **Affection** desire   273 **The coward** i.e.,
even the coward   275 **Respect** prudence   275 **wait on** attend   277 **Sad**
serious

As corn o'ergrown by weeds, so heedful fear
Is almost choked by unresisted lust.
Away he steals with open list'ning ear,
Full of foul hope and full of fond mistrust;
285   Both which, as servitors to the unjust,
      So cross him with their opposite persuasion
      That now he vows a league, and now invasion.

Within his thought her heavenly image sits,
And in the selfsame seat sits Collatine.
290   That eye which looks on her confounds his wits;
That eye which him beholds, as more divine,
Unto a view so false will not incline;
      But with a pure appeal seeks to the heart,
      Which once corrupted takes the worser part;

295   And therein heartens up his servile powers,
Who, flatt'red by their leader's jocund show,
Stuff up his lust, as minutes fill up hours;
And as their captain, so their pride doth grow,
Paying more slavish tribute than they owe.
300   By reprobate desire thus madly led,
      The Roman lord marcheth to Lucrece' bed.

The locks between her chamber and his will,
Each one by him enforced, retires his ward;
But as they open, they all rate his ill,
305   Which drives the creeping thief to some regard.
The threshold grates the door to have him heard;
      Night-wand'ring weasels shriek to see him there;
      They fright him, yet he still pursues his fear.

---

281 **corn** grain   286 **cross** thwart   287 **league** peace   293 **seeks to** applies to   295 **his servile powers** i.e., the senses   303 **retires his ward** draws back its bolt ("ward")   304 **rate his ill** condemn his evil intentions (by creaking)   305 **regard** caution   307 **weasels** (kept in Roman houses in place of cats to catch rats)

As each unwilling portal yields him way,
310 Through little vents and crannies of the place
The wind wars with his torch to make him stay,
And blows the smoke of it into his face,
Extinguishing his conduct in this case;
　　But his hot heart, which fond desire doth scorch,
315 　　Puffs forth another wind that fires the torch;

And being lighted, by the light he spies
Lucretia's glove, wherein her needle sticks;
He takes it from the rushes where it lies,
And griping it, the needle his finger pricks,
320 As who should say, "This glove to wanton tricks
　　Is not inured; return again in haste;
　　Thou seest our mistress' ornaments are chaste."

But all these poor forbiddings could not stay him;
He in the worst sense consters their denial:
325 The doors, the wind, the glove, that did delay him,
He takes for accidental things of trial;
Or as those bars which stop the hourly dial,
　　Who with a ling'ring stay his course doth let,
　　Till every minute pays the hour his debt.

330 "So, so," quoth he, "these lets attend the time,
Like little frosts that sometime threat the spring
To add a more rejoicing to the prime
And give the sneapèd birds more cause to sing.
Pain pays the income of each precious thing:
335 　　Huge rocks, high winds, strong pirates, shelves and sands,
　　The merchant fears ere rich at home he lands."

---

313 **conduct** conductor (i.e., the torch)　318 **rushes** (used as floor coverings)　321 **inured** accustomed　324 **consters** construes　326 **accidental things of trial** chance happenings　327 **bars** lines on the face of a clock　328 **Who** which　328 **let** delay　330 **lets** hindrances　332 **prime** spring　333 **sneapèd** chilled　334 **income** harvest, gain

Now is he come unto the chamber door
That shuts him from the heaven of his thought,
Which with a yielding latch, and with no more,
340   Hath barred him from the blessèd thing he sought.
So from himself impiety hath wrought
    That for his prey to pray he doth begin,
    As if the heavens should countenance his sin.

But in the midst of his unfruitful prayer,
345   Having solicited th' eternal power
That his foul thoughts might compass his fair fair,
And they would stand auspicious to the hour,
Even there he starts; quoth he, "I must deflow'r.
    The powers to whom I pray abhor this fact;
350   How can they then assist me in the act?

"Then Love and Fortune be my gods, my guide:
My will is backed with resolution.
Thoughts are but dreams till their effects be tried;
The blackest sin is cleared with absolution;
355   Against love's fire fear's frost hath dissolution.
    The eye of heaven is out, and misty night
    Covers the shame that follows sweet delight."

This said, his guilty hand plucked up the latch,
And with his knee the door he opens wide.
360   The dove sleeps fast that this night owl will catch.
Thus treason works ere traitors be espied.
Who sees the lurking serpent steps aside;
    But she, sound sleeping, fearing no such thing,
    Lies at the mercy of his mortal sting.

365   Into the chamber wickedly he stalks
And gazeth on her yet unstainèd bed.
The curtains being close, about he walks,
Rolling his greedy eyeballs in his head.
By their high treason is his heart misled,
370   Which gives the watchword to his hand full soon
    To draw the cloud that hides the silver moon.

341 **wrought** i.e., wrought him   346 **compass his fair fair** possess his
virtuous beauty   364 **sting** (1) lust (2) penis

Look as the fair and fiery-pointed sun,
Rushing from forth a cloud, bereaves our sight,
Even so, the curtain drawn, his eyes begun
375 To wink, being blinded with a greater light.
    Whether it is that she reflects so bright
        That dazzleth them, or else some shame supposèd;
        But blind they are, and keep themselves enclosèd.

O, had they in that darksome prison died,
380 Then had they seen the period of their ill!
Then Collatine again by Lucrece' side
In his clear bed might have reposèd still.
    But they must ope, this blessèd league to kill,
        And holy-thoughted Lucrece to their sight
385   Must sell her joy, her life, her world's delight.

Her lily hand her rosy cheek lies under,
Coz'ning the pillow of a lawful kiss;
Who, therefore angry, seems to part in sunder,
Swelling on either side to want his bliss;
390 Between whose hills her head entombèd is;
        Where like a virtuous monument she lies,
        To be admired of lewd unhallowed eyes.

Without the bed her other fair hand was,
On the green coverlet; whose perfect white
395 Showed like an April daisy on the grass,
With pearly sweat resembling dew of night.
    Her eyes like marigolds had sheathed their light,
        And canopied in darkness sweetly lay
        Till they might open to adorn the day.

400 Her hair like golden threads played with her breath—
O modest wantons, wanton modesty—
Showing life's triumph in the map of death,
And death's dim look in life's mortality.
    Each in her sleep themselves so beautify
405   As if between them twain there were no strife,
        But that life lived in death, and death in life.

372 Look as as   373 bereaves takes away   375 wink close   377 supposèd
imagined   380 period end   380 ill evil   382 clear unstained   387 Coz'n-
ing cheating   402 map image

Her breasts like ivory globes circled with blue,
A pair of maiden worlds unconquerèd,
Save of their lord no bearing yoke they knew,
410 And him by oath they truly honorèd.
These worlds in Tarquin new ambition bred,
  Who like a foul usurper went about
  From this fair throne to heave the owner out.

What could he see but mightily he noted?
415 What did he note but strongly he desirèd?
What he beheld, on that he firmly doted,
And in his will his willful eye he tirèd.
With more than admiration he admirèd
  Her azure veins, her alablaster skin,
420 Her coral lips, her snow-white dimpled chin.

As the grim lion fawneth o'er his prey,
Sharp hunger by the conquest satisfied,
So o'er this sleeping soul doth Tarquin stay,
His rage of lust by gazing qualified;
425 Slacked, not suppressed; for, standing by her side,
  His eye, which late this mutiny restrains,
  Unto a greater uproar tempts his veins.

And they, like straggling slaves for pillage fighting,
Obdurate vassals fell exploits effecting,
430 In bloody death and ravishment delighting,
Nor children's tears nor mothers' groans respecting,
Swell in their pride, the onset still expecting.
  Anon his beating heart, alarum striking,
  Gives the hot charge and bids them do their liking.

435 His drumming heart cheers up his burning eye,
His eye commends the leading to his hand;
His hand, as proud of such a dignity,
Smoking with pride, marched on to make his stand
On her bare breast, the heart of all her land;
440 Whose ranks of blue veins, as his hand did scale,
  Left their round turrets destitute and pale.

417 will lust   421 fawneth rejoices   431 Nor ... nor neither ... nor   432
pride lust   433 alarum call to attack in battle   435 cheers up
encourages   436 commends entrusts

They, must'ring to the quiet cabinet
Where their dear governess and lady lies,
Do tell her she is dreadfully beset
445 And fright her with confusion of their cries.
She, much amazed, breaks ope her locked-up eyes,
    Who, peeping forth this tumult to behold,
    Are by his flaming torch dimmed and controlled.

Imagine her as one in dead of night,
450 From forth dull sleep by dreadful fancy waking,
That thinks she hath beheld some ghastly sprite,
Whose grim aspect sets every joint a-shaking.
What terror 'tis! but she, in worser taking,
    From sleep disturbèd, heedfully doth view
455   The sight which makes supposèd terror true.

Wrapped and confounded in a thousand fears,
Like to a new-killed bird she trembling lies.
She dares not look; yet winking there appears
Quick-shifting antics, ugly in her eyes.
460 Such shadows are the weak brain's forgeries,
    Who, angry that the eyes fly from their lights,
    In darkness daunts them with more dreadful sights.

His hand, that yet remains upon her breast
(Rude ram, to batter such an ivory wall),
465 May feel her heart (poor citizen) distressed,
Wounding itself to death, rise up and fall,
Beating her bulk, that his hand shakes withal.
    This moves in him more rage and lesser pity,
    To make the breach and enter this sweet city.

---

442 **must'ring** rallying   442 **the quiet cabinet** i.e., the heart   448 **con-trolled** over-powered   453 **taking** fear   459 **antics** grotesque figures   460 **shadows** shapes   464 **ram** battering-ram   467 **bulk** body

470 First like a trumpet doth his tongue begin
To sound a parley to his heartless foe;
Who o'er the white sheet peers her whiter chin,
The reason of this rash alarm to know,
Which he by dumb demeanor seeks to show;
475 But she with vehement prayers urgeth still
Under what color he commits this ill.

Thus he replies: "The color in thy face,
That even for anger makes the lily pale
And the red rose blush at her own disgrace,
480 Shall plead for me and tell my loving tale.
Under that color am I come to scale
Thy never-conquered fort; the fault is thine,
For those thine eyes betray thee unto mine.

"Thus I forestall thee, if thou mean to chide:
485 Thy beauty hath ensnared thee to this night,
Where thou with patience must my will abide,
My will that marks thee for my earth's delight,
Which I to conquer sought with all my might;
But as reproof and reason beat it dead,
490 By thy bright beauty was it newly bred.

"I see what crosses my attempt will bring,
I know what thorns the growing rose defends,
I think the honey guarded with a sting:
All this beforehand counsel comprehends.
495 But Will is deaf, and hears no heedful friends;
Only he hath an eye to gaze on Beauty,
And dotes on what he looks, 'gainst law or duty.

"I have debated even in my soul,
What wrong, what shame, what sorrow I shall breed;
500 But nothing can affection's course control
Or stop the headlong fury of his speed.
I know repentant tears ensue the deed,
Reproach, disdain, and deadly enmity;
Yet strive I to embrace mine infamy."

---

471 **heartless** frightened   474 **dumb demeanor** dumbshow   476 **color**
(1) pretext (2) flag (3) anger (choler)   485 **to this night** i.e., tonight   486
will sexual desire   500 **affection's** passion's

505 This said, he shakes aloft his Roman blade,
Which, like a falcon tow'ring in the skies,
Coucheth the fowl below with his wings' shade,
Whose crooked beak threats if he mount he dies.
So under his insulting falchion lies
510   Harmless Lucretia, marking what he tells
   With trembling fear, as fowl hear falcons' bells.

"Lucrece," quoth he, "this night I must enjoy thee.
If thou deny, then force must work my way;
For in thy bed I purpose to destroy thee.
515 That done, some worthless slave of thine I'll slay,
To kill thine honor with thy life's decay;
   And in thy dead arms do I mean to place him,
   Swearing I slew him, seeing thee embrace him.

"So thy surviving husband shall remain
520 The scornful mark of every open eye;
Thy kinsmen hang their heads at this disdain,
Thy issue blurred with nameless bastardy;
And thou, the author of their obloquy,
   Shalt have thy trespass cited up in rhymes
525   And sung by children in succeeding times.

"But if thou yield, I rest thy secret friend;
The fault unknown is as a thought unacted.
A little harm done to a great good end
For lawful policy remains enacted.
530 The poisonous simple sometime is compacted
   In a pure compound; being so applied,
   His venom in effect is purified.

---

507 **Coucheth** makes cower   509 **falchion** curved sword (with play on "falcon")   521 **disdain** disgrace   529 **enacted** recorded   530 **simple** medicine   530 **compacted** compounded

"Then, for thy husband and thy children's sake,
Tender my suit; bequeath not to their lot
535 The shame that from them no device can take,
The blemish that will never be forgot;
Worse than a slavish wipe or birth-hour's blot;
　　For marks descried in men's nativity
　　Are nature's faults, not their own infamy."

540 Here with a cockatrice' dead-killing eye
He rouseth up himself and makes a pause;
While she, the picture of pure piety,
Like a white hind under the gripe's sharp claws,
Pleads, in a wilderness where are no laws,
545 　　To the rough beast that knows no gentle right
　　Nor aught obeys but his foul appetite.

But when a black-faced cloud the world doth threat,
In his dim mist th' aspiring mountains hiding,
From earth's dark womb some gentle gust doth get,
550 Which blows these pitchy vapors from their biding,
Hind'ring their present fall by this dividing,
　　So his unhallowed haste her words delays,
　　And moody Pluto winks while Orpheus plays.

Yet, foul night-waking cat, he doth but dally,
555 While in his hold-fast foot the weak mouse panteth.
Her sad behavior feeds his vulture folly,
A swallowing gulf that even in plenty wanteth.
His ear her prayers admits, but his heart granteth
　　No penetrable entrance to her plaining.
560 　　Tears harden lust, though marble wear with raining.

534 Tender regard　537 slavish wipe i.e., brand mark on a slave　537
birth-hour's blot birth mark　540 cockatrice' basilisk's (mythical serpent
which killed with a glance)　543 hind doe　543 gripe's griffin's (?) eagle's (?)
549 doth get makes its way　551 present immediate　553 Pluto ...
Orpheus Pluto, the ruler of the underworld, charmed by Orpheus' music,
shut his eyes and allowed Orpheus to lead his wife, Eurydice, back toward the
world　556 vulture folly ravenous madness　557 wanteth hungers　559
plaining lament

Her pity-pleading eyes are sadly fixèd
In the remorseless wrinkles of his face.
Her modest eloquence with sighs is mixèd,
Which to her oratory adds more grace.
565 She puts the period often from his place,
    And midst the sentence so her accent breaks
    That twice she doth begin ere once she speaks.

She conjures him by high almighty Jove,
By knighthood, gentry, and sweet friendship's oath,
570 By her untimely tears, her husband's love,
By holy human law and common troth,
By heaven and earth, and all the power of both,
    That to his borrowed bed he make retire
    And stoop to honor, not to foul desire.

575 Quoth she, "Reward not hospitality
With such black payment as thou hast pretended;
Mud not the fountain that gave drink to thee;
Mar not the thing that cannot be amended.
End thy ill aim before thy shoot be ended.
580   He is no woodman that doth bend his bow
    To strike a poor unseasonable doe.

"My husband is thy friend; for his sake spare me.
Thyself art mighty; for thine own sake leave me.
Myself a weakling; do not then ensnare me.
585 Thou look'st not like deceit; do not deceive me.
My sighs like whirlwinds labor hence to heave thee.
    If ever man were moved with woman's moans,
    Be movèd with my tears, my sighs, my groans;

562 **remorseless wrinkles** pitiless frowns   565 **She puts ... place** she
often makes a pause in the middle of a sentence   566 **accent** speech   574
stoop to submit to   576 **pretended** proposed   579 **shoot** act of shooting
(with pun on "suit"?)   580 **woodman** hunter   586 **heave** move

"All which together, like a troubled ocean,
590 Beat at thy rocky and wrack-threat'ning heart,
To soften it with their continual motion;
For stones dissolved to water do convert.
O, if no harder than a stone thou art,
    Melt at my tears and be compassionate!
595   Soft pity enters at an iron gate.

"In Tarquin's likeness I did entertain thee;
Hast thou put on his shape to do him shame?
To all the host of heaven I complain me.
Thou wrong'st his honor, wound'st his princely name.
600 Thou art not what thou seem'st; and if the same,
    Thou seem'st not what thou art, a god, a king;
    For kings like gods should govern everything.

"How will thy shame be seeded in thine age
When thus thy vices bud before thy spring?
605 If in thy hope thou dar'st do such outrage,
What dar'st thou not when once thou art a king?
O, be rememb'red, no outrageous thing
    From vassal actors can be wiped away;
    Then kings' misdeeds cannot be hid in clay.

610 "This deed will make thee only loved for fear;
But happy monarchs still are feared for love.
With foul offenders thou perforce must bear
When they in thee the like offenses prove.
If but for fear of this, thy will remove;
615   For princes are the glass, the school, the book,
    Where subjects' eyes do learn, do read, do look.

592 **convert** change   603 **seeded** matured   608 **vassal actors** i.e., subjects, acting on orders   609 **in clay** i.e., in death   614 **If but for** if only for   614 **thy will remove** dissuade your lust   615 **glass** looking glass

"And wilt thou be the school where Lust shall learn?
Must be in thee read lectures of such shame?
Wilt thou be glass wherein it shall discern
620   Authority for sin, warrant for blame,
    To privilege dishonor in thy name?
        Thou back'st reproach against long-living laud
        And mak'st fair reputation but a bawd.

"Hast thou command? By him that gave it thee,
625   From a pure heart command thy rebel will!
Draw not thy sword to guard iniquity,
For it was lent thee all that brood to kill.
Thy princely office how canst thou fulfill
        When, patterned by thy fault, foul Sin may say,
630   He learned to sin, and thou didst teach the way?

"Think but how vile a spectacle it were
To view thy present trespass in another.
Men's faults do seldom to themselves appear;
Their own transgressions partially they smother.
635   This guilt would seem death-worthy in thy brother.
        O, how are they wrapped in with infamies
        That from their own misdeeds askaunce their eyes!

"To thee, to thee, my heaved-up hands appeal,
Not to seducing lust, thy rash relier.
640   I sue for exiled majesty's repeal;
Let him return, and flatt'ring thoughts retire.
His true respect will prison false desire
        And wipe the dim mist from thy doting eyne,
        That thou shalt see thy state, and pity mine."

622 Thou back'st you support   622 laud praise   624 him i.e., God   637 askaunce turn aside   639 lust, thy rash relier i.e., lust which you rashly rely on   640 repeal return from exile   642 respect respectfulness   642 prison imprison   643 eyne eyes

645   "Have done," quoth he. "My uncontrollèd tide
Turns not, but swells the higher by this let.
Small lights are soon blown out; huge fires abide
And with the wind in greater fury fret.
The petty streams that pay a daily debt
650   To their salt sovereign with their fresh falls' haste,
Add to his flow, but alter not his taste."

"Thou art," quoth she, "a sea, a sovereign king;
And, lo, there falls into thy boundless flood
Black lust, dishonor, shame, misgoverning,
655   Who seek to stain the ocean of thy blood.
If all these petty ills shall change thy good,
Thy sea within a puddle's womb is hearsèd,
And not the puddle in thy sea dispersèd.

"So shall these slaves be king, and thou their slave;
660   Thou nobly base, they basely dignified;
Thou their fair life, and they thy fouler grave;
Thou loathèd in their shame, they in thy pride.
The lesser thing should not the greater hide.
The cedar stoops not to the base shrub's foot,
665   But low shrubs wither at the cedar's root.

"So let thy thoughts, low vassals to thy state"—
"No more," quoth he. "By heaven, I will not hear thee!
Yield to my love; if not, enforcèd hate,
Instead of love's coy touch, shall rudely tear thee.
670   That done, despitefully I mean to bear thee
Unto the base bed of some rascal groom,
To be thy partner in this shameful doom."

646 let hindrance   650 salt sovereign i.e., the ocean   650 falls'
flows'   657 hearsèd entombed   669 coy gentle   670 despitefully cruelly

This said, he sets his foot upon the light,
For light and lust are deadly enemies;
675   Shame folded up in blind concealing night,
When most unseen, then most doth tyrannize.
The wolf hath seized his prey; the poor lamb cries,
     Till with her own white fleece her voice controlled
     Entombs her outcry in her lips' sweet fold;

680   For with the nightly linen that she wears
He pens her piteous clamors in her head,
Cooling his hot face in the chastest tears
That ever modest eyes with sorrow shed.
O, that prone lust should stain so pure a bed,
685   The spots whereof, could weeping purify,
     Her tears should drop on them perpetually!

But she hath lost a dearer thing than life,
And he hath won what he would lose again.
This forcèd league doth force a further strife;
690   This momentary joy breeds months of pain;
This hot desire converts to cold disdain;
     Pure Chastity is rifled of her store,
     And Lust, the thief, far poorer than before.

Look as the full-fed hound or gorgèd hawk,
695   Unapt for tender smell or speedy flight,
Make slow pursuit, or altogether balk
The prey wherein by nature they delight,
So surfeit-taking Tarquin fares this night:
     His taste delicious, in digestion souring,
700   Devours his will, that lived by foul devouring.

---

678 **white fleece** i.e., bedclothes   678 **controlled** overwhelmed   680
nightly linen turban (?)   684 **prone** (1) impulsive (2) prostrate   695
tender smell weak scent   696 **balk** neglect to pursue

O, deeper sin than bottomless conceit
Can comprehend in still imagination!
Drunken Desire must vomit his receipt
Ere he can see his own abomination.
750 While Lust is in his pride, no exclamation
    Can curb his heat or rein his rash desire
    Till, like a jade, Self-will himself doth tire.

And then with lank and lean discolored cheek,
With heavy eye, knit brow, and strengthless pace,
710 Feeble Desire, all recreant, poor, and meek,
Like to a bankrout beggar wails his case.
    The flesh being proud, Desire doth fight with Grace,
    For there it revels; and when that decays,
    The guilty rebel for remission prays.

715 So fares it with this fault-full lord of Rome,
Who this accomplishment so hotly chasèd;
For now against himself he sounds this doom,
That through the length of times he stands disgracèd.
Besides, his soul's fair temple is defacèd;
720   To whose weak ruins muster troops of cares,
    To ask the spotted princess how she fares.

She says her subjects with foul insurrection
Have battered down her consecrated wall,
And by their mortal fault brought in subjection
725 Her immortality and made her thrall
To living death and pain perpetual;
    Which in her prescience she controllèd still,
    But her foresight could not forestall their will.

701 bottomless conceit infinite imagination 703 his receipt what it has
received 705 exclamation exhortation 710 recreant cowed 713 that
i.e., lust 721 the spotted princess i.e., Tarquin's defiled soul 722
subjects i.e., the senses 724 mortal deadly 727 Which i.e., her subjects
727 prescience foreknowledge (i.e., in theory)

Ev'n in this thought through the dark night he stealeth,
730 A captive victor that hath lost in gain;
Bearing away the wound that nothing healeth,
The scar that will despite of cure remain;
Leaving his spoil perplexed in greater pain.
   She bears the load of lust he left behind,
735   And he the burden of a guilty mind.

He like a thievish dog creeps sadly thence;
She like a wearied lamb lies panting there.
He scowls, and hates himself for his offense;
She desperate with her nails her flesh doth tear.
740 He faintly flies, sweating with guilty fear;
   She stays, exclaiming on the direful night;
   He runs, and chides his vanished loathed delight.

He thence departs a heavy convertite;
She there remains a hopeless castaway.
745 He in his speed looks for the morning light;
She prays she never may behold the day,
"For day," quoth she, "night's scapes doth open lay,
   And my true eyes have never practiced how
   To cloak offenses with a cunning brow.

750 "They think not but that every eye can see
The same disgrace which they themselves behold;
And therefore would they still in darkness be,
To have their unseen sin remain untold;
For they their guilt with weeping will unfold
755   And grave, like water that doth eat in steel,
   Upon my cheeks what helpless shame I feel."

Here she exclaims against repose and rest,
And bids her eyes hereafter still be blind.
She wakes her heart by beating on her breast,
760 And bids it leap from thence, where it may find
Some purer chest to close so pure a mind.
   Frantic with grief thus breathes she forth her spite
   Against the unseen secrecy of night:

733 **spoil** victim   743 **heavy convertite** sad penitent   744 **castaway** lost
soul   747 **scapes** transgressions   755 **grave** engrave   755 **water** i.e., acid
761 **close** enclose

"O comfort-killing Night, image of hell,
765 Dim register and notary of shame,
Black stage for tragedies and murders fell,
Vast sin-concealing chaos, nurse of blame,
Blind muffled bawd, dark harbor for defame!
    Grim cave of death, whisp'ring conspirator
770 With close-tongued treason and the ravisher!

"O hateful, vaporous, and foggy Night,
Since thou art guilty of my cureless crime,
Muster thy mists to meet the eastern light,
Make war against proportioned course of time;
775 Or if thou wilt permit the sun to climb
    His wonted height, yet ere he go to bed,
    Knit poisonous clouds about his golden head.

"With rotten damps ravish the morning air;
Let their exhaled unwholesome breaths make sick
780 The life of purity, the supreme fair,
Ere he arrive his weary noontide prick;
And let thy musty vapors march so thick
    That in their smoky ranks his smoth'red light
    May set at noon and make perpetual night.

785 "Were Tarquin Night, as he is but Night's child,
The silver-shining queen he would distain;
Her twinkling handmaids too, by him defiled,
Through Night's black bosom should not peep again.
So should I have co-partners in my pain;
790   And fellowship in woe doth woe assuage,
    As palmers' chat makes short their pilgrimage;

---

765 notary recorder 768 defame disgrace 770 **close-tongued**
secretive 774 **proportioned** orderly 780 **the supreme fair** i.e., the sun
781 **Ere he arrive ... prick** before he reaches wearied at the point of noon (on
a sun dial) 785 **Night's child** i.e., wicked 786 **distain** defile 791
palmers' pilgrims' (those who had been to the Holy Land wore a palm leaf)

"Where now I have no one to blush with me,
To cross their arms and hang their heads with mine,
To mask their brows and hide their infamy;
795 But I alone, alone must sit and pine,
Seasoning the earth with show'rs of silver brine,
  Mingling my talk with tears, my grief with groans,
  Poor wasting monuments of lasting moans.

"O Night, thou furnace of foul reeking smoke,
800 Let not the jealous Day behold that face
Which underneath thy black all-hiding cloak
Immodestly lies martyred with disgrace!
Keep still possession of thy gloomy place,
  That all the faults which in thy reign are made
805   May likewise be sepulchered in thy shade!

"Make me not object to the telltale Day.
The light will show, charactered in my brow,
The story of sweet chastity's decay,
The impious breach of holy wedlock vow.
810 Yea, the illiterate, that know not how
  To cipher what is writ in learnèd books,
  Will quote my loathsome trespass in my looks.

"The nurse to still her child will tell my story
And fright her crying babe with Tarquin's name.
815 The orator to deck his oratory
Will couple my reproach to Tarquin's shame.
Feast-finding minstrels, tuning my defame,
  Will tie the hearers to attend each line,
  How Tarquin wrongèd me, I Collatine.

792 **Where now** whereas   793 **To cross their arms** (folded arms were a sign of melancholy)   794 **To mask their brows** (a hat pulled down over one's face was a sign of melancholy)   800 **jealous** watchful   807 **charactered** lettered (accent on second syllable)   811 **cipher** decipher   812 **quote** mark   818 **tie** hold

820   "Let my good name, that senseless reputation,
      For Collatine's dear love be kept unspotted.
      If that be made a theme for disputation,
      The branches of another root are rotted,
      And undeserved reproach to him allotted
825   That is as clear from this attaint of mine
       As I ere this was pure to Collatine.

      "O unseen shame, invisible disgrace!
      O unfelt sore, crest-wounding private scar!
      Reproach is stamped in Collatinus' face,
830   And Tarquin's eye may read the mot afar,
      How he in peace is wounded, not in war.
       Alas, how many bear such shameful blows
       Which not themselves, but he that gives them knows!

      "If, Collatine, thine honor lay in me,
835   From me by strong assault it is bereft;
      My honey lost, and I, a drone-like bee,
      Have no perfection of my summer left,
      But robbed and ransacked by injurious theft.
       In thy weak hive a wand'ring wasp hath crept
840   And sucked the honey which thy chaste bee kept.

      "Yet am I guilty of thy honor's wrack;
      Yet for thy honor did I entertain him:
      Coming from thee, I could not put him back,
      For it had been dishonor to disdain him.
845   Besides, of weariness he did complain him
       And talked of virtue: O unlooked-for evil,
       When virtue is profaned in such a devil!

---

820 **senseless** (1) impalpable (2) free from sensuality   825 **attaint** disgrace   828 **crest-wounding** i.e., disgraceful to the family crest   830 **mot** motto (with allusion to the parable of the mote and the beam, Matthew 7:3)

"Why should the worm intrude the maiden bud?
Or hateful cuckoos hatch in sparrows' nests?
850 Or toads infect fair founts with venom mud?
Or tyrant folly lurk in gentle breasts?
Or kings be breakers of their own behests?
　　But no perfection is so absolute
　　That some impurity doth not pollute.

855 "The agèd man that coffers up his gold
Is plagued with cramps and gouts and painful fits,
And scarce hath eyes his treasure to behold,
But like still-pining Tantalus he sits
And useless barns the harvest of his wits,
860 　　Having no other pleasure of his gain
　　But torment that it cannot cure his pain.

"So then he hath it when he cannot use it,
And leaves it to be mast'red by his young,
Who in their pride do presently abuse it;
865 Their father was too weak, and they too strong,
To hold their cursèd-blessèd fortune long.
　　The sweets we wish for turn to loathèd sours
　　Even in the moment that we call them ours.

"Unruly blasts wait on the tender spring;
870 Unwholesome weeds take root with precious flow'rs;
The adder hisses where the sweet birds sing;
What virtue breeds iniquity devours.
We have no good that we can say is ours,
　　But ill-annexèd opportunity
875 　　Or kills his life or else his quality.

852 **behests** commands 858 **Tantalus** (in Hades, Tantalus was surrounded
by food and drink that he could never touch) 859 **barns** stores 864
presently immediately 874 **ill-annexèd opportunity** disastrously con-
nected chance 875 **Or … quality** either kills its (good's) life or its nature

"O Opportunity, thy guilt is great!
'Tis thou that execut'st the traitor's treason;
Thou sets the wolf where he the lamb may get;
Whoever plots the sin, thou point'st the season.
880 'Tis thou that spurn'st at right, at law, at reason;
    And in thy shady cell, where none may spy him,
    Sits Sin, to seize the souls that wander by him.

"Thou mak'st the vestal violate her oath;
Thou blow'st the fire when temperance is thawed;
885 Thou smother'st honesty, thou murd'rest troth.
Thou foul abettor, thou notorious bawd,
Thou plantest scandal and displacest laud.
    Thou ravisher, thou traitor, thou false thief,
    Thy honey turns to gall, thy joy to grief.

890 "Thy secret pleasure turns to open shame,
Thy private feasting to a public fast,
Thy smoothing titles to a ragged name,
Thy sug'red tongue to bitter wormwood taste:
Thy violent vanities can never last.
895   How comes it then, vile Opportunity,
    Being so bad, such numbers seek for thee?

"When wilt thou be the humble suppliant's friend
And bring him where his suit may be obtainèd?
When wilt thou sort an hour great strifes to end?
900 Or free that soul which wretchedness hath chainèd?
Give physic to the sick, ease to the painèd?
    The poor, lame, blind, halt, creep, cry out for thee;
    But they ne'er meet with Opportunity.

"The patient dies while the physician sleeps;
905 The orphan pines while the oppressor feeds;
Justice is feasting while the widow weeps;
Advice is sporting while infection breeds.
Thou grant'st no time for charitable deeds:
    Wrath, envy, treason, rape, and murder's rages,
910   Thy heinous hours wait on them as their pages.

887 laud praise   892 smoothing flattering   899 sort choose   907 Advice
(medical) knowledge

"When Truth and Virtue have to do with thee,
A thousand crosses keep them from thy aid.
They buy thy help; but Sin ne'er gives a fee,
He gratis comes; and thou art well apaid
915 As well to hear as grant what he hath said.
    My Collatine would else have come to me
    When Tarquin did, but he was stayed by thee.

"Guilty thou art of murder and of theft,
Guilty of perjury and subornation,
920 Guilty of treason, forgery, and shift,
Guilty of incest, that abomination:
An accessary by thine inclination
    To all sins past and all that are to come,
    From the creation to the general doom.

925 "Misshapen Time, copesmate of ugly Night,
Swift subtle post, carrier of grisly care,
Eater of youth, false slave to false delight,
Base watch of woes, sin's packhorse, virtue's snare!
Thou nursest all, and murd'rest all that are.
930   O, hear me then, injurious shifting Time;
    Be guilty of my death, since of my crime.

"Why hath thy servant Opportunity
Betrayed the hours thou gav'st me to repose?
Canceled my fortunes, and enchainèd me
935 To endless date of never-ending woes?
Time's office is to fine the hate of foes,
    To eat up errors by opinion bred,
    Not spend the dowry of a lawful bed.

912 **crosses** hindrances 919 **subornation** bribing someone to commit a
crime 920 **shift** cheating 925 **copesmate** companion, paramour 926
subtle post sly post-rider 928 **watch** watchman 936 **fine** end

"Time's glory is to calm contending kings,
940   To unmask falsehood and bring truth to light,
To stamp the seal of time in agèd things,
To wake the morn and sentinel the night,
To wrong the wronger till he render right,
    To ruinate proud buildings with thy hours,
945   And smear with dust their glitt'ring golden tow'rs;

"To fill with wormholes stately monuments,
To feed oblivion with decay of things,
To blot old books and alter their contents,
To pluck the quills from ancient ravens' wings,
950   To dry the old oak's sap and cherish springs,
    To spoil antiquities of hammered steel
    And turn the giddy round of Fortune's wheel;

"To show the beldame daughters of her daughter,
To make the child a man, the man a child,
995   To slay the tiger that doth live by slaughter,
To tame the unicorn and lion wild,
To mock the subtle in themselves beguiled,
    To cheer the ploughman with increaseful crops
    And waste huge stones with little water-drops.

960   "Why work'st thou mischief in thy pilgrimage,
Unless thou couldst return to make amends?
One poor retiring minute in an age
Would purchase thee a thousand thousand friends,
Lending him wit that to bad debtors lends.
965   O this dread night, wouldst thou one hour come back,
    I could prevent this storm and shun thy wrack!

942 **sentinel** guard   944 **ruinate** reduce to ruin   950 **cherish springs**
renew (1) the water of springs, of (2) young saplings (i.e., new growth of any
kind)   953 **beldame** old woman   959 **waste** wear away   962 **retiring**
returning

"Thou ceaseless lackey to Eternity,
With some mischance cross Tarquin in his flight.
Devise extremes beyond extremity
970 To make him curse this cursèd crimeful night.
Let ghastly shadows his lewd eyes affright,
　　And the dire thought of his committed evil
　　Shape every bush a hideous shapeless devil.

"Disturb his hours of rest with restless trances;
975 Afflict him in his bed with bedrid groans;
Let there bechance him pitiful mischances
To make him moan, but pity not his moans.
Stone him with hard'nèd hearts harder than stones,
　　And let mild women to him lose their mildness,
980 　　Wilder to him than tigers in their wildness.

"Let him have time to tear his curlèd hair,
Let him have time against himself to rave,
Let him have time of Time's help to despair,
Let him have time to live a loathèd slave,
985 Let him have time a beggar's orts to crave,
　　And time to see one that by alms doth live
　　Disdain to him disdainèd scraps to give.

"Let him have time to see his friends his foes
And merry fools to mock at him resort;
990 Let him have time to mark how slow time goes
In time of sorrow, and how swift and short
His time of folly and his time of sport;
　　And ever let his unrecalling crime
　　Have time to wail th' abusing of his time.

967 **ceaseless lackey** ever-present servant　985 **orts** scraps　993 **unrecalling** irrevocable

995 "O Time, thou tutor both to good and bad,
Teach me to curse him that thou taught'st this ill.
At his own shadow let the thief run mad,
Himself himself seek every hour to kill.
Such wretched hands such wretched blood should spill,
1000   For who so base would such an office have
    As sland'rous deathsman to so base a slave?

"The baser is he, coming from a king,
To shame his hope with deeds degenerate.
The mightier man, the mightier is the thing
1005 That makes him honored or begets him hate;
For greatest scandal waits on greatest state.
    The moon being clouded presently is missed,
    But little stars may hide them when they list.

"The crow may bathe his coal-black wings in mire
1010 And unperceived fly with the filth away;
But if the like the snow-white swan desire,
The stain upon his silver down will stay.
Poor grooms are sightless night, kings glorious day;
    Gnats are unnoted wheresoe'er they fly,
1015   But eagles gazed upon with every eye.

"Out, idle words, servants to shallow fools,
Unprofitable sounds, weak arbitrators!
Busy yourselves in skill-contending schools;
Debate where leisure serves with dull debaters;
1020 To trembling clients be you mediators:
    For me, I force not argument a straw,
    Since that my case is past the help of law.

1001 **sland'rous deathsman** disgraced executioner 1003 **hope** expectations (as heir) 1013 **grooms** servants 1013 **sightless** invisible 1017 **arbitrators** arbiters (or compromisers) 1018 **in skill-contending schools** i.e., in mere debates 1020 **clients** suitors at law 1021 **force not argument a straw** care not a straw for argument

"In vain I rail at Opportunity,
At Time, at Tarquin, and uncheerful Night;
1025 In vain I cavil with mine infamy;
In vain I spurn at my confirmed despite:
This helpless smoke of words doth me no right.
    The remedy indeed to do me good
    Is to let forth my foul defilèd blood.

1030 "Poor hand, why quiver'st thou at this decree?
Honor thyself to rid me of this shame;
For if I die, my honor lives in thee;
But if I live, thou liv'st in my defame.
Since thou couldst not defend thy loyal dame
1035   And wast afeared to scratch her wicked foe,
    Kill both thyself and her for yielding so."

This said, from her betumbled couch she starteth,
To find some desp'rate instrument of death;
But this no slaughterhouse no tool imparteth
1040 To make more vent for passage of her breath,
Which, thronging through her lips, so vanisheth
    As smoke from Aetna that in air consumes
    Or that which from dischargèd cannon fumes.

"In vain," quoth she, "I live, and seek in vain
1045 Some happy mean to end a hapless life.
I feared by Tarquin's falchion to be slain,
Yet for the selfsame purpose seek a knife;
But when I feared I was a loyal wife.
    So am I now—O no, that cannot be:
1050   Of that true type hath Tarquin rifled me.

"O, that is gone for which I sought to live,
And therefore now I need not fear to die.
To clear this spot by death, at least I give
A badge of fame to slander's livery,
1055 A dying life to living infamy.
    Poor helpless help, the treasure stol'n away,
    To burn the guiltless casket where it lay!

1026 **spurn** kick 1026 **despite** wrong 1027 **smoke of words** mere talk
1039 **imparteth** provides 1050 **true type** stamp 1054 **badge** mark
(crest, coat of arms) worn on a servant's sleeve 1054 **livery** garment

"Well, well, dear Collatine, thou shalt not know
The stainèd taste of violated troth.
1060 I will not wrong thy true affection so,
To flatter thee with an infringèd oath.
This bastard graff shall never come to growth:
    He shall not boast, who did thy stock pollute
    That thou art doting father of his fruit.

1065 "Nor shall he smile at thee in secret thought,
Nor laugh with his companions at thy state;
But thou shalt know thy int'rest was not bought
Basely with gold, but stol'n from forth thy gate.
For me, I am the mistress of my fate,
1070   And with my trespass never will dispense
    Till life to death acquit my forced offense.

"I will not poison thee with my attaint
Nor fold my fault in cleanly coined excuses;
My sable ground of sin I will not paint
1075 To hide the truth of this false night's abuses.
My tongue shall utter all; mine eyes, like sluices,
    As from a mountain spring that feeds a dale,
    Shall gush pure streams to purge my impure tale."

By this lamenting Philomel had ended
1080 The well-tuned warble of her nightly sorrow,
And solemn night with slow sad gait descended
To ugly hell; when, lo, the blushing morrow
Lends light to all fair eyes that light will borrow;
    But cloudy Lucrece shames herself to see
1085   And therefore still in night would cloist'red be.

1062 **graff** graft, shoot   1067 **int'rest** property   1070 **dispense**
pardon   1074 **sable** black   1079 **Philomel** the nightingale (who, according
to legend, had originally been a woman, ravished by Tereus—see lines
1128–34)

Revealing day through every cranny spies
And seems to point her out where she sits weeping;
To whom she sobbing speaks, "O eye of eyes
Why pry'st thou through my window? Leave thy peeping.
1090　Mock with thy tickling beams eyes that are sleeping.
　　Brand not my forehead with thy piercing light.
　　For day hath naught to do what's done by night."

Thus cavils she with everything she sees.
True grief is fond and testy as a child,
1095　Who wayward once, his mood with naught agrees.
Old woes, not infant sorrows, bear them mild:
Continuance tames the one; the other wild,
　　Like an unpracticed swimmer plunging still,
　　With too much labor drowns for want of skill.

1100　So she, deep drenchèd in a sea of care,
Holds disputation with each thing she views,
And to herself all sorrow doth compare;
No object but her passion's strength renews;
And as one shifts, another straight ensues.
1105　　Sometime her grief is dumb and hath no words;
　　Sometime 'tis mad and too much talk affords.

The little birds that tune their morning's joy
Make her moans mad with their sweet melody:
For mirth doth search the bottom of annoy;
1110　Sad souls are slain in merry company;
Grief best is pleased with grief's society:
　　True sorrow then is feelingly sufficed
　　When with like semblance it is sympathized.

1090 **tickling** lightly touching　1094 **fond and testy** foolish and
irritable　1095 **wayward once** once becoming angry　1096 **them**
themselves　1104 **straight ensues** straightway follows　1107 **tune** sing
1109 **search the bottom of annoy** pierce to the depths of grief　1112
sufficed contented

'Tis double death to drown in ken of shore;
1115 He ten times pines that pines beholding food;
To see the salve doth make the wound ache more;
Great grief grieves most at that would do it good;
Deep woes roll forward like a gentle flood,
  Who, being stopped, the bounding banks o'erflows;
1120 Grief dallied with, nor law nor limit knows.

"You mocking birds," quoth she, "your tunes entomb
Within your hollow swelling feath'red breasts,
And in my hearing be you mute and dumb;
My restless discord loves no stops nor rests.
1125 A woeful hostess brooks not merry guests.
  Relish your nimble notes to pleasing ears;
  Distress likes dumps when time is kept with tears.

"Come, Philomel, that sing'st of ravishment,
Make thy sad grove in my disheveled hair.
1130 As the dank earth weeps at thy languishment,
So I at each sad strain will strain a tear
And with deep groans the diapason bear;
  For burden-wise I'll hum on Tarquin still,
  While thou on Tereus descants better skill.

1135 "And whiles against a thorn thou bear'st thy part
To keep thy sharp woes waking, wretched I,
To imitate thee well, against my heart
Will fix a sharp knife to affright mine eye,
Who if it wink shall thereon fall and die.
1140   These means, as frets upon an instrument,
  Shall tune our heartstrings to true languishment.

1114 ken sight 1120 dallied with trifled with 1124 stops, rests (1)
cessation of discord (2) musical pauses 1126 Relish make pleasant
(sauce) 1127 dumps slow mournful tunes 1132 diapason bass accom-
paniment 1133 burden-wise a burden was (1) a bass accompaniment (2)
the refrain of a song 1134 descants better skill (1) sings better (2) sings
more intricately 1139 Who which (i.e., her heart) 1139 it wink i.e., her
eye closes 1140 frets ridges fastened across the fingerboard of a stringed
instrument to regulate fingering

"And for, poor bird, thou sing'st not in the day,
As shaming any eye should thee behold,
Some dark deep desert, seated from the way,
1145 That knows not parching heat nor freezing cold,
Will we find out; and there we will unfold
    To creatures stern sad tunes, to change their kinds.
    Since men prove beasts, let beasts bear gentle minds."

As the poor frighted deer that stands at gaze,
1150 Wildly determining which way to fly,
Or one encompassed with a winding maze,
That cannot tread the way out readily;
So with herself is she in mutiny,
    To live or die which of the twain were better,
1155   When life is shamed and death reproach's debtor.

"To kill myself," quoth she, "alack, what were it
But with my body my poor soul's pollution?
They that lose half with greater patience bear it
Than they whose whole is swallowed in confusion.
1160 That mother tries a merciless conclusion
    Who, having two sweet babes, when death takes one,
    Will slay the other and be nurse to none.

"My body or my soul, which was the dearer
When the one pure, the other made divine?
1165 Whose love of either to myself was nearer
When both were kept for heaven and Collatine?
Ay me, the bark pilled from the lofty pine,
    His leaves will wither and his sap decay:
    So must my soul, her bark being pilled away.

1142 **And for** and because 1143 **shaming** being ashamed 1144 **desert,
seated from the way** deserted place situated away from a path 1147 **kinds**
natures 1149 **at gaze** i.e., bewildered 1155 **death reproach's debtor** i.e.,
her death (suicide) would be the occasion of reproach 1159 **confusion**
destruction 1160 **conclusion** experiment 1167 **pilled** peeled

1170 "Her house is sacked, her quiet interrupted,
Her mansion battered by the enemy;
Her sacred temple spotted, spoiled, corrupted,
Grossly engirt with daring infamy.
Then let it not be called impiety
1175   If in this blemished fort I make some hole
   Through which I may convey this troubled soul.

"Yet die I will not till my Collatine
Have heard the cause of my untimely death,
That he may vow, in that sad hour of mine,
1180 Revenge on him that made me stop my breath.
My stainèd blood to Tarquin I'll bequeath,
   Which, by him tainted, shall for him be spent
   And as his due writ in my testament.

"My honor I'll bequeath unto the knife
1185 That wounds my body so dishonorèd.
'Tis honor to deprive dishonored life:
The one will live, the other being dead.
So of shame's ashes shall my fame be bred,
   For in my death I murder shameful scorn;
1190   My shame so dead, mine honor is new born.

"Dear lord of that dear jewel I have lost,
What legacy shall I bequeath to thee?
My resolution, love, shall be thy boast,
By whose example thou revenged mayst be.
1195 How Tarquin must be used, read it in me:
   Myself thy friend will kill myself thy foe,
   And for my sake serve thou false Tarquin so.

"This brief abridgment of my will I make:
My soul and body to the skies and ground;
1200 My resolution, husband, do thou take;
Mine honor be the knife's that makes my wound;
My shame be his that did my fame confound;
   And all my fame that lives disbursèd be
   To those that live and think no shame of me.

1173 **engirt** besieged   1175 **fort** i.e., her body   1186 **deprive** take away

1205 "Thou, Collatine, shalt oversee this will.
How was I overseen that thou shalt see it!
My blood shall wash the slander of mine ill;
My life's foul deed my life's fair end shall free it.
Faint not, faint heart, but stoutly say, 'So be it.'
1210   Yield to my hand, my hand shall conquer thee:
    Thou dead, both die, and both shall victors be."

This plot of death when sadly she had laid
And wiped the brinish pearl from her bright eyes,
With untuned tongue she hoarsely calls her maid,
1215 Whose swift obedience to her mistress hies;
For fleet-winged duty with thought's feathers flies.
    Poor Lucrece' cheeks unto her maid seem so
    As winter meads when sun doth melt their snow.

Her mistress she doth give demure good-morrow
1220 With soft-slow tongue, true mark of modesty,
And sorts a sad look to her lady's sorrow,
For why her face wore sorrow's livery;
But durst not ask of her audaciously
    Why her two suns were cloud-eclipsèd so,
1225 Nor why her fair cheeks overwashed with woe.

But as the earth doth weep, the sun being set,
Each flower moist'ned like a melting eye,
Even so the maid with swelling drops 'gan wet
Her circled eyne, enforced by sympathy
1230 Of those fair suns set in her mistress' sky,
    Who in a salt-waved ocean quench their light,
    Which makes the maid weep like the dewy night.

1205 oversee execute 1206 overseen deceived 1207 **wash** wash away
1207 **ill** sin 1214 **untuned** discordant 1219 **demure** modest 1221
sorts fits 1222 **For why** because 1229 **circled eyne** rounded eyes (?) eyes
encircled with dark rings (?)

A pretty while these pretty creatures stand,
Like ivory conduits coral cisterns filling.
1235 One justly weeps, the other takes in hand
No cause, but company, of her drops spilling.
Their gentle sex to weep are often willing,
    Grieving themselves to guess at others' smarts,
    And then they drown their eyes or break their hearts.

1240 For men have marble, women waxen minds,
And therefore are they formed as marble will;
The weak oppressed, th' impression of strange kinds
Is formed in them by force, by fraud, or skill.
Then call them not the authors of their ill,
1245   No more than wax shall be accounted evil
    Wherein is stamped the semblance of a devil.

Their smoothness, like a goodly champain plain,
Lays open all the little worms that creep;
In men, as in a rough-grown grove, remain
1250 Cave-keeping evils that obscurely sleep.
Through crystal walls each little mate will peep.
    Though men can cover crimes with bold stern looks,
    Poor women's faces are their own faults' books.

No man inveigh against the with'red flow'r,
1255 But chide rough winter that the flow'r hath killed.
Nor that devoured, but that which doth devour,
Is worthy blame; O, let it not be hild
Poor women's faults that they are so fulfilled
    With men's abuses! those proud lords to blame
1260   Make weak-made women tenants to their shame.

1234 **coral cisterns** i.e., their reddened eyes (?) 1235 **takes in hand** acknowledges 1241 **will** i.e., as marble will have them formed 1247 **champain** level 1248 **Lays open** reveals 1250 **Cave-keeping** dwelling in caves 1251 **mote** speck 1254 **No man** let no man 1257 **hild** held 1258 **fulfilled** filled

The precedent whereof in Lucrece view,
Assailed by night with circumstances strong
Of present death, and shame that might ensue
By that her death, to do her husband wrong.
1265 Such danger to resistance did belong
    That dying fear through all her body spread;
    And who cannot abuse a body dead?

By this, mild patience bid fair Lucrece speak
To the poor counterfeit of her complaining.
1270 "My girl," quoth she, "on what occasion break
Those tears from thee that down thy cheeks are raining?
If thou dost weep for grief of my sustaining,
    Know, gentle wench, it small avails my mood;
    If tears could help, mine own would do me good.

1275 "But tell me, girl, when went" (and there she stayed
Till after a deep groan) "Tarquin from hence?"
"Madam, ere I was up," replied the maid,
"The more to blame my sluggard negligence.
Yet with the fault I thus far can dispense:
1280   Myself was stirring ere the break of day,
    And ere I rose was Tarquin gone away.

"But, lady, if your maid may be so bold,
She would request to know your heaviness."
"O, peace," quoth Lucrece. "If it should be told,
1285 The repetition cannot make it less;
For more it is than I can well express,
    And that deep torture may be called a hell
    When more is felt than one hath power to tell.

1261 **precedent** example   1266 **dying** i.e., unnerving   1269 **counterfeit**
image   1272 **of my sustaining** that I sustain   1273 **mood** grief   1283
heaviness cause of grief

"Go get me hither paper, ink, and pen;
1290   Yet save that labor, for I have them here.
What should I say? One of my husband's men
Bid thou be ready by and by to bear
A letter to my lord, my love, my dear.
    Bid him with speed prepare to carry it;
1295   The cause craves haste, and it will soon be writ."

Her maid is gone, and she prepares to write,
First hovering o'er the paper with her quill.
Conceit and grief an eager combat fight;
What wit sets down is blotted straight with will.
1300   This is too curious good, this blunt and ill.
    Much like a press of people at a door,
    Throng her inventions, which shall go before.

At last she thus begins: "Thou worthy lord
Of that unworthy wife that greeteth thee,
1305   Health to thy person! next vouchsafe t' afford
(If ever, love, thy Lucrece thou wilt see)
Some present speed to come and visit me.
    So I commend me, from our house in grief.
    My woes are tedious, though my words are brief."

1310 Here folds she up the tenure of her woe,
Her certain sorrow writ uncertainly.
By this short schedule Collatine may know
Her grief, but not her grief's true quality;
She dares not thereof make discovery,
1315   Lest he should hold it her own gross abuse
    Ere she with blood had stained her stained excuse.

1292 **by and by** immediately   1298 **Conceit** thought   1300 **curious** cleverly   1302 **which shall go before** which one shall enter first   1310 **tenure** statement   1312 **schedule** summary   1316 **her stained excuse** her account of her stain

Besides, the life and feeling of her passion
She hoards, to spend when he is by to hear her,
When sighs and groans and tears may grace the fashion
1320 Of her disgrace, the better so to clear her
From that suspicion which the world might bear her.
    To shun this blot, she would not blot the letter
    With words till action might become them better.

To see sad sights moves more than hear them told,
1325 For then the eye interprets to the ear
The heavy motion that it doth behold
When every part a part of woe doth bear.
'Tis but a part of sorrow that we hear.
    Deep sounds make lesser noise than shallow fords,
1330   And sorrow ebbs, being blown with winds of words.

Her letter now is sealed, and on it writ,
"At Ardea to my lord with more than haste."
The post attends, and she delivers it,
Charging the sour-faced groom to hie as fast
1335 As lagging fowls before the Northern blast;
    Speed more than speed but dull and slow she deems:
    Extremity still urgeth such extremes.

The homely villein curtsies to her low;
And, blushing on her, with a steadfast eye,
1340 Receives the scroll without or yea or no
And forth with bashful innocence doth hie.
But they whose guilt within their bosoms lie
    Imagine every eye beholds their blame,
    For Lucrece thought he blushed to see her shame,

1317 **passion** suffering   1326 **heavy motion** melancholy action   1329
sounds soundings (naval term)   1334 **sour-faced** sad-faced (?) long-faced
(out of respect)   1338 **homely villein curtsies** simple servant bows   1339
blushing on her i.e., blushing toward her

1345 When, seely groom (God wot), it was defect
      Of spirit, life, and bold audacity;
      Such harmless creatures have a true respect
      To talk in deeds, while others saucily
      Promise more speed, but do it leisurely.
1350   Even so this pattern of the worn-out age
          Pawned honest looks, but laid no words to gage.

      His kindled duty kindled her mistrust,
      That two red fires in both their faces blazèd.
      She thought he blushed as knowing Tarquin's lust,
1355 And, blushing with him, wistly on him gazèd;
      Her earnest eye did make him more amazèd.
          The more she saw the blood his cheeks replenish,
          The more she thought he spied in her some blemish.

      But long she thinks till he return again,
1360 And yet the duteous vassal scarce is gone;
      The weary time she cannot entertain,
      For now 'tis stale to sigh, to weep and groan:
      So woe hath wearied woe, moan tirèd moan,
          That she her plaints a little while doth stay,
1365   Pausing for means to mourn some newer way.

      At last she calls to mind where hangs a piece
      Of skillful painting, made for Priam's Troy,
      Before the which is drawn the power of Greece,
      For Helen's rape the city to destroy,
1370 Threat'ning cloud-kissing Ilion with annoy;
          Which the conceited painter drew so proud
          As heaven, it seemed, to kiss the turrets bowed.

1345 seely simple   1345 wot knows   1346 life liveliness   1347 **respect**
aspect   1348 **To talk in deeds** to act and not to talk   1350 **worn-out**
past   1351 **Pawned** pledged   1351 **gage** i.e., to bind him (as by an
oath)   1355 **wistly** earnestly   1359 **long she thinks** i.e., she thinks time
passes slowly   1361 **entertain** occupy   1364 **stay** stop   1367 **made for**
depicting   1367 **Priam's Troy** Priam was the king of Troy during the
Trojan War   1368 **is drawn the power of Greece** the Greek army is
assembled   1369 **Helen's rape** the abduction of Helen   1370 **Ilion**
Troy   1370 **annoy** destruction   1371 **conceited** ingenious   1372 **As that**

A thousand lamentable objects there,
In scorn of nature, art gave lifeless life;
1375 Many a dry drop seemed a weeping tear
Shed for the slaught'red husband by the wife,
The red blood reeked, to show the painter's strife,
    And dying eyes gleamed forth their ashy lights,
    Like dying coals burnt out in tedious nights.

1380 There might you see the laboring pioner
Begrimed with sweat, and smearèd all with dust;
And from the tow'rs of Troy there would appear
The very eyes of men through loopholes thrust,
Gazing upon the Greeks with little lust:
1385   Such sweet observance in this work was had
    That one might see those far-off eyes look sad.

In great commanders grace and majesty
You might behold triumphing in their faces;
In youth, quick bearing and dexterity;
1390 And here and there the painter interlaces
Pale cowards marching on with trembling paces,
    Which heartless peasants did so well resemble
    That one would swear he saw them quake and tremble.

In Ajax and Ulysses, O, what art
1395 Of physiognomy might one behold!
The face of either ciphered either's heart;
Their face their manners most expressly told:
In Ajax' eyes blunt rage and rigor rolled;
    But the mild glance that sly Ulysses lent
1400   Showed deep regard and smiling government.

1374 In scorn of to rival 1377 strife effort 1380 pioner engineer 1384
lust pleasure 1385 sweet observance loving accuracy 1389 quick lively
1392 heartless cowardly 1394 Ajax and Ulysses Greek leaders 1396
ciphered depicted 1400 deep regard ... government profound wisdom
and successful rule

There pleading might you see grave Nestor stand,
As 'twere encouraging the Greeks to fight,
Making such sober action with his hand
That it beguiled attention, charmed the sight.
1405 In speech it seemed his beard, all silver white,
    Wagged up and down, and from his lips did fly
    Thin winding breath which purled up to the sky.

About him were a press of gaping faces,
Which seemed to swallow up his sound advice,
1410 All jointly list'ning, but with several graces,
As if some mermaid did their ears entice,
Some high, some low—the painter was so nice.
    The scalps of many, almost hid behind,
    To jump up higher seemed, to mock the mind.

1415 Here one man's hand leaned on another's head,
His nose being shadowed by his neighbor's ear;
Here one, being thronged, bears back, all boll'n and red;
Another, smothered, seems to pelt and swear;
And in their rage such signs of rage they bear
1420   As, but for loss of Nestor's golden words,
    It seemed they would debate with angry swords.

For much imaginary work was there;
Conceit deceitful, so compact, so kind,
That for Achilles' image stood his spear,
1425 Griped in an armèd hand; himself behind
Was left unseen, save to the eye of mind:
    A hand, a foot, a face, a leg, a head
    Stood for the whole to be imaginèd.

1401 **Nestor** an aged Greek leader 1407 **purled** curled 1410 **several**
distinct 1412 **nice** precise 1417 **thronged** crushed in the crowd 1417
boll'n swollen 1418 **pelt** scold 1423 **Conceit** conception 1423 **kind**
natural 1424 **Achilles** chief warrior of the Greeks

And from the walls of strong-besiegèd Troy
1430　When their brave hope, bold Hector, marched to field,
Stood many Troyan mothers, sharing joy
To see their youthful sons bright weapons wield;
And to their hope they such odd action yield
　　That through their light joy seemèd to appear
1435　(Like bright things stained) a kind of heavy fear.

And from the strond of Dardan, where they fought,
To Simois' reedy banks the red blood ran,
Whose waves to imitate the battle sought
With swelling ridges, and their ranks began
1440　To break upon the gallèd shore, and than
　　Retire again, till, meeting greater ranks,
　　They join, and shoot their foam at Simois' banks.

To this well-painted piece is Lucrece come,
To find a face where all distress is stelled.
1445　Many she sees where cares have carvèd some,
But none where all distress and dolor dwelled
Till she despairing Hecuba beheld,
　　Staring on Priam's wounds with her old eyes,
　　Which bleeding under Pyrrhus' proud foot lies.

1450　In her the painter had anatomized
Time's ruin, beauty's wrack, and grim care's reign;
Her cheeks with chops and wrinkles were disguised;
Of what she was no semblance did remain.
Her blue blood, changed to black in every vein,
1455　　Wanting the spring that those shrunk pipes had fed,
　　Showed life imprisoned in a body dead.

1430 **Hector** son of Priam and chief warrior of the Trojans　1433 **odd
action yield** contrary gestures express　1436 **strond of Dardan** shore of
Troas (the country of which Troy was the chief city)　1437 **Simois'** river
near Troy　1440 **gallèd** eroded　1440 **than** then　1444 **stelled** portrayed
1447 **Hecuba** wife of Priam　1449 **Pyrrhus** Greek warrior, slayer of Priam
1450 **anatomized** dissected　1452 **chops** cracks　1452 **disguised** disfigured

On this sad shadow Lucrece spends her eyes
And shapes her sorrow to the beldame's woes,
Who nothing wants to answer her but cries
1460 And bitter words to ban her cruel foes.
The painter was no god to lend her those;
    And therefore Lucrece swears he did her wrong
    To give her so much grief and not a tongue.

"Poor instrument," quoth she, "without a sound:
1465 I'll tune thy woes with my lamenting tongue,
And drop sweet balm in Priam's painted wound,
And rail on Pyrrhus that hath done him wrong,
And with my tears quench Troy that burns so long,
    And with my knife scratch out the angry eyes
1470 Of all the Greeks that are thine enemies.

"Show me the strumpet that began this stir,
That with my nails her beauty I may tear.
Thy heat of lust, fond Paris, did incur
This load of wrath that burning Troy doth bear.
1475 Thy eye kindled the fire that burneth here,
    And here in Troy, for trespass of thine eye,
    The sire, the son, the dame and daughter die.

"Why should the private pleasure of some one
Become the public plague of many moe?
1480 Let sin, alone committed, light alone
Upon his head that hath transgressèd so;
Let guiltless souls be freed from guilty woe:
    For one's offense why should so many fall,
    To plague a private sin in general?

1485 "Lo, here weeps Hecuba, here Priam dies,
Here manly Hector faints, here Troilus sounds,
Here friend by friend in bloody channel lies,
And friend to friend gives unadvisèd wounds,
And one man's lust these many lives confounds.
1490   Had doting Priam checked his son's desire,
    Troy had been bright with fame, and not with fire."

1460 ban curse 1465 tune sing 1471 stir action (i.e., war) 1479 moe
more 1484 in general on the general public 1486 Troilus a son of
Priam 1486 sounds swoons 1488 unadvisèd unintentional 1489 con-
founds destroys

Here feelingly she weeps Troy's painted woes,
For sorrow, like a heavy hanging bell,
Once set on ringing, with his own weight goes;
1495 Then little strength rings out the doleful knell.
So Lucrece, set awork, sad tales doth tell
To penciled pensiveness and colored sorrow:
She lends them words, and she their looks doth borrow.

She throws her eyes about the painting round,
1500 And who she finds forlorn, she doth lament.
At last she sees a wretched image bound
That piteous looks to Phrygian shepherds lent.
His face, though full of cares, yet showed content;
Onward to Troy with the blunt swains he goes,
1505 So mild that patience seemed to scorn his woes.

In him the painter labored with his skill
To hide deceit, and give the harmless show
An humble gait, calm looks, eyes wailing still,
A brow unbent that seemed to welcome woe,
1510 Cheeks neither red nor pale, but mingled so
That blushing red no guilty instance gave
Nor ashy pale the fear that false hearts have;

But, like a constant and confirmèd devil,
He entertained a show so seeming just,
1515 And therein so ensconced his secret evil,
That jealousy itself could not mistrust
False creeping craft and perjury should thrust
Into so bright a day such black-faced storms
Or blot with hell-born sin such saintlike forms.

1497 **penciled, colored** painted   1499 **round** all around   1501 **wretched image** i.e., Sinon, the Trojan traitor   1502 **piteous ... lent** i.e., aroused compassionate looks from the Phrygian shepherds   1504 **blunt** simple   1505 **patience** i.e., his patience   1507 **show** appearance   1509 **unbent** unfurrowed   1514 **entertained a show** kept up an appearance   1516 **jealousy** suspicion

1520 The well-skilled workman this mild image drew
For perjured Sinon, whose enchanting story
The credulous old Priam after slew;
Whose words like wildfire burnt the shining glory
Of rich-built Ilion, that the skies were sorry,
1525   And little stars shot from their fixèd places
    When their glass fell, wherein they viewed their faces.

This picture she advisedly perused
And chid the painter for his wondrous skill,
Saying, some shape in Sinon's was abused;
1530 So fair a form lodged not a mind so ill.
And still on him she gazed, and gazing still,
    Such signs of truth in his plain face she spied,
    That she concludes the picture was belied.

"It cannot be," quoth she, "that so much guile"—
1535 She would have said "can lurk in such a look";
But Tarquin's shape came in her mind the while,
And from her tongue "can lurk" from "cannot" took.
"It cannot be" she in that sense forsook
    And turned it thus: "It cannot be, I find,
1540   But such a face should bear a wicked mind;

"For even as subtile Sinon here is painted,
So sober-sad, so weary, and so mild
(As if with grief or travail he had fainted),
To me came Tarquin armèd, to beguiled
1545 With outward honesty, but yet defiled
    With inward vice. As Priam him did cherish,
    So did I Tarquin; so my Troy did perish.

1521 **enchanting story** i.e., bewitching lie   1526 **glass** mirror (i.e., shining Troy)   1527 **advisedly** thoughtfully   1529 **some shape ... abused** some other person's form had been falsely represented as Sinon's   1533 **belied** proved false   1544 **beguiled** beguile

"Look, look, how list'ning Priam wets his eyes,
To see those borrowed tears that Sinon sheeds!
1550 Priam, why art thou old, and yet not wise?
For every tear he falls a Troyan bleeds.
His eye drops fire, no water thence proceeds:
    Those round clear pearls of his that move thy pity
    Are balls of quenchless fire to burn thy city.

1555 "Such devils steal effects from lightless hell,
For Sinon in his fire doth quake with cold,
And in that cold hot burning fire doth dwell.
These contraries such unity do hold
Only to flatter fools and make them bold.
1560   So Priam's trust false Sinon's tears doth flatter
    That he finds means to burn his Troy with water."

Here, all enraged, such passion her assails
That patience is quite beaten from her breast.
She tears the senseless Sinon with her nails,
1565 Comparing him to that unhappy guest
Whose deed hath made herself herself detest.
    At last she smilingly with this gives o'er:
    "Fool, fool!" quoth she, "his wounds will not be sore."

Thus ebbs and flows the current of her sorrow,
1570 And time doth weary time with her complaining.
She looks for night, and then she longs for morrow,
And both she thinks too long with her remaining.
Short time seems long in sorrow's sharp sustaining;
    Though woe be heavy, yet it seldom sleeps,
1575   And they that watch see time how slow it creeps;

1549 borrowed i.e., false 1549 sheeds sheds 1551 falls lets fall 1559
flatter deceive 1559 make them bold give them confidence 1565
unhappy unfortunate 1567 gives o'er ceases 1574 heavy (1) distressing
(2) sleepy

Which all this time hath overslipped her thought
That she with painted images hath spent,
Being from the feeling of her own grief brought
By deep surmise of others' detriment,
1580   Losing her woes in shows of discontent.
    It easeth some, though none it ever curèd,
    To think their dolor others have endurèd.

But now the mindful messenger, come back,
Brings home his lord and other company;
1585   Who finds his Lucrece clad in mourning black,
And round about her tear-distainèd eye
Blue circles streamed, like rainbows in the sky.
    These water-galls in her dim element
    Foretell new storms to those already spent.

1590   Which when her sad-beholding husband saw,
Amazedly in her sad face he stares.
Her eyes, though sod in tears, looked red and raw,
Her lively color killed with deadly cares.
He hath no power to ask her how she fares;
1595   Both stood like old acquaintance in a trance,
    Met far from home, wond'ring each other's chance.

At last he takes her by the bloodless hand,
And thus begins; "What uncouth ill event
Hath thee befall'n, that thou dost trembling stand?
1600   Sweet love, what spite hath thy fair color spent?
Why are thou thus attired in discontent?
    Unmask, dear dear, this moody heaviness,
    And tell thy grief, that we may give redress."

1576 **overslipped her thought** i.e., gone unnoticed   1579 **surmise**
contemplation   1580 **shows** representations   1586 **tear-distainèd**
tear-stained   1588 **water-galls** atmospheric conditions attendant upon
rainbows   1588 **element** sky   1592 **sod** sodden   1596 **chance**
fortune   1598 **uncouth** unknown   1600 **spite** feeling of annoyance   1602
Unmask disclose

THE RAPE OF LUCRECE

Three times with sighs she gives her sorrow fire,
1605 Ere once she can discharge one word of woe.
At length addressed to answer his desire,
She modestly prepares to let them know
Her honor is ta'en prisoner by the foe,
    While Collatine and his consorted lords
1610 With sad attention long to hear her words.

And now this pale swan in her wat'ry nest
Begins the sad dirge of her certain ending:
"Few words," quoth she, "shall fit the trespass best,
Where no excuse can give the fault amending.
1615 In me moe woes than words are now depending,
    And my laments would be drawn out too long
    To tell them all with one poor tirèd tongue.

"Then be this all the task it hath to say:
Dear husband, in the interest of thy bed
1620 A stranger came and on that pillow lay
Where thou wast wont to rest thy weary head;
And what wrong else may be imaginèd
    By foul enforcement might be done to me,
    From that, alas, thy Lucrece is not free.

1625 "For in the dreadful dead of dark midnight,
With shining falchion in my chamber came
A creeping creature with a flaming light
And softly cried, 'Awake, thou Roman dame,
And entertain my love; else lasting shame
1630 On thee and thine this night I will inflict,
    If thou my love's desire do contradict.

1604 **fire** i.e., fire to ignite a discharge (from a cannon) 1606 **addressed** prepared 1609 **consorted** associated 1612 **ending** death 1615 **moe** more 1615 **depending** impending 1619 **interest** possession 1629 **entertain** receive

188

" 'For some hard-favored groom of thine,' quoth he,
'Unless thou yoke thy liking to my will,
I'll murder straight, and then I'll slaughter thee
1635 And swear I found you where you did fulfill
The loathsome act of lust, and so did kill
 The lechers in their deed: this act will be
 My fame and thy perpetual infamy.'

"With this I did begin to start and cry;
1640 And then against my heart he set his sword,
Swearing, unless I took all patiently,
I should not live to speak another word.
So should my shame still rest upon record,
 And never be forgot in mighty Rome
1645 Th' adulterate death of Lucrece and her groom.

"Mine enemy was strong, my poor self weak
And far the weaker with so strong a fear.
My bloody judge forbod my tongue to speak;
No rightful plea might plead for justice there.
1650 His scarlet lust came evidence to swear
 That my poor beauty had purloined his eyes;
 And when the judge is robbed, the prisoner dies.

"O, teach me how to make mine own excuse,
Or (at the least) this refuge let me find:
1655 Though my gross blood be stained with this abuse,
Immaculate and spotless is my mind;
That was not forced, that never was inclined
 To accessary yieldings, but still pure
 Doth in her poisoned closet yet endure."

1660 Lo, here, the hopeless merchant of this loss,
With head declined and voice dammed up with woe,
With sad-set eyes and wreathèd arms across,
From lips new-waxen pale begins to blow
The grief away that stops his answer so.
1665 But, wretched as he is, he strives in vain;
 What he breathes out his breath drinks up again.

1633 **yoke** submit 1648 **forbod** forbade 1660 **merchant** i.e.,
Collatine 1662 **wreathèd arms** (arms folded were a sign of melancholy)

189

As through an arch the violent roaring tide
Outruns the eye that doth behold his haste,
Yet in the eddy boundeth in his pride
1670 Back to the strait that forced him on so fast;
In rage sent out, recalled in rage being past:
     Even so his sighs, his sorrows, make a saw,
     To push grief on, and back the same grief draw.

Which speechless woe of his poor she attendeth
1675 And his untimely frenzy thus awaketh:
"Dear lord, thy sorrow to my sorrow lendeth
Another power; no flood by raining slaketh;
My woe too sensible thy passion maketh
     More feeling-painful. Let it then suffice
1680 To drown one woe, one pair of weeping eyes.

"And for my sake when I might charm thee so,
For she that was thy Lucrece (now attend me)
Be suddenly revengèd on my foe—
Thine, mine, his own. Suppose thou dost defend me
1685 From what is past; the help that thou shalt lend me
     Comes all too late, yet let the traitor die;
     For sparing justice feeds iniquity.

"But ere I name him, you fair lords," quoth she,
Speaking to those that came with Collatine,
1690 "Shall plight your honorable faiths to me
With swift pursuit to 'venge this wrong of mine;
For 'tis a meritorious fair design
     To chase injustice with revengeful arms:
     Knights by their oaths should right poor ladies' harms."

1695 At this request, with noble disposition
Each present lord began to promise aid,
As bound in knighthood to her imposition,
Longing to hear the hateful foe bewrayed.
But she, that yet her sad task hath not said,
1700 The protestation stops. "O, speak!" quoth she,
     "How may this forcèd stain be wiped from me?

1672 **saw** i.e., sawlike motion 1675 **frenzy** trance 1678 **sensible**
sensitive 1681 **so** in such things 1698 **bewrayed** revealed

"What is the quality of my offense,
Being constrained with dreadful circumstance?
May my pure mind with the foul act dispense,
1705 My low-declinèd honor to advance?
May any terms acquit me from this chance?
    The poisoned fountain clears itself again;
    And why not I from this compellèd stain?"

With this they all at once began to say,
1710 Her body's stain her mind untainted clears;
While with a joyless smile she turns away
The face, that map which deep impression bears
Of hard misfortune, carved in it with tears.
    "No, no!" quoth she, "no dame hereafter living
1715   By my excuse shall claim excuse's giving."

Here with a sigh as if her heart would break
She throws forth Tarquin's name: "He, he!" she says,
But more than "he" her poor tongue could not speak,
Till after many accents and delays,
1720 Untimely breathings, sick and short assays,
    She utters this: "He, he! fair lords, 'tis he
    That guides this hand to give this wound to me."

Even here she sheathèd in her harmless breast
A harmful knife, that thence her soul unsheathèd.
1725 That blow did bail it from the deep unrest
Of that polluted prison where it breathèd.
Her contrite sighs unto the clouds bequeathèd
    Her wingèd sprite, and through her wounds doth fly
    Life's lasting date from canceled destiny.

1702 **quality** nature 1704 **dispense** be reconciled 1705 **advance**
raise 1719 **accents** emphasized sounds 1720 **assays** attempts 1723
harmless innocent 1725 **bail** release 1729 **Life's ... canceled destiny**
i.e., eternal life is freed (canceled) by flying from life on earth (destiny)

1730 Stone-still, astonished with this deadly deed,
Stood Collatine and all his lordly crew,
Till Lucrece' father, that beholds her bleed,
Himself on her self-slaught'red body threw,
And from the purple fountain Brutus drew
1735 The murd'rous knife, and as it left the place,
Her blood, in poor revenge, held it in chase;

And bubbling from her breast, it doth divide
In two slow rivers, that the crimson blood
Circles her body in on every side,
1740 Who like a late-sacked island vastly stood
Bare and unpeopled in this fearful flood.
Some of her blood still pure and red remained,
And some looked black, and that false Tarquin stained.

About the mourning and congealèd face
1745 Of that black blood a wat'ry rigoll goes,
Which seems to weep upon the tainted place;
And ever since, as pitying Lucrece' woes,
Corrupted blood some watery token shows,
And blood untainted still doth red abide,
1750 Blushing at that which is so putrefied.

"Daughter, dear daughter!" old Lucretius cries,
"That life was mine which thou hast here deprivèd;
If in the child the father's image lies,
Where shall I live now Lucrece is unlivèd?
1755 Thou wast not to this end from me derivèd.
If children predecease progenitors,
We are their offspring, and they none of ours.

1740 **vastly** like a waste   1745 **wat'ry rigoll** (when blood coagulates it
separates into a congealed blot and a serum, "wat'ry rigoll")

"Poor broken glass, I often did behold
In thy sweet semblance my old age new born;
1760 But now that fair fresh mirror, dim and old,
Shows me a bare-boned death by time outworn.
O, from thy cheeks my image thou hast torn
    And shivered all the beauty of my glass,
    That I no more can see what once I was.

1765 "O time, cease thou thy course, and last no longer,
If they surcease to be that should survive.
Shall rotten death make conquest of the stronger
And leave the falt'ring feeble souls alive?
The old bees die, the young possess their hive;
1770   Then live, sweet Lucrece, live again and see
    Thy father die, and not thy father thee."

By this, starts Collatine as from a dream
And bids Lucretius give his sorrow place;
And then in key-cold Lucrece' bleeding stream
1775 He falls, and bathes the pale fear in his face,
And counterfeits to die with her a space;
    Till manly shame bids him possess his breath,
    And live to be revengèd on her death.

The deep vexation of his inward soul
1780 Hath served a dumb arrest upon his tongue;
Who, mad that sorrow should his use control,
Or keep him from heart-easing words so long,
Begins to talk; but through his lips do throng
    Weak words, so thick come in his poor heart's aid
1785   That no man could distinguish what he said.

1758 glass mirror 1761 death skull 1763 shivered shattered 1766
surcease cease 1774 key-cold i.e., cold as metal 1776 counterfeits to
die swoons (and seems transported as by an orgasm) 1780 served a dumb
arrest enforced a silence (as if by a warrant) 1784 thick quickly

Yet sometime "Tarquin" was pronouncèd plain,
But through his teeth, as if the name he tore.
This windy tempest, till it blow up rain,
Held back his sorrow's tide, to make it more.
1790   At last it rains, and busy winds give o'er;
      Then son and father weep with equal strife
      Who should weep most, for daughter or for wife.

The one doth call her his, the other his;
Yet neither may possess the claim they lay.
1795   The father says, "She's mine." "O, mine, she is!"
Replies her husband, "do not take away
My sorrow's interest; let no mourner say
      He weeps for her, for she was only mine,
      And only must be wailed by Collatine."

1800   "O," quoth Lucretius, "I did give that life
Which she too early and too late hath spilled."
"Woe, woe!" quoth Collatine, "she was my wife,
I owed her, and 'tis mine that she hath killed."
"My daughter" and "my wife" with clamors filled
1805   The dispersed air, who, holding Lucrece' life,
      Answered their cries, "my daughter" and "my wife."

Brutus, who plucked the knife from Lucrece' side,
Seeing such emulation in their woe,
Began to clothe his wit in state and pride,
1810   Burying in Lucrece' wound his folly's show.
He with the Romans was esteemèd so
      As seely jeering idiots are with kings,
      For sportive words and utt'ring foolish things;

1797 **sorrow's interest** right to sorrow   1801 **late** recently   1803 **owed** owned   1805 **The dispersed air** i.e., the boundless air (which has received Lucrece's "life" or spirit upon her death)   1810 **folly's show** appearance of folly   1812 **seely** simple   1813 **sportive** merry

But now he throws that shallow habit by
1815 Wherein deep policy did him disguise,
And armed his long-hid wits advisedly
To check the tears in Collatinus' eyes.
"Thou wrongèd lord of Rome," quoth he, "arise!
Let my unsounded self, supposed a fool,
1820 Now set thy long-experienced wit to school.

"Why, Collatine, is woe the cure for woe?
Do wounds help wounds, or grief help grievous deeds?
Is it revenge to give thyself a blow
For his foul act by whom thy fair wife bleeds?
1825 Such childish humor from weak minds proceeds;
Thy wretched wife mistook the matter so,
To slay herself that should have slain her foe.

"Courageous Roman, do not steep thy heart
In such relenting dew of lamentations;
1830 But kneel with me, and help to bear thy part
To rouse our Roman gods with invocations
That they will suffer these abominations
(Since Rome herself in them doth stand disgracèd)
By our strong arms from forth her fair streets chasèd.

1835 "Now, by the Capitol that we adore,
And by this chaste blood so unjustly stainèd,
By heaven's fair sun that breeds the fat earth's store,
By all our country rights in Rome maintainèd,
And by chaste Lucrece' soul that late complainèd
1840 Her wrongs to us, and by his bloody knife,
We will revenge the death of this true wife."

1814 **habit** cloak (here, of a king's jester) 1815 **policy** calculation 1819
unsounded unplumbed 1821 **Why** (exclamation of impatience) 1829
relenting melting 1832 **suffer** allow 1834 **chasèd** i.e., to be chased
1837 **fat earth's store** fertile earth's abundance

This said, he strook his hand upon his breast
And kissed the fatal knife to end his vow;
And to his protestation urged the rest,
1845 Who, wond'ring at him, did his words allow,
Then jointly to the ground their knees they bow,
    And that deep vow which Brutus made before,
    He doth again repeat, and that they swore.

When they had sworn to this advisèd doom,
1850 They did conclude to bear dead Lucrece thence,
To show her bleeding body thorough Rome,
And so to publish Tarquin's foul offense;
Which being done with speedy diligence,
    The Romans plausibly did give consent
1855   To Tarquin's everlasting banishment.

FINIS

1842 **strook** struck 1844 **protestation** vow 1845 **allow** approve 1849
advisèd doom considered judgment 1854 **plausibly** with applause (i.e.,
with a "general acclamation"; see Argument, page 92, lines 43-44)

THE PHOENIX AND THE TURTLE

Let the bird of loudest lay
On the sole Arabian tree
Herald sad and trumpet be,
To whose sound chaste wings obey.

5 But thou shrieking harbinger,
Foul precurrer of the fiend,
Augur of the fever's end,
To this troop come thou not near.

From this session interdict
10 Every fowl of tyrant wing,
Save the eagle, feath'red king:
Keep the obsequy so strict.

Let the priest in surplice white,
That defunctive music can,
15 Be the death-divining swan,
Lest the requiem lack his right.

The Phoenix and the Turtle the phoenix, a unique legendary bird, was said to fly periodically to Arabia, where, after building a nest of spices, it was consumed in flame, and from its ashes a new phoenix arose; it is a symbol of immortality. The turtle, i.e., the turtle dove, is a symbol of true love. 1 **lay** song 2 **sole** unique 3 **sad** serious 3 **trumpet** trumpeter 4 **chaste wings** i.e., other good birds 5 **shrieking harbinger** screech owl (?) 6 **precurrer** precursor (apparently Shakespeare's coinage) 7 **Augur of the fever's end** prophet of death 9 **session** formal gathering, as of a parliament or a court 9 **interdict** ban 10 **fowl of tyrant wing** bird of prey, unsocial bird (in contrast to those of "chaste wings," line 4) 12 **obsequy** funeral rite 14 **defunctive music can** is skilled in funeral music 15 **death-divining** foretelling death (the swan allegedly sang only once, just before it died) 16 **his right** its due (?) his (i.e., the swan's) rite of requiem (?)

THE PHOENIX AND THE TURTLE

And thou treble-dated crow,
That thy sable gender mak'st
With the breath thou giv'st and tak'st,
20　　'Mongst our mourners shalt thou go.

Here the anthem doth commence:
Love and constancy is dead,
Phoenix and the turtle fled
In a mutual flame from hence.

25　　So they loved, as love in twain
Had the essence but in one;
Two distincts, division none:
Number there in love was slain.

Hearts remote, yet not asunder;
30　　Distance and no space was seen
'Twixt this turtle and his queen;
But in them it were a wonder.

So between them love did shine
That the turtle saw his right
35　　Flaming in the phoenix' sight:
Either was the other's mine.

Property was thus appallèd,
That the self was not the same;
Single nature's double name
40　　Neither two nor one was callèd.

---

17 **treble-dated** long-lived 18-19 **That thy ... tak'st** that breeds your black offspring with the breath you exhale and inhale (alluding to a belief that some birds conceived and laid eggs at the bill) 25 **as** that 26 **essence** nature 27 **distincts** distinct or separate things 28 **Number ... slain** i.e., because the two were one, and Elizabethan proverbial love held that "one is no number" 29 **remote** apart 32 **But ... wonder** i.e., in any others except them it would have been a marvel 34 **his right** what was due to him 36 **mine** (1) my own property (2) source of precious metals 37 **Property** essential nature, peculiar quality

Reason, in itself confounded,
Saw division grow together,
To themselves yet either neither,
Simple were so well compounded;

45 That it cried, "How true a twain
Seemeth this concordant one!
Love hath reason, reason none,
If what parts can so remain."

Whereupon it made this threne
50 To the phoenix and the dove,
Co-supremes and stars of love,
As chorus to their tragic scene.

THRENOS

Beauty, truth, and rarity,
Grace in all simplicity,
55 Here enclosed, in cinders lie.

Death is now the phoenix' nest,
And the turtle's loyal breast
To eternity doth rest,

Leaving no posterity:
60 'Twas not their infirmity,
It was married chastity.

Truth may seem, but cannot be;
Beauty brag, but 'tis not she:
Truth and Beauty buried be.

---

41 **confounded** perplexed   44 **Simple** i.e., simples, elementary elements (?)
individual ingredients (?)   44 **compounded** made into a new unity   45 **it**
i.e., Reason   48 **If ... remain** i.e., if what divides into two can remain
one   49 **threne** funeral song (Greek: *threnos*)   51 **Co-supremes** joint
rulers   53 **rarity** excellence   55 **cinders** ashes   61 **married chastity**
faithful married love (?) abstinence (?)   63 **she** i.e., true Beauty

65 To this urn let those repair
That are either true or fair;
For these dead birds sigh a prayer.

FINIS

A LOVER'S COMPLAINT

From off a hill whose concave womb reworded
A plaintful story from a sist'ring vale,
My spirits t' attend this double voice accorded,
And down I laid to list the sad-tuned tale;
5 Ere long espied a fickle maid full pale,
Tearing of papers, breaking rings atwain,
Storming her world with sorrow's wind and rain.

Upon her head a platted hive of straw,
Which fortified her visage from the sun,
10 Whereon the thought might think sometime it saw
The carcass of a beauty spent and done.
Time had not scythèd all that youth begun,
Nor youth all quit; but, spite of heaven's fell rage,
Some beauty peeped through lattice of seared age.

15 Oft did she heave her napkin to her eyne,
Which on it had conceited characters,
Laund'ring the silken figures in the brine
That seasoned woe had pelleted in tears,
And often reading what contents it bears;
20 As often shrieking undistinguished woe,
In clamours of all size, both high and low.

Sometimes her leveled eyes their carriage ride,
As they did batt'ry to the spheres intend;
Sometime diverted their poor balls are tied
25   To th' orbèd earth; sometimes they do extend
Their view right on; anon their gazes lend
To every place at once, and, nowhere fixed,
The mind and sight distractedly commixed.

Her hair, nor loose nor tied in formal plat,
30   Proclaimed in her a careless hand of pride;
For some, untucked, descended her sheaved hat,
Hanging her pale and pinèd cheek beside;
Some in her threaden fillet still did bide
And, true to bondage, would not break from thence,
35   Though slackly braided in loose negligence.

A thousand favors from a maund she drew,
Of amber, crystal, and of bedded jet,
Which one by one she in a river threw,
Upon whose weeping margent she was set,
40   Like usury, applying wet to wet,
Or monarch's hands that lets not bounty fall
Where want cries some but where excess begs all.

Of folded schedules had she many a one
Which she perused, sighed, tore, and gave the flood;
45   Cracked many a ring of posied gold and bone,
Bidding them find their sepulchers in mud;
Found yet moe letters sadly penned in blood,
With sleided silk feat and affectedly
Enswathed and sealed to curious secrecy.

---

22 **leveled** aimed (the image is of a firearm on a gun-carriage)   23 **As ... intend** as if they intended to direct their fire against the stars   29 **nor ... nor** neither ... nor   29 **plat** not   30 a **careless hand of pride** a hand indifferent to show   31 **sheaved** straw   33 **threaden fillet** headband   37 **bedded** inlaid (emendation to "beaded" is plausible)   39 **weeping margent** wet bank   40 **Like usury** i.e., adding to the original amount   42 **cries some** cries out for some   43 **schedules** papers with writing   45 **posied** inscribed with mottoes   47 **moe** more   48 **sleided** raveled   48-49 **feat and affectedly/Enswathed** tied neatly and elaborately (or neatly and lovingly)   49 **curious** painstaking

50 These often bathed she in her fluxive eyes,
And often kissed, and often gave to tear;
Cried, "O false blood, thou register of lies,
What unapprovèd witness dost thou bear!
Ink would have seemed more black and damnèd here!"
55 This said, in top of rage the lines she rents,
Big discontent so breaking their contents.

A reverend man that grazed his cattle nigh,
Sometime a blusterer that the ruffle knew
Of court, of city, and had let go by
60 The swiftest hours, observèd as they flew,
Towards this afflicted fancy fastly drew,
And, privileged by age, desires to know
In brief the grounds and motives of her woe.

So slides he down upon his grainèd bat,
65 And comely-distant sits he by her side;
When he again desires her, being sat,
Her grievance with his hearing to divide:
If that from him there may be aught applied
Which may her suffering ecstasy assuage,
70 'Tis promised in the charity of age.

"Father," she says, "though in me you behold
The injury of many a blasting hour,
Let it not tell your judgment I am old;
Not age, but sorrow, over me hath power.
75 I might as yet have been a spreading flower,
Fresh to myself, if I had self-applied
Love to myself, and to no love beside.

50 **fluxive** flowing   53 **unapprovèd** unconfirmed, not proved by deeds   57 **reverend** aged   58 **ruffle** bustle   59-60 **had ... flew** i.e., had learned about the world through observation during the busy days of youth   61 **fancy** love-sick lady   61 **fastly** near (?) quickly (?)   64 **grainèd bat** shepherd's staff on which the grain was showing   65 **comely-distant** at an appropriate distance   69 **ecstasy** fit, passion

"But, woe is me, too early I attended
A youthful suit—it was to gain my grace—
80 Of one by nature's outwards so commended,
That maidens' eyes stuck over all his face:
Love lacked a dwelling, and made him her place;
And when in his fair parts she did abide,
She was new lodged and newly deified.

85 "His browny locks did hang in crooked curls,
And every light occasion of the wind
Upon his lips their silken parcels hurls.
What's sweet to do, to do will aptly find;
Each eye that saw him did enchant the mind,
90 For on his visage was in little drawn
What largeness thinks in Paradise was sawn.

"Small show of man was yet upon his chin;
His phoenix down began but to appear,
Like unshorn velvet, on that termless skin
95 Whose bare out-bragged the web it seemed to wear.
Yet showed his visage by that cost more dear;
And nice affections wavering stood in doubt
If best were as it was, or best without.

"His qualities were beauteous as his form,
100 For maiden-tongued he was, and thereof free;
Yet, if men moved him, was he such a storm
As oft 'twixt May and April is to see,
When winds breathe sweet, unruly though they be.
His rudeness so with his authorized youth
105 Did livery falseness in a pride of truth.

78 **attended** heeded 86 **occasion** chance movement 91 **What ... sawn**
what was seen (or possibly "sown") in large in paradise 93 **phoenix down**
i.e., newborn fuzz 94 **termless** young (?) indescribable (?) 95 **Whose ...
wear** i.e., the skin excelled the covering (?) 96 **cost** display, ornament 97
nice affections delicate tastes 100 **maiden-tongued** modestly spoken
100 **thereof free** not shy in speaking 104-05 **His rudeness ... truth** his
agitated behavior, with his privilege of youth, covered falseness with the
appearance of honesty

"Well could he ride, and often men would say,
'That horse his mettle from his rider takes.
Proud of subjection, noble by the sway,
What rounds, what bounds, what course, what stop he makes!'
110 And controversy hence a question takes,
Whether the horse by him became his deed,
Or he his manage by th' well-doing steed.

"But quickly on this side the verdict went:
His real habitude gave life and grace
115 To appertainings and to ornament,
Accomplished in himself, not in his case.
All aids, themselves made fairer by their place,
Came for additions; yet their purposed trim
Pieced not his grace but were all graced by him.

120 "So on the tip of his subduing tongue
All kind of arguments and question deep,
All replication prompt and reason strong,
For his advantage still did wake and sleep.
To make the weeper laugh, the laugher weep,
125 He had the dialect and different skill,
Catching all passions in his craft of will,

"That he did in the general bosom reign
Of young, of old, and sexes both enchanted
To dwell with him in thoughts, or to remain
130 In personal duty, following where he haunted.
Consents bewitched, ere he desire, have granted,
And dialogued for him what he would say,
Asked their own wills and made their wills obey.

109 **rounds, bounds, stop** (terms of horsemanship, or "manage") 111–12
Whether ... steed whether the horse showed his good qualities because of
the man, or whether the man showed his skill at horsemanship ("manage")
because of the horse's skill 113 **this** i.e., the following 114 **real habitude**
true character 116 **case** outside, belongings 118 **for** as 119 **Pieced not**
did not add to 122 **replication** reply, repartee 126 **craft of will** skill to
persuade 127 **That** so that 130 **In personal duty** i.e., as servants to
him 130 **haunted** frequented

"Many there were that did his picture get,
135   To serve their eyes, and in it put their mind,
      Like fools that in th' imagination set
      The goodly objects which abroad they find
      Of lands and mansions, theirs in thought assigned,
      And laboring in moe pleasures to bestow them
140   Than the true gouty landlord which doth owe them.

      "So many have, that never touched his hand,
      Sweetly supposed them mistress of his heart.
      My woeful self, that did in freedom stand
      And was my own fee-simple, not in part,
145   What with his art in youth and youth in art,
      Threw my affections in his charmèd power,
      Reserved the stalk and gave him all my flower.

      "Yet did I not, as some my equals did,
      Demand of him, nor being desirèd yielded;
150   Finding myself in honor so forbid,
      With safest distance I mine honor shielded.
      Experience for me many bulwarks builded
      Of proofs new-bleeding, which remained the foil
      Of this false jewel, and his amorous spoil.

155   "But, ah, who ever shunned by precedent
      The destined ill she must herself assay?
      Or forced examples, 'gainst her own content,
      To put the by-past perils in her way?
      Counsel may stop awhile what will not stay;
160   For when we rage, advice is often seen
      By blunting us to make our wits more keen.

140 **gouty** rheumatic, i.e., old   140 **owe** own   144 **fee-simple, not in part**
absolute possession, without restriction   146 **charmèd** enchanting   148
my equals i.e., girls of my age   152 **Experience** knowledge   153 **proofs
new-bleeding** examples of others newly ruined   153 **foil** dark background
(to display a jewel)   156 **assay** experience   157 **forced examples** compari-
sons with her own case which seem to her far-fetched, though she is made to
consider them   160 **rage** are impassioned

"Nor gives it satisfaction to our blood,
That we must curb it upon others' proof,
To be forbod the sweets that seems so good
165   For fear of harms that preach in our behoof.
O appetite, from judgment stand aloof!
The one a palate hath that needs will taste,
Though Reason weep and cry, 'It is thy last.'

"For further I could say this man's untrue,
170   And knew the patterns of his foul beguiling;
Heard where his plants in others' orchards grew;
Saw how deceits were gilded in his smiling;
Knew vows were ever brokers to defiling;
Thought characters and words merely but art,
175   And bastards of his foul adulterate heart.

"And long upon these terms I held my city,
Till thus he 'gan besiege me: 'Gentle maid,
Have of my suffering youth some feeling pity
And be not of my holy vows afraid.
180   That's to ye sworn to none was ever said;
For feasts of love I have been called unto,
Till now did ne'er invite nor never woo.

" 'All my offenses that abroad you see
Are errors of the blood, none of the mind.
185   Love made them not. With acture they may be,
Where neither party is nor true nor kind.
They sought their shame that so their shame did find,
And so much less of shame in me remains
By how much of me their reproach contains.

---

162 **blood** passion 163 **others' proof** the experience of others 164 **forbod** forbidden 169 **say this man's untrue** tell of this man's untruth 173 **brokers** panders 174 **characters and words** written and spoken words 180 **That's** what's 184 **blood** lust 185 **acture** action (as opposed to volition)

190 " 'Among the many that mine eyes have seen,
Not one whose flame my heart so much as warmèd,
Or my affection put to th' smallest teen,
Or any of my leisures ever charmèd.
Harm have I done to them, but ne'er was harmèd;
195 Kept hearts in liveries, but mine own was free
And reigned commanding in his monarchy.

" 'Look here what tributes wounded fancies sent me
Of pallid pearls and rubies red as blood,
Figuring that they their passions likewise lent me
200 Of grief and blushes, aptly understood
In bloodless white and the encrimsoned mood;
Effects of terror and dear modesty,
Encamped in hearts, but fighting outwardly.

" 'And, lo, behold these talents of their hair,
205 With twisted metal amorously empleached,
I have received from many a several fair,
Their kind acceptance weepingly beseeched,
With th' annexions of fair gems enriched,
And deep-brained sonnets that did amplify
210 Each stone's dear nature, worth, and quality.

" 'The diamond, why, 'twast beautiful and hard,
Whereto his invised properties did tend;
The deep-green em'rald, in whose fresh regard
Weak sights their sickly radiance do amend:
215 The heaven-hued sapphire, and the opal blend
With objects manifold: each several stone,
With wit well blazoned, smiled or made some moan.

192 **teen** distress   195 **in liveries** as servants   201 **mood** mode   204
talents treasures   205 **empleached** intertwined   206 **several fair** different
lady   208 **annexions** additions   210 **dear** valuable   212 **invised** inward-
looking, self-regarding (?) (Latin *invisus* = secret)   214 **radiance** power of
vision   215-16 **opal ... manifold** blended opal, with many other
objects (?)   216 **several** separate   217 **blazoned** proclaimed

" 'Lo, all these trophies of affections hot,
Of pensived and subdued desires the tender,
220 Nature hath charged me that I hoard them not,
But yield them up where I myself must render,
That is, to you, my origin and ender.
For these of force must your oblations be,
Since I their altar, you enpatron me.

225 " 'O, then, advance of yours that phraseless hand,
Whose white weighs down the airy scale of praise!
Take all these similes to your own command,
Hollowed with sighs that burning lungs did raise.
What me, your minister, for you obeys,
230 Works under you; and to your audit comes
Their distract parcels in combinèd sums.

" 'Lo, this device was sent me from a nun,
Or sister sanctified, of holiest note,
Which late her noble suit in court did shun,
235 Whose rarest havings made the blossoms dote;
For she was sought by spirits of richest coat,
But kept cold distance, and did thence remove
To spend her living in eternal love.

" 'But, O my sweet, what labor is't to leave
240 The thing we have not, mast'ring what not strives,
Paling the place which did no form receive,
Playing patient sports in unconstrainèd gyves?
She that her fame so to herself contrives,
The scars of battle 'scapeth by the flight
245 And makes her absence valiant, not her might.

219 **tender** offering   223 **oblations** offerings   224 **Since ... enpatron me**
i.e., I am the altar at which they are offered to you, my patron saint   225
phraseless indescribable   227 **similes** love-tokens (jewels and sonnets)
228 **Hollowed** (1) blown up, shaped (2) hallowed   229 **What ... obeys**
whatever obeys me, your servant ("minister")   230 **audit** accounting   231
distract parcels separate items   234 **suit** wooing   235 **havings** personal
qualities   235 **blossoms** i.e., flower of the nobility   236 **coat** coats of
arms   238 **eternal love** love of things heavenly   241 **Paling** fencing (but
"Paling" is an emendation for "Playing"; "Leaving" and "Flying" have also
been suggested)   241 **the place** i.e., the nun's heart, which had never
received the impression of love   242 **unconstrainèd gyves** fetters that do
not constrain (because willingly put on)   243 **her ... contrives** creates for
herself a reputation (for renouncing love)   245 **might** power

" 'O, pardon me, in that my boast is true:
The accident which brought me to her eye
Upon the moment did her force subdue,
And now she would the cagèd cloister fly.
250 Religious love put out religion's eye.
Not to be tempted, would she be inured,
And now, to tempt all, liberty procured.

" 'How mighty then you are, O hear me tell:
The broken bosoms that to me belong
255 Have emptied all their fountains in my well,
And mine I pour your ocean all among.
I strong o'er them, and you o'er me being strong,
Must for your victory us all congest,
As compound love to physic your cold breast.

260 " 'My parts had pow'r to charm a sacred nun,
Who, disciplined, ay, dieted in grace,
Believed her eyes when they t' assail begun,
All vows and consecrations giving place.
O most potential love! vow, bond, nor space
265 In thee hath neither sting, knot, nor confine,
For thou art all, and all things else are thine.

" 'When thou impressest, what are precepts worth
Of stale example? When thou wilt inflame,
How coldly those impediments stand forth
270 Of wealth, of filial fear, law, kindred, fame!
Love's arms are peace, 'gainst rule, 'gainst sense, 'gainst shame;
And sweetens, in the suff'ring pangs it bears,
The aloes of all forces, shocks, and fears.

250 **Religious** devoted   251 **inured** hardened   252 **And ... procured** and now she has procured liberty to try ("tempt") all things (?)   254 **bosoms** hearts   258 **congest** gather together   259 **physic** cure   262 **Believed ... begun** trusted her eyes when, filled with his image, they assailed her chastity   264 **potential** powerful   267 **impressest** conscripts   271 **arms are** warfare produces   273 **aloes** bitterness

" 'Now all these hearts that do on mine depend,
275 Feeling it break, with bleeding groans they pine;
And supplicant their sighs to you extend,
To leave the batt'ry that you make 'gainst mine,
Lending soft audience to my sweet design,
And credent soul to that strong-bonded oath
280 That shall prefer and undertake my troth.'

"This said, his wat'ry eyes he did dismount,
Whose sights till then were leveled on my face;
Each cheek a river running from a fount
With brinish current downward flowed apace.
285 O, how the channel to the stream gave grace!
Who glazed with crystal gate the glowing roses
That flame through water which their hue encloses.

"O father, what a hell of witchcraft lies
In the small orb of one particular tear!
290 But with the inundation of the eyes
What rocky heart to water will not wear?
What breast so cold that is not warmèd here?
O cleft effect! Cold modesty, hot wrath,
Both fire from hence and chill extincture hath.

295 "For, lo, his passion, but an art of craft,
Even there resolved my reason into tears;
There my white stole of chastity I daffed,
Shook off my sober guards and civil fears;
Appear to him as he to me appears,
300 All melting, though our drops this diff'rence bore:
His poisoned me, and mine did him restore.

275 **bleeding groans** (every sigh was thought to lessen life by drawing blood
from the heart) 279 **credent** believing 280 **prefer** advance, promote
280 **undertake my troth** support my love 281 **dismount** lower 286
Who which 286 **gate** barrier (the idea is that his cheeks beneath his ears are
like roses beneath glass) 293 **cleft** double 296 **resolved** dissolved 297
daffed doffed, put off 298 **civil** moral 299 **Appear** I appear 300 **drops**
medicinal drops

"In him a plenitude of subtle matter,
Applied to cautels, all strange forms receives,
Of burning blushes, or of weeping water,
305   Or sounding paleness; and he takes and leaves,
In either's aptness, as it best deceives,
To blush at speeches rank, to weep at woes,
Or to turn white and sound at tragic shows;

"That not a heart which in his level came
310   Could 'scape the hail of his all-hurting aim,
Showing fair nature as both kind and tame;
And, veiled in them, did win whom he would maim.
Against the thing he sought he would exclaim:
When he most burned in heart-wished luxury,
315   He preached pure maid and praised cold chastity.

"Thus merely with the garment of a Grace,
The naked and concealèd fiend he covered,
That th' unexperient gave the tempter place,
Which, like a cherubin, above them hovered.
320   Who, young and simple, would not be so lovered?
Ay me! I fell, and yet do question make
What I should do again for such a sake.

"O, that infected moisture of his eye,
O, that false fire which in his cheek so glowed,
325   O, that forced thunder from his heart did fly,
O, that sad breath his spongy lungs bestowed,
O, all that borrowed motion, seeming owed,
Would yet again betray the fore-betrayed
And new-pervert a reconcilèd maid!"

FINIS

303 **cautels** tricks   305 **sounding** swooning   305 **takes and leaves** alternately uses   306 **In either's aptness** i.e., according as it serves his purpose
307 **rank** lustful   308 **sound** swoon   309 **level** range of eye (literally: aim, line of fire)   310 **hail** bullets   311 **Showing … tame** appearing to be harmless and friendly   312 **them** i.e., kindness and tameness (or possibly the "strange forms" of line 303)   314 **luxury** lechery   318 **unexperient** inexperienced   319 **Which** who   323 **infected** unnatural   327 **borrowed … owed** assumed behavior that seemed his own   329 **reconcilèd** penitent

THE PASSIONATE PILGRIM

IV

Sweet Cytherea, sitting by a brook
With young Adonis, lovely, fresh, and green,
Did court the lad with many a lovely look,
Such looks as none could look but beauty's queen.
5 She told him stories, to delight his ear;
She showed him favors, to allure his eye;
To win his heart she touched him here and there—
Touches so soft still conquer chastity.
But whether unripe years did want conceit,
10 Or he refused to take her figured proffer,
The tender nibbler would not touch the bait,
But smile and jest at every gentle offer.
    Then fell she on her back, fair queen, and toward.
    He rose and ran away. Ah, fool too froward!

IV 1 **Cytherea** Venus 2 **green** young 3 **lovely** loving 9 **conceit**
understanding 13 **toward** willing 14 **froward** refractory

THE PASSIONATE PILGRIM

VI

Scarce had the sun dried up the dewy morn,
And scarce the herd gone to the hedge for shade,
When Cytherea (all in love forlorn),
A longing tarriance for Adonis made
5 Under an osier growing by a brook,
A brook where Adon used to cool his spleen.
Hot was the day; she hotter that did look
For his approach that often there had been.
Anon he comes, and throws his mantle by,
10 And stood stark naked on the brook's green brim.
The sun looked on the world with glorious eye,
Yet not so wistly as this queen on him.
    He, spying her, bounced in whereas he stood.
    "O Jove," quoth she, "why was not I a flood!"

VII

Fair is my love, but not so fair as fickle;
Mild as a dove, but neither true nor trusty;
Brighter than glass, and yet as glass is, brittle;
Softer than wax, and yet as iron rusty:
5   A lily pale, with damask dye to grace her;
    None fairer, nor none falser to deface her.

Her lips to mine how often hath she joinèd,
Between each kiss her oaths of true love swearing!
How many tales to please me hath she coinèd,
10 Dreading my love, the loss whereof still fearing!
    Yet, in the midst of all her pure protestings,
    Her faith, her oaths, her tears, and all were jestings.

VI 3 **Cytherea** Venus 4 **tarriance** awaiting 5 **osier** willow 6 **spleen** hot
temper 12 **wistly** eagerly 13 **whereas** where
VII 5 **damask** pale red 6 **to deface her** to her discredit 9 **coinèd**
counterfeited

She burnt with love, as straw with fire flameth;
She burnt out love, as soon as straw outburneth;
15 She framed the love, and yet she foiled the framing;
She bade love last, and yet she fell a-turning.
    Was this a lover, or a lecher, whether?
    Bad in the best, though excellent in neither.

IX

Fair was the morn when the fair queen of love,
          . . .
Paler for sorrow than her milk-white dove,
For Adon's sake, a youngster proud and wild,
5 Her stand she takes upon a steep-up hill.
Anon Adonis comes with horn and hounds.
She, silly queen, with more than love's good will,
Forbade the boy he should not pass those grounds.
"Once," quoth she, "did I see a fair sweet youth
10 Here in these brakes deep-wounded with a boar,
Deep in the thigh, a spectacle of ruth!
See, in my thigh," quoth she, "here was the sore."
    She showèd hers; he saw more wounds than one,
    And blushing fled and left her all alone.

X

Sweet rose, fair flower, untimely plucked, soon vaded,
Plucked in the bud, and vaded in the spring!
Bright orient pearl, alack, too timely shaded!
Fair creature, killed too soon by death's sharp sting!
5   Like a green plum that hangs upon a tree,
    And falls, through wind, before the fall should be.

---

13 fire (two syllables) 15 framed formed 15 foiled thwarted 16 fell a-
turning i.e., turned to others (for sex) 17 whether which of the two 18
neither (also, the sexual organs are "nether" parts) IX 2 (a line rhyming
with "wild" is lost) 11 ruth pity X 1, 2 vaded (1) departed (2) faded
3 timely soon

THE PASSIONATE PILGRIM

I weep for thee, and yet no cause I have;
For why, thou left'st me nothing in thy will.
And yet thou left'st me more than I did crave,
10   For why, I cravèd nothing of thee still.
    O yes, dear friend, I pardon crave of thee:
    Thy discontent thou didst bequeath to me.

XII

Crabbèd age and youth cannot live together;
Youth is full of pleasance, age is full of care;
Youth like summer morn, age like winter weather;
Youth like summer brave, age like winter bare.
5 Youth is full of sport, age's breath is short;
  Youth is nimble, age is lame;
  Youth is hot and bold, age is weak and cold;
  Youth is wild, and age is tame.
  Age, I do abhor thee; youth, I do adore thee:
10 O, my love, my love is young!
  Age, I do defy thee. O sweet shepherd hie thee,
  For methinks thou stays too long.

XIII

Beauty is but a vain and doubtful good;
A shining gloss that vadeth suddenly;
A flower that dies when first it 'gins to bud;
A brittle that's broken presently;
5   A doubtful good, a gloss, a glass, a flower,
    Lost, vaded, broken, dead within an hour.

8, 10 **For why** because   XII 2 **pleasance** gaiety   4 **brave** splendid
11 **defy** reject   11 **hie thee** hurry   XIII 2 **vadeth** (1) departs (2) fades
4 **presently** soon

And as goods lost are seld or never found,
As vaded gloss no rubbing will refresh,
As flowers dead lie witherèd on the ground,
10   As broken glass no cement can redress:
     So beauty blemished once, for ever lost,
     In spite of physic, painting, pain, and cost.

XIV

Good night, good rest; ah, neither be my share!
She bade good night that kept my rest away,
And daffed me to a cabin hanged with care
To descant on the doubts of my decay.
5   "Farewell," quoth she, "and come again tomorrow."
     Fare well I could not, for I supped with sorrow.

Yet at my parting sweetly did she smile,
In scorn or friendship, nill I conster whether.
'T may be she joyed to jest at my exile;
10   'T may be, again to make me wander thither:
     "Wander"—a word for shadows like myself
     As take the pain but cannot pluck the pelf.

Lord, how mine eyes throw gazes to the east!
My heart doth charge the watch; the morning rise
15   Doth cite each moving sense from idle rest,
Not daring trust the office of mine eyes,
     While Philomela sits and sings, I sit and mark,
     And wish her lays were tunèd like the lark;

---

7 **seld** seldom   10 **cement** (stress on first syllable)   12 **physic** medicine   12 **cost** expenditure   XIV 3 **daffed me** sent me off   4 **descant** lament (literally, compose musical variations)   8 **nill I conster whether** I do not know which   12 **As** who   12 **pelf** reward   14 **charge the watch** order the watchman to proclaim day (?)   15 **cite** summon   17 **Philomela** the nightingale   18 **lays** songs

For she doth welcome daylight with her ditty
20 And drives away dark dreaming night.
The night so packed, I post unto my pretty;
Heart hath his hope, and eyes their wishèd sight;
    Sorrow changed to solace and solace mixed with sorrow;
    For why, she sighed and bade me come tomorrow.

25 Were I with her, the night would post too soon,
But now are minutes added to the hours;
To spite me now, each minute seems a moon;
Yet not for me, shine sun to succor flowers!
    Pack night, peep day! Good day, of night now borrow:
30   Short, night, tonight, and length thyself tomorrow.

XV

It was a lording's daughter, the fairest one of three,
That likèd of her master as well as well might be,
Till looking on an Englishman, the fair'st that eye could see,
    Her fancy fell a-turning.
5 Long was the combat doubtful that love with love did fight,
To leave the master loveless, or kill the gallant knight:
To put in practice either, alas, it was a spite
    Unto the silly damsel!
But one must be refusèd; more mickle was the pain
10 That nothing could be usèd to turn them both to gain,
For of the two the trusty knight was wounded with disdain:
    Alas, she could not help it!
Thus art with arms contending was victor of the day,
Which by a gift of learning did bear the maid away:
15 Then, lullaby, the learned man hath got the lady gay;
    For now my song is ended.

21 **packed** disposed of 21 **post** hurry 24 **For why** because 26 **added to** i.e., like 27 **moon** month 30 **Short … length** shorten … lengthen
XV 1 **lording's** lord's 2 **master** teacher 8 **silly** inexperienced 9 **more mickle** greater 13 **art** learning

THE PASSIONATE PILGRIM

XVII

My flocks feed not, my ewes breed not,
My rams speed not, all is amiss:
Love is dying, faith's defying,
Heart's denying, causer of this.
5 All my merry jigs are quite forgot,
All my lady's love is lost, God wot.
Where her faith was firmly fixed in love,
There a nay is placed without remove.
One silly cross wrought all my loss.
10   O frowning Fortune, cursèd fickle dame!
For now I see inconstancy
     More in women than in men remain.

In black mourn I, all fears scorn I,
Love hath forlorn me, living in thrall.
15 Heart is bleeding, all help needing—
O cruel speeding, fraughted with gall!
My shepherd's pipe can sound no deal;
My wether's bell rings doleful knell;
My curtail dog, that wont to have played,
20 Plays not at all, but seems afraid;
With sighs so deep procures to weep,
     In howling wise, to see my doleful plight.
How sighs resound through heartless ground,
     Like a thousand vanquished men in bloody fight!

XVII 3 defying rejection 4 denying (perhaps it should be emended to
renying = disowning) 5 jigs songs or dance tunes 6 wot knows 8 nay
denial 9 cross misfortune 16 speeding lot 16 fraughted laden 17 no
deal not at all 19 curtail dog dog with docked tail 23 heartless (1)
pitiless (2) cowardly

25 Clear wells spring not, sweet birds sing not,
    Green plants bring not forth their dye.
    Herds stands weeping, flocks all sleeping,
    Nymphs back peeping fearfully.
    All our pleasure known to us poor swains,
30 All our merry meetings on the plains,
    All our evening sport from us is fled,
    All our love is lost, for Love is dead.
    Farewell, sweet lass! Thy like ne'er was
      For a sweet content, the cause of all my moan.
35 Poor Corydon must live alone.
      Other help for him I see that there is none.

                      XVIII

    When as thine eye hath chose the dame
    And stalled the deer that thou shouldst strike,
    Let reason rule things worthy blame,
    As well as fancy's partial might;
5   Take counsel of some wiser head,
        Neither too young, nor yet unwed.

    And when thou com'st thy tale to tell,
    Smooth not thy tongue with filèd talk,
    Lest she some subtile practice smell—
10   A cripple soon can find a halt;
        But plainly say thou lov'st her well,
        And set thy person forth to sell.

    And to her will frame all thy ways.
    Spare not to spend, and chiefly there
15 Where thy desert may merit praise
    By ringing in thy lady's ear.
        The strongest castle, tower, and town,
        The golden bullet beats it down.

XVIII 2 **stalled the deer** got the deer within range (with pun on "dear")
4 **fancy's partial might** (a desperate emendation for the text's "fancy
[partyall might]" which seems meaningless. The emendation, and its context,
means that sexual behavior ["things worthy blame"] should be governed by
impartial reason and by the partial power of love ["fancy"]) 8 **filèd**
polished 9 **practice** deception 10 **A cripple ... halt** a cripple knows a
limp (and so a woman can recognize a deceiver)

Serve always with assurèd trust
20 And in thy suit be humble-true.
Unless thy lady prove unjust,
Press never thou to choose a new.
    When time shall serve, be thou not slack
    To proffer, though she put thee back.

25 What though her frowning brows be bent,
Her cloudy looks will calm ere night;
And then too late she will repent
That thus dissembled her delight,
    And twice desire, ere it be day,
30   That which with scorn she put away.

What though she strive to try her strength,
And ban and brawl and say thee nay,
Her feeble force will yield at length,
When craft hath taught her thus to say:
35   "Had women been so strong as men,
    In faith, you had not had it then."

The wiles and guiles that women work,
Dissembled wth an outward show,
The tricks and toys that in them lurk,
40 The cock that treads them shall not know.
    Have you not heard it said full oft,
    A woman's nay doth stand for naught?

32 ban curse

Think women still to strive with men
To sin and never for to saint.
45 There is no heaven: be holy then
When time with age shall them attaint.
Were kisses all the joys in bed,
One woman would another wed.

But soft, enough! too much, I fear,
50 Lest that my mistress hear my song.
She will not stick to round me on th' ear,
To teach my tongue to be so long.
Yet will she blush, here be it said,
To hear her secrets so bewrayed.

FINIS

45 **There is no heaven** i.e., there is no heavenly bliss in serving women (?)
49 **soft** stop 51 **stick to round me on th' ear** hesitate to scold me
54 **bewrayed** revealed

Textual Note

Three nondramatic poems (other than the sonnets) are regularly attributed to Shakespeare: *Venus and Adonis, The Rape of Lucrece*, and "The Phoenix and the Turtle." *Venus and Adonis* was first published in a quarto dated 1593, *Lucrece* (thus the title page, but the heading at the beginning of the poem, and on all the following pages, is *The Rape of Lucrece*) in a quarto dated 1594. Both quartos are dedicated to Shakespeare's patron, the Earl of Southampton. These two books were Shakespeare's first publications, and they were destined for a nobleman's eye; Shakespeare apparently read the proofs, and the texts are remarkably clean. There is no reason to believe that he had anything to do with the later quartos, which introduce numerous changes.

The third canonical poem, "The Phoenix and the Turtle," appears (without a title) attributed to Shakespeare in a quarto (1601) whose title page reads in part: "*Love's Martyr* ... allegorically shadowing the truth of Love, in the constant fate of the phoenix and turtle. ... A poem ... by Robert Chester. ... To these [Chester's poem and other materials] are added some new compositions, of several modern writers, whose names are subscribed to their several works, upon the first subject, viz. the phoenix and turtle."

"A Lover's Complaint" appears at the end of the 1609 volume of Shakespeare's sonnets, published by Thomas Thorpe. No one doubts that the sonnets are Shakespeare's, but many doubt that "A Lover's Complaint" is his. The usual view is that the poem does not sound like Shakespeare, and that the publisher's ascription is of no value. The poem does not do Shakespeare great credit, and a fair number of its words do not appear elsewhere in Shakespeare; still, there is no evidence that anyone else wrote it. Thorpe's attribution is not compelling, but it is all of the evidence that there is.

Departures from the copy-texts are listed below. The adopted reading is given first, in bold type, followed by the original reading, in roman type. The copy-text for *Venus and Adonis* and *The Rape of Lucrece* is of course the first quarto of each poem. The copy-text of "The Phoenix and the Turtle" is

TEXTUAL NOTE

Love's Martyr (1601), that of "A Lover's Complaint" is the quarto of 1609. The earliest known complete text of *The Passionate Pilgrim* is the second edition (1599), but some pages of the first edition (perhaps also 1599) survive at the Folger Library.

Venus and Adonis 19 satiety sacietie 231, 239 deer deare 432 **Ear's** Eares 616 javelin's iauelings 644 Saw'st Sawest 680 **overshoot** ouer-shut 748 th' the th' 754 sons suns 873 twine twin'd 940 **dost** doest 1031 as are 1054 **was** had

The Rape of Lucrece 550 **blows** blow 833 mak'st makest 884 blow'st blowest 1227 **flower** flowre 1312 **schedule** Cedule 1662 wreathèd wretched 1680 one woe on woe 1713 in it it in

A Lover's Complaint 14 lattice lettice 80 Of O 95 wear were 112 **manage** mannad'g 118 Came Can 182 woo vow 241 **Paling** Playing 252 procured procure 160 nun Sunne 293 O Or 311 as is*

The Passionate Pilgrim IV 5 ear eares 10 her his
VII 11 midst mids
X 8, 9 left'st lefts
XIV 24 **sighed** sight 27 a moon an houre
XV 3 fair'st fairest
XVII 38 **back** blacke 33 lass loue 34 **moan** woe
XVIII 4 **fancy's partial might** fancy (partyall might) 12 thy her 12 sel sale 22 **Press** Prease 26, 29 ere yer 45 be by 51 ear are

*William Empson suggests emending "A Lover's Complaint," line 311, which reads: "Showing fair nature is both kind and tame." Mr. Empson writes: It seems better, though not necessary, to emend *is* to *as*, an easy change in itself. Otherwise *kind and tame* has to mean "the fact that he could seduce *any* virgin makes them all look like sheep." Maybe this was Shakespeare's opinion, but he does not express it so bleakly. Besides, *them* in the next line has to refer back to *strange forms* (line 303), the pretenses of tenderness which the seducer was skilled at adopting; if your mind is cluttered with tame ladies you miss the grammar. *Nature* here is chiefly the sexual experience, and he shows it to the virgins *as* not alarming; it really is *fair*, we are told by the author and the wronged lady, and this should content us. They can hardly want to assert that it is always *tame*.

APPENDIX

W . H . A U D E N

I N T R O D U C T I O N

Probably, more nonsense has been talked and written, more intellectual and emotional energy expended in vain, on the sonnets of Shakespeare than on any other literary work in the world. Indeed, they have become the best touchstone I know of for distinguishing the sheep from the goats, those, that is, who love poetry for its own sake and understand its nature, from those who only value poems either as historical documents or because they express feelings or beliefs of which the reader happens to approve.

It so happens that we know almost nothing about the historical circumstances under which Shakespeare wrote these sonnets: we don't know to whom they are addressed or exactly when they were written, and, unless entirely new evidence should turn up, which is unlikely, we never shall.

This has not prevented many very learned gentlemen from displaying their scholarship and ingenuity in conjecture. Though it seems to me rather silly to spend much time upon conjectures which cannot be proved true or false, that is not my real objection to their efforts. What I really object to is their illusion that, if they were successful, if the identity of the Friend, the Dark Lady, the Rival Poet, etc., could be established beyond doubt, this would in any way illuminate our understanding of the sonnets themselves.

Their illusion seems to me to betray either a complete misunderstanding of the nature of the relation between art and life or an attempt to rationalize and justify plain vulgar idle curiosity.

Idle curiosity is an ineradicable vice of the human mind. All of us like to discover the secrets of our neighbours, particularly the ugly ones. This has always been so, and, probably, always will be. What is relatively new, however – it is scarcely to be found before the latter half of the eighteenth century – is a blurring of the borderline between the desire for truth and idle curiosity, until, today, it has been so thoroughly erased that we can indulge in the latter without the slightest pangs of conscience. A great deal of what today passes for scholarly research is an activity no different from that of reading somebody's private correspondence when he is out of the room, and it doesn't really make it morally any better if he is out of the room because he is in his grave.

In the case of a man of action – a ruler, a statesman, a general – the man is identical with his biography. In the case of any kind of artist, however, who is a maker not a doer, his biography, the story of his life, and the history of his works are distinct. In the case of a man of action, we can distinguish in a rough and ready way between his private personal life and his public life, but both are lives of action and, therefore, capable of affecting each other. The political interests of a king's mistress, for example, may influence his decisions on national policy. Consequently, the historian, in his search for truth, is justified in investigating the private life of a man of action to the degree that such discoveries throw light upon the history of his times which he had a share in shaping, even if the victim would prefer such secrets not to be known.

The case of any artist is quite different. Art history, the comparison of one work with another, one artistic epoch with another, the study of influences and changes of style is a legitimate study. The late J. B. Leishman's book, *Themes and Variations in Shakespeare's Sonnets*, is an admirable example of such an enquiry. Even the biography of an artist, if his life as a man was sufficiently interesting, is permissible, provided that the biographer and his readers realize that such an account throws no light whatsoever upon the artist's work. The relation between his life and his works is at one and the same time too self-evident to require comment – every work of art is, in one sense, a self-disclosure – and too complicated ever to unravel. Thus, it is self-evident that Catullus's love for Lesbia was the experience which inspired his love poems, and that, if either of them had had a different character, the poems would have been different, but no amount of research into their lives can tell us why Catullus wrote the actual poems he did, instead of an infinite number of similar poems he might have written instead, why, indeed he wrote any, or why those he did are good. Even if one could question a poet himself about the relation between some poem of his and the events which provoked him to write it, he could not give a satisfactory answer, because even the most 'occasional' poem, in the Goethean sense, involves not only the occasion but the whole life experience of the poet, and he himself cannot identify all the contributing elements.

Further, it should be borne in mind that most genuine artists would prefer that no biography be written. A genuine artist believes he has been put on earth to fulfil a certain function determined by the talent with which he has been entrusted. His personal life is, naturally, of concern to himself and, he hopes, to his personal friends, but he does not think it is or ought to be of any concern to the public. The one thing a writer, for example, hopes for, is attentive readers of his writings. He hopes they will study the text closely enough to spot misprints. Shakespeare would be grateful to many scholars, beginning with Malone, who have suggested sensible emendations to the Q text. And he hopes that they will read with patience and intelligence so as to extract as much meaning from the text as possible. If the shade of Shakespeare has read Professor William Empson's explication of 'They that have power to hurt and will do none' (Sonnet 94), he may have wondered to himself, 'Now, did I *really* say all that?', but he will certainly be grateful to Mr Empson for his loving care.

Not only would most genuine writers prefer to have no biography written; they would also prefer, were it practically feasible, that their writings were published anonymously.

Shakespeare is in the singularly fortunate position of being, to all intents and purposes, anonymous. Hence the existence of persons who spend their lives trying to prove that his plays were written by someone else. (How odd it is that Freud should have been a firm believer in the Earl of Oxford theory.)

So far as the sonnets are concerned, the certain facts are just two in number. Two of the sonnets, 'When my love swears that she is made of truth' (138), and 'Two loves I have, of comfort and despair' (144), appeared in *The Passionate Pilgrim*, a poetic miscellany printed in 1599, and the whole collection was

published by G. Eld for T. T. in 1609 with a dedication
'To.The.Onlie.Begetter.Of.These.Insuing.Sonnets. Mr. W.H.'
Meres's reference in 1598 to 'sugred Sonnets' by Shakespeare
is inconclusive: the word *sonnet* was often used as a general
term for a lyric, and even if Meres was using it in the stricter
sense, we do not know if the sonnets he was referring to are the
ones we have.

Aside from the text itself, this is all we know for certain and
all we are ever likely to know. On philological grounds, I am
inclined to agree with those scholars who take the word *begetter*
to mean procurer, so that Mr. W.H. is not the friend who
inspired most of the sonnets, but the person who secured the
manuscript for the publisher.

So far as the date of their composition is concerned, all we
know for certain is that the relation between Shakespeare and
the Friend lasted at least three years:

> Three April perfumes in three hot Junes burned,
> Since first I saw you fresh, which yet are green. (104)

The fact that the style of the sonnets is nearer to that of the
earlier plays than the later is not conclusive proof that their
composition was contemporary with the former, because a
poet's style is always greatly influenced by the particular verse
form he is employing. As Professor C. S. Lewis has said: 'If
Shakespeare had taken an hour off from the composition of
Lear to write a sonnet, the sonnet might not have been in the
style of *Lear*.' On the whole, I think an early date is a more
plausible conjecture than a late one, because the experiences
the sonnets describe seem to me to be more likely to befall a
younger man than an older.

Let us, however, forget all about Shakespeare the man,
leave the speculations about the persons involved, the names,
already or in the future to be put forward, Southampton,
Pembroke, Hughes, etc., to the foolish and the idle, and
consider the sonnets themselves.

The first thing which is obvious after reading through the one
hundred and fifty-four sonnets as we have them, is that they
are not in any kind of planned sequence. The only semblance

of order is a division into two unequal heaps – Sonnets 1 to 126 are addressed to a young man, assuming, which is probable but not certain, that there is only one young man addressed, and Sonnets 127–154 are addressed to a dark-haired woman. In both heaps, a triangle situation is referred to in which Shakespeare's friend and his mistress betray him by having an affair together, which proves that the order is not chronological. Sonnets 40 and 42, 'Take all my loves, my love, yea take them all', 'That thou hast her, it is not all my grief', must be more or less contemporary with 144 and 152, 'Two loves I have, of comfort and despair', 'In loving thee thou know'st I am forsworn'.

Nor in the two sets considered separately is it possible to believe that the order is chronological. Sometimes batches of sonnets occur which clearly belong together – for example, the opening series 1–17, in which the friend is urged to marry, though, even here, 15 seems not to belong, for marriage is not mentioned in it. At other times, sonnets which are similar in theme are widely separated. To take a very trivial example. In 77 Shakespeare speaks of giving his friend a commonplace book:

> Look what thy memory cannot contain,
> Commit to these waste blanks.

And in 122, he speaks of a similar gift from his friend to him,

> Thy gift, thy tables, are within my brain.

Surely, it is probable that they exchanged gifts and that these sonnets belong together.

The serious objection, however, to the order of Sonnets 1–126 as the Q text prints them is psychological. Sonnets expressing feelings of unalloyed happiness and devotion are mixed with others expressing grief and estrangement. Some speak of injuries done to Shakespeare by his friend, others of some scandal in which the friend was involved, others again of some infidelity on Shakespeare's part in a succession which makes no kind of emotional sense.

Any passionate relationship can go through and survive

painful crises, and become all the stronger for it. As Shakespeare writes in Sonnet 119:

> O, benefit of ill: now I find true
> That better is by evil still made better;
> And ruined love, when it is built anew,
> Grows fairer than at first, more strong, far greater.

But forgiveness and reconciliation do not obliterate memory of the past. It is not possible to return to the innocent happiness expressed before any cloud appeared on the sky. It is not, it seems to me, possible to believe that, *after* going through the experiences described in Sonnets 40–42, Shakespeare would write either Sonnet 53,

> In all external grace, you have some part,
> But you like none, none you, for constant heart

or 105,

> Let not my love be called idolatry,
> Nor my beloved as an idol show,
> Since all alike my songs and praises be
> To one, of one, still such, and ever so.
> Kind is my love today, tomorrow kind,
> Still constant in a wondrous excellence.

If the order is not chronological, it cannot, either, be a sequence planned by Shakespeare for publication. Any writer with an audience in mind knows that a sequence of poems must climax with one of the best. Yet the sequence as we have it concludes with two of the worst of the sonnets, trivial conceits about, apparently, going to Bath to take the waters. Nor, when preparing for publication, will an author leave unrevised what is obviously a first draft, like Sonnet 99 with its fifteen lines.

A number of scholars have tried to rearrange the sonnets into some more logical order, but such efforts can never be more than conjecture, and it is best to accept the jumble we have been given.

If the first impression made by the sonnets is of their

haphazard order, the second is of their extremely uneven poetic value.

After the 1609 edition, the sonnets were pretty well forgotten for over a century and a half. In 1640 Benson produced an extraordinary hodgepodge in which one hundred and forty-six of them were arranged into seventy-two poems with invented titles, and some of the *he*'s and *him*'s changed to *she*'s and *her*'s. It was not until 1780 that a significant critical text was made by Malone. This happened to be a period when critics condemned the sonnet as a form. Thus Stevens could write in 1766:

Quaintness, obscurity, and tautology are to be regarded at the constituent parts of this exotic species of composition ... I am one of those who should have wished it to have expired in the country where it was born ... [A sonnet] is composed in the highest strain of affectation, pedantry, circumlocution, and nonsense.

And of Shakespeare's essays in this form:

The strongest act of Parliament that could be framed would fail to compel readers unto their service.

Even when this prejudice against the sonnet as such had begun to weaken, and even after Bardolatry had begun, adverse criticism of the sonnets continued.

Thus Wordsworth, who was as responsible as anyone for rehabilitating the sonnet as a form (though he employed the Petrarchan, not the Shakespearian, kind), remarked:

These sonnets beginning at CXXVII to his mistress are worse than a puzzle-peg. They are abominably harsh, obscure, and worthless. The others are for the most part much better, have many fine lines and passages. They are also in many places warm with passion. Their chief faults – and heavy ones they are – are sameness, tediousness, quaintness, and elaborate obscurity.

Hazlitt:

If Shakespeare had written nothing but his sonnets ... he would ... have been assigned to the class of cold, artificial writers, who had no genuine sense of nature or passion.

Keats:

They seem to be full of fine things said unintentionally – in the intensity of working out conceits.

Landor:

Not a single one is very admirable ... They are hot and pothery: there is much condensation, little delicacy; like raspberry jam without cream, without crust, without bread; to break its viscidity.

In this century we have reacquired a taste for the conceit, as we have for baroque architecture, and no longer think that artifice is incompatible with passion. Even so, no serious critic of poetry can possibly think that all the sonnets are equally good.

On going through the hundred and fifty-four of them, I find forty-fine which seem to me excellent throughout, a good number of the rest have one or two memorable lines, but there are also several which I can only read out of a sense of duty. For the inferior ones we have no right to condemn Shakespeare unless we are prepared to believe, a belief for which there is no evidence, that he prepared or intended them all to be published.

Considered in the abstract, as if they were Platonic Ideas, the Petrarchan sonnet seems to be a more aesthetically satisfying form than the Shakespearian. Having only two different rhymes in the octave and two in the sestet, each is bound by rhyme into a closed unity, and the asymmetrical relation of 8 to 6 is pleasing. The Shakespearian form, on the other hand, with its seven different rhymes, almost inevitably becomes a lyric of three symmetrical quatrains, finished off with an epigrammatic couplet. As a rule Shakespeare shapes his rhetorical argument in conformity with this, that is to say, there is usually a major pause after the fourth, the eighth, and the twelfth line. Only in one case, Sonnet 86, 'Was it the proud full sail of his great verse', does the main pause occur in the middle of the second quatrain, so that the sonnet divides into 6.6.2.

It is the concluding couplet in particular which, in the Shakespearian form, can be a snare. The poet is tempted to use it, either to make a summary of the preceding twelve lines which is unnecessary, or to draw a moral which is too glib and trite. In the case of Shakespeare himself, though there are some wonderful couplets, for example the conclusion of 61,

> For thee watch I, whilst thou dost wake elsewhere,
> From me far off, with others all too near,

or 87,

> Thus have I had thee as a dream doth flatter,
> In sleep a king, but waking no such matter,

all too often, even in some of the best, the couplet lines are the weakest and dullest in the sonnet, and, coming where they do at the end, the reader has the sense of a disappointing anticlimax.

Despite all this, it seems to me wise of Shakespeare to have chosen the form he did rather than the Petrarchan. Compared with Italian, English is so poor in rhymes that it is almost impossible to write a Petrarchan sonnet in it that sounds effortless throughout. In even the best examples from Milton, Wordsworth, Rossetti, for example, one is almost sure to find at least one line the concluding word of which does not seem inevitable, the only word which could accurately express the poet's meaning; one feels it is only there because the rhyme demanded it.

In addition, there are certain things which can be done in the Shakepearian form which the Petrarchan, with its sharp division between octave and sestet, cannot do. In Sonnet 66, 'Tired with all these, for restful death I cry', and 129, 'Th' expense of spirit in a waste of shame', Shakespeare is able to give twelve single-line *exempla* of the wretchedness of this world and the horrors of lust, with an accumulative effect of great power.

In their style, two characteristics of the sonnets stand out. Firstly, their *cantabile*. They are the work of someone whose ear is unerring. In his later blank verse, Shakespeare became a master of highly complicated effects of sound and rhythm, and the counterpointing of these with the sense, but in the sonnets he is intent upon making his verse as melodious, in the simplest

235

and most obvious sense of the word, as possible, and there is
scarcely a line, even in the dull ones, which sounds harsh or
awkward. Occasionally, there are lines which foreshadow the
freedom of his later verse. For example:

> Not mine own fears nor the prophetic soul
> Of the wide world dreaming on things to come.   (107)

But, as a rule, he keeps the rhythm pretty close to the metrical
base. Inversion, except in the first foot, is rare, and so is
trisyllabic substitution. The commonest musical devices are
alliteration –

> Then were not summer's distillation left,
> A liquid prisoner pent in walls of glass   (5)

> Let me not to the marriage of true minds
> Admit impediments ...   (116)

and the careful patterning of long and short vowels –

> How many a holy and obsequious tear   (31)

> Nor think the bitterness of absence sour   (57)

> So far from home into my deeds to pry.   (61)

The second characteristic they display is a mastery of every
possible rhetorical device. The reiteration, for example, of
words with either an identical or a different meaning –

> love is not love
> Which alters when it alteration finds,
> Or bends with the remover to remove.   (116)

Or the avoidance of monotony by an artful arithmetical
variation of theme or illustration.

Here, I cannot do better than to quote (interpolating lines
where appropriate) Professor C. S. Lewis on Sonnet 18. 'As
often,' he says, 'the theme begins at line 9,

> But thy eternal summer shall not fade,

occupying four lines, and the application is in the couplet:

APPENDIX

> So long as men can breathe or eyes can see,
> So long lives this, and this gives life to thee.

Line 1

> Shall I compare thee to a summer's day

proposes a simile. Line 2

> Thou art more lively and more temperate

corrects it. Then we have two one-line *exempla* justifying the correction

> Rough winds do shake the darling buds of May,
> And summer's lease hath all too short a date:

then a two-line *exemplum* about the sun

> Sometime too hot the eye of heaven shines,
> And often is his gold complexion dimmed:

then two more lines

> And every fair from fair sometime declines,
> By chance, or nature's changing course, untrimmed

which do not, as we expected, add a fourth *exemplum* but generalize. Equality of length in the two last variations is thus played off against difference of function."[1]

The visual imagery is usually drawn from the most obviously beautiful natural objects, but, in a number, a single metaphorical conceit is methodically worked out, as in 87,

> Farewell, thou art too dear for my possessing,

where the character of an emotional relationship is worked out in terms of a legal contract.

In the inferior sonnets, such artifices may strike the reader as artificial, but he must reflect that, without the artifice, they might be much worse than they are. The worst one can say, I

---

[1]. *English Literature in the Sixteenth Century.* Clarendon Press, Oxford, 1954, p.507.

think, is that rhetorical skill enables a poet to write a poem for which genuine inspiration is lacking which, had he lacked such skill, he would not have written at all.

On the other hand those sonnets which express passionate emotions, whether of adoration or anger or grief or disgust, owe a very great deal of their effect precisely to Shakespeare's artifice, for without the restraint and distancing which the rhetorical devices provide, the intensity and immediacy of the emotion might have produced, not a poem, but an embarrassing 'human document'. Wordsworth defined poetry as emotion recollected in tranquillity. It seems highly unlikely that Shakespeare wrote many of these sonnets out of recollected emotion. In his case, it is the artifice that makes up for the lack of tranquillity.

If the vagueness of the historical circumstances under which the sonnets were written has encouraged the goats of idle curiosity, their matter has given the goats of ideology a wonderful opportunity to display their love of simplification at the expense of truth. Confronted with the extremely odd story they tell, with the fact that, in so many of them, Shakespeare addresses a young man in terms of passionate devotion, the sound and sensible citizen, alarmed at the thought that our Top-Bard could have had any experience with which he is unfamiliar, has either been shocked and wished that Shakespeare had never written them, or, in defiance of common sense, tried to persuade himself that Shakespeare was merely expressing in somewhat hyperbolic terms, such as an Elizabethan poet might be expected to use, what any normal man feels for a friend of his own sex. The homosexual reader, on the other hand, determined to secure our Top-Bard as a patron saint of the Homintern, has been uncritically enthusiastic about the first one hundred and twenty-six of the sonnets, and preferred to ignore those to the Dark Lady in which the relationship is unequivocally sexual, and the fact that Shakespeare was a married man and a father.

Dag Hammerskjöld, in a diary found after his death and just recently published in Sweden, makes an observation to which both the above types would do well to listen:

APPENDIX

How easy Psychology has made it for us to dismiss the perplexing mystery with a label which assigns it a place in the list of common aberrations.

That we are confronted in the sonnets by a mystery rather than by an aberration is evidenced for me by the fact that men and women whose sexual tastes are perfectly normal, but who enjoy and understand poetry, have always been able to read them as expressions of what they understand by the word *love*, without finding the masculine pronoun an obstacle.

I think that the *primary* experience – complicated as it became later – out of which the sonnets to the friend spring was a mystical one.

All experiences which may be called mystical have certain characteristics in common.

(1) The experience is 'given'. That is to say, it cannot be induced or prolonged by an effort of will, though the openness of any individual to receive it is partly determined by his age, his psychophysical make-up, and his cultural milieu.

(2) Whatever the contents of the experience, the subject is absolutely convinced that it is a revelation of reality. When it is over, he does not say, as one says when one awakes from a dream: 'Now I am awake and conscious again of the real world.' He says, rather: 'For a while the veil was lifted and a reality revealed which in my "normal" state is hidden from me.'

(3) With whatever the vision is concerned, things, human beings, or God, they are experienced as numinous, clothed in glory, charged with an intense beingthereness.

(4) Confronted by the vision, the attention of the subject, in awe, joy, dread, is absolutely absorbed in contemplation and, while the vision lasts, his self, its desires and needs, are completely forgotten.

Natural mystical experiences, visions that is to say, concerned with created beings, not with a creator God, and without overt religious content, are of two kinds, which one might call the Vision of Dame Kind and the Vision of Eros.

The classic descriptions of the first are to be found, of course, in certain of Wordsworth's poems, like *The Prelude*, the Immortality Ode, 'Tintern Abbey', and 'The Ruined Cottage'. It is concerned with a multiplicity of creatures, inanimate and animate, but not with persons, though it may include human artifacts. If human beings do appear in it, they are always, I believe, total strangers to the subject, so that, so far as he is concerned, they are not persons. It would seem that, in our culture, this vision is not uncommon in childhood, but rare in adults.

The Vision of Eros, on the other hand, is concerned with a single person, who is revealed to the subject as being of infinite sacred importance. The classic descriptions of it are to be found in Plato's *Symposium*, Dante's *La Vita Nuova*, and some of these sonnets by Shakespeare.

It can, it seems, be experienced before puberty. If it occurs later, though the subject is aware of it erotic nature, his own desire is always completely subordinate to the sacredness of the beloved person who is felt to be infinitely superior to the lover. Before anything else, the lover desires the happiness of the beloved.

The Vision of Eros is probably a much rarer experience than most people in our culture suppose, but, when it is genuine, I do not think it makes any sense to apply to it terms like heterosexual or homosexual. Such terms can only be legitimately applied to the profane erotic experiences with which we are all familiar, to lust, for example, an interest in another solely as a sexual object, and that combination of sexual desire and *philia*, affection based upon mutual interests, values, and shared experiences which is the securest basis for a happy marriage.

That, in the Vision of Eros, the erotic is the medium, not the cause, is proved, I think, by the fact, on which all who have written about it with authority agree, that it cannot long survive an actual sexual relationship. Indeed, it is very doubtful if the Vision can ever be mutual: the story of Tristan and Isolde is a myth, not an instance of what can historically occur. To be receptive to it, it would seem that the subject must be exceptionally imaginative. Class feelings also seem to play a role; no one, apparently, can have such a vision about an individual who belongs to a social group which he has been brought up to regard as inferior to his own, so that its members are not, for him, fully persons.

The medium of the Vision is, however, undoubtedly erotic. Nobody who was unconscious of an erotic interest on his part would use the frank, if not brutal, sexual image which Shakespeare employs in speaking of his friend's exclusive interest in women.

> But since she pricked thee out for women's pleasure,
> Mine be thy love, and thy love's use their treasure.   (20)

The beloved is always beautiful in the impersonal sense of the word as well as the personal. It is unfortunate that we have to use the same words, beauty and beautiful, to mean two quite different things. If I say: 'Elizabeth has a beautiful figure' or 'a beautiful profile', I am referring to an objective, publicly recognizable property, and, so long as the objects are members of the same class, I can compare one with another and arrange them along a scale of beauty. That is why it is possible to hold dog shows, beauty competitions, etc., or for a sculptor to state in mathematical terms the proportions of the ideal male or female figure. This kind of beauty is a gift of Nature's, depending upon a lucky combination of genes and the luck of good health, and a gift which Nature can, and, in due time, alway does, take away. The reaction of the spectactor to it is either impersonal admiration or impersonal sexual desire. Moral approval is not involved. It is perfectly possible for me to say: 'Elizabeth has a beautiful figure, but she is a monster.'

If, on the other hand, I say: 'Elizabeth has a beautiful face or a beautiful expression', though I am still referring to something physical – I could not make the statement if I were blind – I am speaking of something which is personal, a unique face which cannot be compared with that of anyone else, and for which I hold Elizabeth personally responsible. Nature has had nothing to do with it. This kind of beauty is always associated with the notion of moral goodness. It is impossible to imagine circumstances in which I could say: 'Elizabeth has a beautiful expression but she is a monster.' And it is this kind of beauty which arouses in the beholder feelings, not of impersonal admiration or lust, but of personal love.

The Petrarchan distinction, employed by Shakespeare in a number of his sonnets, between the love of the eye and the love of the heart, is an attempt, I think, to express the difference between these two kinds of beauty and our response to them.

In the Vision of Eros, both are always present. The beloved is alway beautiful in both the public and the personal sense. But, to the lover, the second is the more important. Dante certainly thought that Beatrice was a girl whose beauty everybody would admire, but it wouldn't have entered his head to compare her for beauty with other Florentine girls of the same age.

Both Plato and Dante attempt to give a religious explanation of the Vision. Both, that is to say, regard the love inspired by a created human being as intended to lead the lover towards the love of the uncreated source of all beauty. The difference between them is that Plato is without any notion of what we mean by a person, whether human or Divine; he can only think in terms of the individual and the universal, and beauty, for him, is always beauty in the impersonal sense. Consequently, on the Platonic ladder, the love of an individual must be forgotten in the love of the universal; what we should call infidelity becomes a moral duty. How different is Dante's interpretation. Neither he nor Beatrice tell us exactly what he had done which had led him to the brink of perdition, but both speak of it as a lack of fidelity on Dante's part to his love for Beatrice. In Paradise, she is with him up until the final moment when he turns from her towards 'The Eternal Fountain' and, even then, he knows that her eyes are turned in the same direction. Instead of the many rungs of the Platonic ladder, there is only one step for the lover to take, from the person of the beloved creature to the Person of their common Creator.

It is consistent with Shakespeare's cast of mind as we meet it in the plays, where it is impossible to be certain what his personal beliefs were on any subject, that the sonnets should contain no theory of love: Shakespeare contents himself with simply describing the experience.

APPENDIX

Though the primary experience from which they started was, I believe, the Vision of Eros, that is, of course, not all they are about. For the vision to remain undimmed, it is probably necessary that the lover have very little contact with the beloved, however nice a person she (or he) may be. Dante, after all, only saw Beatrice once or twice, and she probably knew little about him. The story of the sonnets seems to me to be the story of an agonized struggle by Shakespeare to preserve the glory of the vision he had been granted in a relationship, lasting at least three years, with a person who seemed intent by his actions upon covering the vision with dirt.

As outsiders, the impression we get of his friend is one of a young man who was not really very nice, very conscious of his good looks, able to switch on the charm at any moment, but essentially frivolous, cold-hearted, and self-centred, aware, probably, that he had some power over Shakespeare – if he thought about it at all, no doubt he gave it a cynical explanation – but with no conception of the intensity of the feelings he had, unwittingly, aroused. Somebody, in fact, rather like Bassanio in *The Merchant of Venice*.

The Sonnets addressed to the Dark Lady are concerned with that most humiliating of all erotic experiences, sexual infatuation – *Vénus toute entière à sa proie attachée*.

Simple lust is impersonal, that is to say the pursuer regards himself as a person but the object of his pursuit as a thing, to whose personal qualities, if she has any, he is indifferent, and, if he succeeds, he expects to be able to make a safe getaway as soon as he becomes bored. Sometimes, however, he gets trapped. Instead of becoming bored, he becomes sexually obsessed, and the girl, instead of conveniently remaining an object, becomes a real person to him, but a person whom he not only does not love, but actively dislikes.

No other poet, not even Catullus, has described the anguish, self-contempt, and rage produced by this unfortunate condition so well as Shakespeare in some of these sonnets, 141, for example, 'In faith I do not love thee with my eyes', or 151, 'Love is too young to know what conscience is'.

Aside from the opening sixteen sonnets urging his friend to marry – which may well, as some scholars have suggested, have been written at the suggestion of some member of the young man's family – aside from these, and half a dozen elegant trifles, what is astonishing about the sonnets, especially when one remembers the age in which they were written, is the impression they make of naked autobiographical confession. The Elizabethans were not given to writing their autobiographies or to 'unlocking their hearts'. Donne's love poems were no doubt inpired by a personal passion, but this is hidden behind the public performance. It is not until Rousseau and the age of *Sturm und Drang* that confession becomes a literary genre. After the sonnets, I cannot think of anything in English poetry so seemingly autobiographical until Meredith's *Modern Love*, and even then, the personal events seem to be very carefully 'posed'.

It is impossible to believe either that Shakespeare wished them to be published or that he can have shown most of them to the young man and woman, whoever they were, to whom they are addressed. Suppose you had written Sonnet 57,

> Being your slave, what should I do but tend
> Upon the hours and times of your desire?

Can you imagine showing it to the person you were thinking of! Vice versa, what on earth would you feel, supposing someone you knew handed you the sonnet and said: 'This is about you'?

Though Shakespeare may have shown the sonnets to one or two intimate literary friends – it would appear that he must have – he wrote them, I am quite certain, as one writes a diary, for himself alone, with no thought of a public.

When the sonnets are really obscure, they are obscure in the way that a diary can be, in which the writer does not bother to explain references which are obvious to him, but an outsider cannot know. For example, in the opening lines of Sonnet 125

> Were't aught to me I bore the canopy,
> With my extern the outward honoring.

It is impossible for the reader to know whether Shakespeare is

simply being figurative or whether he is referring to some
ceremony in which he actually took part, or, if he is, what that
ceremony can have been. Again, the concluding couplet of 124
remains impenetrable.

> To this I witness call the fools of Time,
> Which die for goodness, who have lived for crime.

Some critics have suggested that this is a cryptic reference to
the Jesuits who were executed on charges of high treason. This
may be so, but there is nothing in the text to prove it, and even
if it is so, I fail to understand their relevance as witnesses to
Shakespeare's love which no disaster or self-interest can affect.

How the sonnets came to be published – whether Shake-
speare gave copies to some friend who then betrayed him, or
whether some enemy stole them – we shall probably never
know. Of one thing I am certain: Shakespeare must have been
horrified when they were published.

The Elizabethan age was certainly as worldly-wise and no
more tolerant, perhaps less, than our own. After all, sodomy
was still a capital offence. The poets of the period, like
Marlowe and Barnfield, whom we know to have been homo-
sexual, were very careful not to express their feelings in the
first person, but in terms of classical mythology. Renaissance
Italy had the reputation for being tolerant on this subject, yet,
when Michelangelo's nephew published his sonnets to
Tomasso de Cavalieri, which are much more restrained than
Shakespeare's, for the sake of his uncle's reputation he altered
the sex, just as Benson was to do with Shakespeare in 1640.

Shakespeare must have known that his sonnets would be
read by many readers in 1609 as they are read by many today
– with raised eyebrows. Though I believe such a reaction to be
due to a misunderstanding, one cannot say that it is not
understandable.

In our culture, we have good reason to be sceptical when
anyone claims to have experienced the Vision of Eros, and
even to doubt if it ever occurs, because half our literature,
popular and highbrow, ever since the Provençal poets made
the disastrous mistake of trying to turn a mystical experience
into a social cult, is based on the assumption that what is,

probably, a rare experience, is one which almost everybody has or ought to have; if they don't, then there must be something wrong with them. We know only too well how often, when a person speaks of having 'fallen in love' with X, what he or she really feels could be described in much cruder terms. As La Rochefoucauld observed:

True love is like seeing ghosts: we all talk about it, but few of us have ever seen one.

It does not follow, however, that true love or ghosts cannot exist. Perhaps poets are more likely to experience it than others, or become poets because they have. Perhaps Hannah Arendt is right: 'Poets are the only people to whom love is not only a crucial but an indispensable experience, which entitles them to mistake it for a universal one.' In Shakespeare's case, what happened to his relations with his friend and his mistress, whether they were abruptly broken off in a quarrel, or slowly faded into indifference, is anybody's guess. Did Shakespeare later feel that the anguish at the end was not too great a price to pay for the glory of the initial vision? I hope so and believe so. Anyway, poets are tough and can profit from the most dreadful experiences.

There is a scene in *The Two Noble Kinsmen* which most scholars believe to have been written by Shakespeare and which, if he did, may very well be the last thing he wrote. In it there is a speech by Palamon in which he prays to Venus for her aid. The speech is remarkable, firstly, in its choice of examples of the power of the Goddess – nearly all are humiliating or horrid – and, secondly, for the intensity of the disgust expressed at masculine sexual vanity.

> Hail, Sovereign Queen of secrets, who has power
> To call the fiercest tyrant from his rage,
> And weep unto a girl; that hast the might
> Even with an eye-glance, to choke Mars's drum
> And turn th' alarm to whispers; that canst make
> A cripple flourish with his crutch, and cure him
> Before Apollo; that mayst force the King
> To be his subjects' vassal, and induce
> Stale gravity to dance; the polled bachelor –
> Whose youth, like wanton boys through bonfires,

Have skipped thy flame – at seventy thou canst catch
And make him, to the scorn of his hoarse throat,
Abuse young lays of love: what godlike power
Hast thou not power upon? ...
           ... Take to thy grace
Me, thy vowed soldier, who do bear thy yoke
As 'twere a wreath of roses, yet is heavier
Than lead itself, stings more than nettles.
I have never been foul-mouthed against thy law,
Nev'r revealed secret, for I knew none; would not
Had I kenned all that were; I never practised
Upon man's wife, nor would the libels read
Of liberal wits; I never at great feasts
Sought to betray a beauty, but have blushed
At simp'ring Sirs that did; I have been harsh
To large confessors, and have hotly asked them
If they had mothers: I had one, a woman,
And women 'twere they wronged. I knew a man
Of eighty winters, this I told them, who
A lass of fourteen brided. 'Twas thy power
To put life into dust; the aged cramp
Had screwed his square foot round,
The gout had knitted his fingers into knots,
Torturing convulsions from his globy eyes,
Had almost drawn their spheres, that what was life
In him seemed torture: this anatomy
Had by his young fair pheare a boy, and I
Believed it was his, for she swore it was,
And who would not believe her? Brief, I am
To those that prate, and have done, no companion;
To those that boast, and have not, a defier;
To those that would, and cannot, a rejoicer.
Yea, him I do not love, and tells close offices
The foulest way, nor names concealments in
The boldest language. Such a one I am,
And vow that lover never yet made sigh
Truer than I. O, then, most soft, sweet Goddess,
Give me the victory of this question, which
Is true love's merit, and bless me with a sign
Of thy great pleasure.

Here music is heard, doves are seen to flutter; they fall again upon their faces, then on their knees.

Oh thou, that from eleven to ninety reign'st
In mortal bosoms, whose chase is this world,
And we in herds thy game; I give thee thanks
For this fair token, which, being laid unto
Mine innocent true heart, arms in assurance
My body to this business. Let us rise
And bow before the Goddess: Time comes on.

Exeunt. Still music of records.

W. H. Auden

TITLES IN EVERYMAN'S LIBRARY

CHINUA ACHEBE
Things Fall Apart

THE ARABIAN NIGHTS
(tr. Husain Haddawy)

MARCUS AURELIUS
Meditations

JANE AUSTEN
Emma
Mansfield Park
Northanger Abbey
Persuasion
Pride and Prejudice
Sense and Sensibility

HONORÉ DE BALZAC
Cousin Bette
Eugénie Grandet
Old Goriot

WILLIAM BLAKE
Poems and Prophecies

JAMES BOSWELL
The Life of Samuel Johnson

CHARLOTTE BRONTË
Jane Eyre
Villette

EMILY BRONTË
Wuthering Heights

MIKHAIL BULGAKOV
The Master and Margarita

SAMUEL BUTLER
The Way of all Flesh

MIGUEL DE CERVANTES
Don Quixote

GEOFFREY CHAUCER
Canterbury Tales

ANTON CHEKHOV
The Steppe and Other Stories
My Life and Other Stories

KATE CHOPIN
The Awakening

SAMUEL TAYLOR COLERIDGE
Poems

WILLIAM WILKIE COLLINS
The Moonstone
The Woman in White

JOSEPH CONRAD
Lord Jim
Nostromo
Typhoon and Other Stories
Under Western Eyes
The Secret Agent

DANIEL DEFOE
Moll Flanders
Robinson Crusoe

CHARLES DICKENS
Bleak House
David Copperfield
Great Expectations
Hard Times
Little Dorrit
Oliver Twist

DENIS DIDEROT
Memoirs of a Nun

JOHN DONNE
The Complete English Poems

GEORGE ELIOT
Adam Bede
Middlemarch
The Mill on the Floss

WILLIAM FAULKNER
The Sound and the Fury

HENRY FIELDING
Joseph Andrews
Tom Jones

SCOTT FITZGERALD
The Great Gatsby

FORD MADOX FORD
The Good Soldier
Parade's End

E. M. FORSTER
Howards End
A Passage to India

IVAN GONCHAROV
Oblomov

GRAHAM GREENE
The Human Factor

THOMAS HARDY
Far From The Madding Crowd
Jude the Obscure
The Return of the Native
Tess of the d'Urbervilles

NATHANIEL HAWTHORNE
The Scarlet Letter

HINDU SCRIPTURES
(tr. R. C. Zaehner)

JAMES HOGG
Confessions of a Justified Sinner

HOMER
The Iliad
The Odyssey

HENRY JAMES
The Bostonians
The Golden Bowl
The Portrait of a Lady
The Princess Casamassima

JAMES JOYCE
Dubliners
A Portrait of the Artist as a Young
Man
Ulysses

FRANZ KAKFA
The Castle
The Trial

JOHN KEATS
The Poems

THE KORAN
(tr. Marmaduke Pickthall)

CHODERLOS DE LACLOS
Les Liaisons dangereuses

GIUSEPPE TOMASI DI
LAMPEDUSA
The Leopard

D. H. LAWRENCE
Sons and Lovers
Women in Love

MIKHAIL LERMONTOV
A Hero of Our Time

NICCOLÒ MACHIAVELLI
The Prince

THOMAS MANN
Death in Venice and Other Stories
Doctor Faustus

KATHERINE MANSFIELD
The Garden Party and Other
Stories

HERMAN MELVILLE
Moby-Dick

JOHN STUART MILL
On Liberty and Utilitarianism

JOHN MILTON
The Complete English Poems

MARY WORTLEY MONTAGU
Letters

THOMAS MORE
Utopia

MURASAKI SHIKIBU
The Tale of Genji

VLADIMIR NABOKOV
Lolita
Pale Fire

GEORGE ORWELL
Nineteen Eighty-Four

BORIS PASTERNAK
Doctor Zhivago

PLATO
The Republic

EDGAR ALLAN POE
The Complete Stories

ALEXANDER PUSHKIN
The Captain's Daughter
and Other Stories

JEAN-JACQUES ROUSSEAU
Confessions

WILLIAM SHAKESPEARE
Sonnets and Narrative Poems
Tragedies Vol. 1

MARY SHELLEY
Frankenstein

ADAM SMITH
The Wealth of Nations

STENDHAL
The Charterhouse of Parma
Scarlet and Black

LAURENCE STERNE
Tristram Shandy

ROBERT LOUIS STEVENSON
The Master of Ballantrae and Weir of
Hermiston
Dr Jekyll and Mr Hyde
and Other Stories

JONATHAN SWIFT
Gulliver's Travels

WILLIAM MAKEPEACE
THACKERAY
Vanity Fair

LEO TOLSTOY
Anna Karenina
Childhood, Boyhood and Youth
War and Peace

ANTHONY TROLLOPE
Barchester Towers
The Eustace Diamonds
The Warden

IVAN TURGENEV
Fathers and Children
A Sportsman's Notebook

MARK TWAIN
Tom Sawyer
and Huckleberry Finn

HENRY DAVID THOREAU
Walden

VIRGIL
The Aeneid

VOLTAIRE
Candide

EDITH WHARTON
The House of Mirth

OSCAR WILDE
Plays, Prose Writings and Poems

MARY WOLLSTONECRAFT
A Vindication of the Rights of
Woman

VIRGINIA WOOLF
To the Lighthouse

W. B. YEATS
The Poems

ÉMILE ZOLA
Germinal

Everyman's Library, founded in 1906 and relaunched in 1991, aims to offer the most complete library in the English language of the world's classics. Each volume is printed in a classic typeface on acid-free, cream-wove paper with a sewn full cloth binding.